A STORY OF
SIDMOUTH

THE CHURCH AND OLD COTTAGES

A STORY OF
SIDMOUTH

and the villages of
SALCOMBE REGIS, BRANSCOMBE
SIDBURY AND SIDFORD

Written and Illustrated
by
ANNA SUTTON

PHILLIMORE

1953
First edition

1959
Second edition, revised

1973
Reprinted by
PHILLIMORE & CO. LTD.
London and Chichester

Head Office: Shopwyke Hall,
Chichester, Sussex, England

© Mrs. D.E.R. Bellamy, 1973

ISBN 0 85033 113 7

Printed in Great Britain by
Fletcher & Son Ltd., Norwich

CONTENTS

SIDMOUTH

ACKNOWLEDGEMENTS

POLWHELE.

LYSONS.

MR. BUTLER'S "GUIDE TO SIDMOUTH".

MR. P. O. HUTCHINSON.

MR. J. G. ANDERSON MORSHEAD.

MR. CHARLES AND MR. ERNEST COLWILL.

"LETHABY'S JOURNAL" (PER MR. DAVID SELLEK).

"THE SIDMOUTH OBSERVER".

"THE SIDMOUTH HERALD".

MR. GEORGE HORN.

THE REV. VYVYAN HOPE.

MRS. WOLSEY HARRIS.

MR. ELIJAH CHICK.

MR. J. R. W. COXHEAD.

THE REV. F. C. BUTTERS.

MR. PALEY (EXETER CITY LIBRARY).

SIR CHARLES CAVE.

MR. VICTOR CAVE.

PREFACE

THE writer wishes to point out that the collection and arrangement of many points of interest in this book has been a work of time and a labour of love, and has only been possible because of the original researches of others, added to her own happy memories.

THIS book "A Story of Sidmouth" is dedicated to my Grandchildren, Jill (Gillian Anna Eileen), David and Colin Bellamy, who encouraged me to write this book; also to my Great-grand-daughter Anna Belinda Speight.

PROLOGUE

SIDMOUTH, formerly known as SIDEMEW, or SIDEMUIE.

When Julius Caesar invaded Britain in 55–54 B.C., the South was divided between three powerful tribes:—*The Belgae*, from Germany, who had driven away the Ancient Britons and possessed themselves of Hampshire, Wiltshire and Somerset; *The Morini* who conquered the Durotrigues, a Celtic tribe, and seated themselves in Dorset, and *The Dunmonii* or Devonshire Men, who not only retained possession of Devon, but also conquered parts of Cornwall. The name Dunmonii under the Romans is familiar with variations.

In the time of the Heptarchy (i.e. the government of seven rulers in England, A.D. 455–828) it was under the West Saxons, when it received the name of Devonseyre, from the British words deunan and deuphaynt, which signified "deep valleys", most of the towns and villages being in a low situation; and from thence its name is derived.

Opinion is divided as to when the Celtic tribe first set foot on the British Isles. The incoming Celts subdued and drove out the original inhabitants. There is evidence that they perched themselves on a ridge 500 feet high, jutting out from High Peak and towering over a forest extending at least three acres seawards at Chet (Chit Rock and the two Pickets (off Ladram) were probably at that time part of the mainland). In January, 1873, P. O. Hutchinson writes:— "Gales entirely cleared away the shingle beneath Clifton Place and Rock Cottage, and it was bared to the rock. The beach was dotted with numerous trunks of trees never seen before, evidence of a submerged forest !" (One of the tree trunks can be seen at the Museum.)

The names "Rackway", "Pinn", "Lincombe", "Ring-in-the-Mire", etc., go to prove that the Celts dispersed themselves widely over our moors in summer and in winter, grazed their stocks and sowed their corn in our fertile spots at Sidbury, Dunscombe and Berry, where the demesne farms recur in Domesday.

This is our earliest connection with Otterton. *Then came the Roman traders*, as the finding of coins, etc., at the mouth of the Sid goes to prove. An interesting collection of Roman coins found on the beach at Sidmouth date from Vespasian, A.D. 69–79, to Constantine, A.D. 315. Bactrian coins found in 1851 range from A.D. 32 to 351. Recent acquisitions to the Museum include two coins, a groat of Edward III (1327–1377) and a Roman coin. It is worth noting that the Roman coin was found in a garden at Stephens Cross, which is part of the reputed Old Roman Road.

The Sid Road and High Street, Sidford, are said to be Roman roads extending from Lyme through High Street to Stowford. Sidmouth had by then grown into a busy Port, with houses lining the main road (now Old Fore Street), which finally trifurcated to Stowford Fischar Path.

Then came the Saxons (King Alfred, A.D. 849–901), their probable line of march being along this road, then known as "Ston-her-path".

During King Alfred's reign the Danes were constantly descending on England and were driven out in the years 871 and 878. Then in 892 under the Viking, Hastings, they descended in hordes and were soundly beaten and driven out in 901. During their invasion the Danish leaders appropriated all Church Manors. *Canute* (994–1035) re-conveyed the Manors, only on paper. Bishop Leofric had to buy the Danish squatters out. They took the money, yet retained the land for 59 years. When they left, they drove off all the cattle.

The Church property (Bishop's Land) was marked off by stones at Woolbrook, "Hare and Hounds" and "Hangman's", while interior ones, "Bulstone", "Long Stone" and "Manstone" seem limits between copyholders and the wastes.

It was probably the Danes who made pigs a speciality, and these would need salt and "Lardarii" to cure their pork—hence "Larder-ham" (Ladram).

There were fourteen or fifteen salt-works in the district, one factory at Saltcombe (Salcombe).

King Alfred's will, A.D. 901, suggests that Sidbury, Salcombe, Branscombe and Sidmouth were annexed at this time, and that the first Hundred Court was held at Branscombe. In *King Athelstan's charters* the units were hides (a hide was a family holding from 60 to 120 acres) with three adults to the hide, and remained unaltered until the Conquest. At this time Sidmouth consisted of five farms, the value of each being probably £1. This is the average of our Bishop's Estates in Domesday, and seems to represent an "Ancient Rent".

In Stephen's reign (A.D. 1097–1154) we were still protected from the outer world by a kind of forest or waste, a crescent of moorland, from Windgates through "King's Slade", "Long Chimney", etc.

The next century saw a lot of waste land cultivated. Wealthy tenants took and equipped large areas from the lords:—Heatherland, Chelson, Raditch, and they sub-enfeuded them to some agriculturalists. The Chapter was still wealthy and bought the middle man out and made the agriculturalists freeholders. (Survey A.D. 1281.)

Vicars now appear (hitherto they had been only Chaplains) in reference to a house, a glebe, the lease of "Reverend's Close" or "Parson's Hayes" (Parsonage) or Vowson Hill with the tenth bean, Mackerel, or Onion of the Copy-holders.

The names of Clapp and Culverwell (in Sidmouth), Ford and Dean (Branscombe), Carters and Chanons (Salcombe), Parker, King and Pigeon (Sidbury) appear in contemporary documents.

As early as A.D. 1330 the "roozing" of the hills shows a heap of pebbles at the mouth of the Sid, where Mussel Rock had disappeared. Hooke Cape (Hooke Ebb) and Luckness Cape have both gone. Before A.D. 1500 the Southdown enclosure of 100 acres had shrunk to 45, and the tenant had only a right "to parsew the soil that had slipped". Sidmouth, like the Otter and Axe harbours, vanished, and King Hal assigned Sidmouth to Gosnell and his son for 99 years.

The names of Michell, Bartlett, Hooper, Guppy and Manley appear. Things were still old-fashioned. Bullock teams were turned out on task work for a neighbour. No one grumbled if pigs took "common-of-shack" in the Autumn.

Not until A.D. 1770 did our pauper roll show an increase or smuggling become usual. Even then we were good-tempered and pulled together. Sidbury financed, Branscombe landed the goods, Sidmouth found the waggons, and Salcombe the carriers; our "uncorrupt and fearless magistrate" died in the odour of sanctity. His executors discovered his brandy cave!

*   *   *   *

CHAPTER I

THE MANOR

THE town of Sidmouth lies at the mouth of a beautiful valley, facing the south-west, about a mile in breadth from Salcombe Hill to Peak Hill, and four or five miles long from the Honiton range of hills to the sea.

When the Monks of St. Michael de Monte first came over "Pykeswaye", "Pick Hill" (Peak Hill) from Otterton in 1175, to reach St. Peter's Chapel of Ease, in order to carry out their manorial duties, what feelings of wonderment and joy must have filled their hearts, as they descended the hill and beheld our beautiful valley. This path which led to the Chapel and Market Cross was known as "Go Church Path".

At the termination of Saxon rule, before William the Conqueror, the Countess Ghida, wife of Harold of Norway (872–930), became the Lady of the Manor of Sidmouth (then an appendage of Otterton), as appears in Domesday Book, folio 104.

Otterton (Otterington) and Yarticombe, were granted by William de Monte in "Periculo maris" and from the Monasticon we learn that King John founded a Priory for four monks and granted them the Manors of Sidmouth and Budleigh, in consideration of which they were obliged to distribute to the poor the sum of 6/– each week in bread for ever. The Prior of Otterton acted as the Abbot's deputy in England, and had immediate control over the estates of the district and the tenants. He had a list of all the inhabitants of Sidmouth, totalling about 160, with the amount of service or money required from each attached to each name. The manuscript is dated 1260. The first four entries read thus:—

> Adam de Radweye,
> Nicholas de Ascerton,
> Richard Medicus (Doctor) Calley (Cawley),
> Walter Calley.

The common service of the bondman consisted of tilling, mowing and reaping so much land for the Prior every year, helping at the mills and paying 16/– every Giles Mass (1st September). The whole sum raised in this manner was about £18 per year. At the dissolution of the Monasteries, Sidmouth ceased to belong to Otterton Priory, and Sidmouth Manor was bought by Christopher Mainwaring before 1623. Richard Duke was then a clerk in the Augmented

1

Court and he bought Otterton and Budleigh from Henry VIII for £1,727. 4s. 2d.

The Manor

It is not difficult to trace a continued list of owners and lessees of the Manor down to the present day:—

1. Countess Ghida 1066.
2. William the Conqueror took possession 1067.
3. The Abbot and Convent of St. Michael's Mount, Normandy.
4. King Henry V resumed possession and gave it to:
5. The Abbess and Convent of Syon, Isleworth, Middlesex, in 1415.
6. Richard Gosnell took a 99-year lease for £516. 17s. 7d. per annum from 1538.
7. King Henry VIII seized it in 1539.
8. Queen Elizabeth owner in 1558.
9. Thomas Baron
10. John Leigh or Lee

appear as lessees in 1560 and on 10th September of that year they leased it with the tithes of fish, etc., to the three members of the Raleigh family, Walter and his two sons, Carew and Wallis. This deed is in the parish chest, and as it has never been printed is of the greatest local interest. Walter (the future Sir Walter Raleigh) was at that time 8 years of age.

11. Sir William Peryam became possessor of a quarter of the Manor on 15th April, 1578.
12. John Scutt, having an interest in the moiety of the Manor and Rectory and the residue of Gosnell's lease, demised half of his half to Sir William Peryam in 1579.
13. Giles Dottyn
14. William Hakewill } leased the Manor and Rectory in 1598.
15. King James I, Lord of the fee in 1603.
16. Christopher Mainwaring took a lease of the King for £38. 7s. 8d. on 21st December, 1604. He afterwards bought the Manor before 1623. The Manor was in the Prideaux family from 1627.
24. Thomas Jenkins succeeded in 1798.
26. Edward Hughes Ball-Hughes became owner in 1836.
27. George Edmund Balfour purchased the Manor for £80,000 in 1866 and built the present Manor House (details appear later). He died in 1869. His son, Col. John Heugh Balfour, C.M.G., D.S.O., was the last Lord of The Manor.

In 1819 there was an advertisement in a newspaper concerning the Manor of Sidmouth. No information is given as to the motives which may have induced the owner of the Manor to put it up for auction. It reads as follows:—

"Important freehold property, Sidmouth, Devon, by Mr. Phillips, at the York Hotel, on Thursday the 26th and two following days at 11 and noon, in 156 lots. A truly valuable and important estate and the Royalty of the Manor of Sidmouth, comprising 600 acres of common and waste lands, together with upwards of 160 residences, farm houses, cottages, stables and extensive buildings, nursery grounds, shambles, polls of fairs and markets, let to respectable tenants at annual rents amounting to upwards of seven thousand pounds. The Estate is capable of considerable improvements."

In 1825 General Slessor bought a farm at Broadway and built a fine house.

Although it was not on Manor land, Mr. G. E. Balfour bought General Slessor's house, demolished it, and built the present Manor House, residing at Powys during its erection. An enterprising firm of builders, Messrs. Stevens & Barstow of Bristol (who were building at Beer at the time), were engaged by Mr. Balfour to build the Manor House, and in order to overcome the difficulties of transport (there was no railway) it was decided to make the bricks on the spot, so a brickfield was opened nearby on land where the present Path Whorlands Council houses stand. Outside labour was imported, but employment was also given to local men.

RADWAY MANOR AND MILLS

AT a very ancient period a mill, or rather two mills under one roof, stood near Mill Cross. This suggests that the mills and cross were not far from each other. A pillory also stood at these four cross-roads. The use of the pillory was abolished by Act of Parliament in June, 1837.

The mills stood on the eastern side of the street, opposite the Unitarian Chapel (on the site now Fords). The motive power was water, one feeder coming down the road by the old Vicarage, and the other coming down Mill Lane from Cotmaton (it still runs through the lawn at Woodlands), but it was later directed down behind Coburg Terrace into the sewers.

The Radway Manor extended all the way between Mill Lane and the Glebe to Brewery Lane, and eastwards down to the river Sid, then southward to the entrance to Mill Street by the Y.M.C.A. and westward to Powys.

About 1287 Adam de Radwaie lived near Mill Cross, on the site of Sidlands. (In 1826 Sidlands Lodge was built on the site supposed to have been occupied by the ancient Manor of Radway, known as "Ullebroke Radwaie", and everything points to this being so. (It has now been divided into two houses; one is occupied by Dr. Michelmore and the other is the Conservative Club.)) The Manor of Otterton claimed the right in the mills, though on Radway land, and the dispute was brought before the itinerant justices in the year mentioned. A mutual arrangement was reached between the contending parties. The Prior agreed to give Adam de Radwaie twenty shillings sterling and to pay him sixteen pence yearly. He also relinquished to Adam the privilege of grinding his corn first.

He likewise remitted a claim of fourpence concerning a piece of land in Sidmouth, but the Prior demanded the right of cutting turf to keep up the banks of the mill stream, as far as it ran through Adam's land. In 1425 John Hake rented the old mill. He married Jenet, one of the two daughters and co-heiresses of Nicholas de Radwaie, and thus got half the Radway estate. This no doubt explains the title Hake's Mill, which I have found in old books.

In 1540 a valuation of the resources of the Manor and the farm of the mill is set down as £4. 13s. 4d.

Later the mills were looked on as town mills; they appeared to have paid a town rate.

Mr. Hooke built The Mill House and a small triangular piece of the garden was claimed by Salcombe Parish, but the late Mrs. Cornish sold this piece for £10 and when Mr. Hooke built the house he threw down the hedge and turned the whole into a garden. The hedge of the Glebe land is claimed by Sidmouth.

We read that the old mills of 1200 at Radway Cross, opposite the Unitarian Chapel, endured for 600 years and then fell into decay.

In the year 1817 or 1818, a roadway (formerly included in the Radway estate) was cut out of a field belonging to Mr. Joseph Hooke. This land was procured and the road made, partly by subscription, but the bridge was erected by the County. The Act for keeping the road in repair and improving it was dated 21st May, 1816. It was about this time that the weir was made in Salcombe Fields (The Lawn) and the mill stream of the newer mill was constructed.

Before Salcombe Road and Cambridge Terrace, built in 1874, were made, the common route that led to Salcombe Parish was by way of Mill Street and the Y.M.C.A., past the Parish Hall and then by ford through the river. Foot passengers used the wooden bridge leading into Milford Road.

CHAPTER II

THE PARISH CHURCH

THE CHURCH OF ST. NICHOLAS AND ST. GILES

A DEED bearing the date 1156 (from F.87 of the Otterton Cartulary) states that Robert the Abbot gave to William his "clericus", or clerk, at Sidmouth the tenement of his father, viz.: a virgate of land for 4/-, paid annually to the Priory provided that one of his sons should have it for the same rent. This is the earliest known record of a priest in Sidmouth; he is therefore set down as the first Vicar. His name was Gulielmus, styled Capellanus and Clericus; he was succeeded by Ricardus in 1200.

The Church of Sidmouth was granted in 1212 by Bishop Marshall to the Monastery of St. Michael de Monte in Normandy, to which the Priory of Otterton was a cell.

In the register of Bronescombe, Bishop of Exeter, of 1259, we read: "In the morrow of St. Nicholas the Lord Bishop of Exeter dedicated the Church of Sidmouth." It was first dedicated to St. Giles, Abbot. The arcade on the north of the nave belongs to the Perpendicular period; that on the south was placed there in 1822, when the church was restored. An old organ destroyed in Cromwell's days was replaced in 1847.

In 1859–60 the church was rebuilt and everything was renewed, except the tower and arcade on each side of the nave. The fragments of Saxon and Norman sculpture found embedded in the walls were portions of an unrecorded church. From these fragments it can be gathered that four churches have stood in this parish, the first of Saxon and Norman period, the second dedicated in 1259, the third of the Perpendicular period like the tower still standing, and the fourth the present edifice. In 1864 the heating apparatus was added. A new stone pulpit was given by some of the inhabitants and fixed on 24th November, 1866.

In 1869 the bells were re-hung in a new cage.

The octagonal clock-face of 1808, which concealed a window of architectural beauty, was removed and a clock with two faces was presented by Mr. R. N. Thornton and fixed on 24th November, 1866. At the same time he gave two new bells.

Pinnacles were added in 1873 at the four corners, the cost being defrayed by the Earl of Buckinghamshire, the Rev. H. G. J. Clements, Dr. Radford and Mr. Thornton.

Orawae Sutton
april Jan 1952

CHURCH OF ST. NICHOLAS AND ST. GILES
RESTORED 1860

The church contains many very beautiful specimens of coloured glass, especially in the west window, which was a gift from her late Majesty Queen Victoria in memory of her father, H.R.H. The Duke of Kent. It contains upwards of sixty figures.

The living as a vicarage was valued in the King's Books in 1539 at £18. 15s. 5d. The nett annual revenue in 1836 was £481.

Thus the cure of souls ranges over a space of more than 700 years. I shall not give a list of the Vicars, as they can be found in the church. The first in my memory was the Rev. H. G. J. Clements. He was inducted on 15th September, 1865, and died on 12th September, 1913. (The Rev. C. E. Roberts was Curate). The Rev. C. K. Woollcombe followed him, being inducted on 16th November, 1913. He retired through ill health in 1938.

The Rev. E. F. A. Ball, M.A., was inducted on 24th May, 1938. He later became Prebendary. Prebendary Ball died in October, 1956. The Rev. Roderick King, M.A., was inducted on 16th July, 1954.

A Parish Magazine was started in January, 1872. The printer was A. Channon, The Market Place. These were sold for 2d., but only six editions were issued. Amongst much interesting information, it contained a list of the bellringers of that date. Many of the names are still remembered by our oldest inhabitants.

"1st bell, George Connett, 2nd bell, James Saunders, 3rd, George Haycraft, 4th, Robert Newberry, 5th, Stretchley Churchill, Tenor William Colwill."

Sidmouth's present Magazine was started by the late Rev. C. K. Woollcombe in 1912.

FRIENDS OF SIDMOUTH PARISH CHURCH

New Society Formed

"For eight hundred years there have been friends of Sidmouth Parish Church," said the Vicar, the Rev. Roderick King, in a sermon on Sunday last, "and so what we are doing now is to acknowledge an existing fact; and to remind ourselves that Friends of the Church should be Friends one of another."

The first function of the newly-formed "Friends" was held on Monday, 4th May, 1958, when the Chairman, Lady Fleming, entertained members at a Coffee Party at Church House.

The Aims of the Friends

(1) To unite all who love our Parish Church into a society which will kindle and deepen friendship.

(2) To stimulate interest in the history and architecture of the Church.

Peal of Eight Bells—Parish Church of St. Nicholas

The history of the bells is most interesting. In the reign of Edward VI (1553) there were only three bells in the tower. Others were added in 1667, 1708, 1844 and 1875.

The weight of the bells varies between 12 cwt. (tenor) and 4 cwt. (treble) and the notes cover an octave between F$\sharp$ and F$\sharp$ Tenor bell.

> Date 1708. Names of Wardens inscribed on bell; that of donor erased.
>
> Seventh, 1708. Donors Henry Conant, Thos. Stocker, Stephen Stocker, Nich. Auston.
>
> Sixth, undated, supposed to be the oldest in the tower.
>
> Fifth, 1667. Founder and donor John Pitt Exon I.P.
>
> Fourth, 1708. Donors George Cawley, Tom Peryman, Thos. Lyde.
>
> Third, 1844. Donor T. Fish.
>
> Second & Treble, 1875. Donor R. N. Thornton.

The founders of the last three were Messrs. Mears & Stainbank of Whitechapel. Evidence in favour of the existence of a former peal is found in a historical statement that the people of Sidmouth at the time of the Reformation (16th century) gave a bell towards the cost of Ottermouth Haven. The sixth bell mentioned above is possibly a remnant—and if so the last—of the peal.

Space will not permit me to mention many of the old monuments, but I quote from Mr. P. O. Hutchinson, concerning the only vault that he mentions: "At the restoration of the Church on September 23, I went down into the vault of Samuel Cawley, partly opened the day before. On the north side of the Chancel, it is a large vault ten to twelve feet long and 6 to 8 feet wide and high enough to stand up in, being arched over and whitewashed. It was opened to build a new pier at the place. The plate of the coffin was loose." A tablet placed on the wall, evidently over the spot, reads:—"Beneath this place rests the mortal part of Samuel Cawley Esq. who departed this life the 29th June 1811, aged 67 years."

More recent monuments were erected by Mr. F. C. Purcell, who gave a new floor to the Chancel in 1921 in memory of his wife Annie and sister Louisa.

In 1922 Mrs. Blake-Burdekin gave oak Altar rails in memory of William Blake-Burdekin. In 1926 Mr. F. C. Purcell gave the Lych Gate in memory of Rhoda Winifred Purcell.

The brass gates in the Chancel were replaced in 1951 by oak gates in memory of Roy Trench and Mary Ailse Trench.

The richly-carved reading desk was given to the Church by Lady Fleming in memory of her husband, Sir Ambrose Fleming, Kt.

GLEBE LANDS

August, 1634

In the Parish Chest is an account of the property belonging to the Glebe:—A Terrier of all the Glebe lands, meadows, gardens, orchards, houses, stocks, implements, tenements and portion of tithes belonging to the Vicarage Sidmouth, taken by the vow of honest men of the said parish, whose names are hereunder subscribed, the 10th day of August 1634 as followeth Imprimis, One mansion house with appurtenances, one barne, and apple mill with a wringe on it; 2 little orchards and an arbour, one close of land called Culverpark, contayninge 5 akers, one close called Middle Close contayninge 5 akers, one close called 7 akers, one old house called Balsbridge house, and an aker of land lying behinde. The said house and one close of land called Bickwell close contayning 3 akers and all the tithes of the said parish except the tithe of wheat, barley, rye, and otes, and the tithe of fish, the sixth part belongs to the Vicarage.

Samuel Slade $\left.\right\}$ Churchwardens.
Edward Huxtable

A. Steven Stocker $\left.\right\}$ Sidesmen.
William Mander

The Churchwardens' accounts inform us that Elias Cawley was Clerk soon after this period. In 1693 he was paid for keeping the bells and "10/– for clerkship", in 1709 "paid Elias Cawley for Clerkship £3.0.0".

"The Glebe contains two fields lying between the two rivers called The Ham. On the north is Culver-park containing 5 acres with hedges belonging on every side."

It goes on to say that land extended and included an orchard at Cottington. In 1813 Mr. Bernard bought Cottington from Dr. Cawley and wanted to get the orchard near his own land, belonging to the Glebe. He effected the change with the Vicar of that day, the Rev. W. Jenkins.

Sidmouth Parish

Through the courtesy of Felix Knevitt, Esq., the following was copied from the original at Lambeth Palace:—

"Mr. John Minshull incumbent, a preachinge minister supplies the Cure being a Vicaridge and receivith the profitte thereof being the small Tythes of the whole p. it be worth p. Annu thirtie poundes. The house and Glebe land belonginge worth per Annu, Twentye poundes."

John Minshull, the Incumbent, had the living from 1635 to 1664 nominally: that is from the ninth year of Charles I, until the fourth year after the Restoration of Charles II. He was the twenty-third Vicar reckoning from Gulielmus in 1175.

CHAPTER III

SIDMOUTH CHARITIES

FROM feudal times until somewhere about the middle of the 19th century one of the methods of conveying land or buildings was by feoffment. The person making the grant was called the Feoffee, a title which persisted long after the method of Land Transfer ceased to be used, before its final abolition at the end of 1925. In the bad old days (which were perhaps not so bad after all) the relief of the poor was generally a matter for the Church, or for the action of private benevolent individuals.

So far as Sidmouth is concerned, most of the gifts are of very ancient date. One of the oldest deeds relating to a Trust was executed in 1328 and was written in Latin. The first deed, which definitely refers to a trust for the parishioners and Church of Sidmouth, was signed on the 15th of June, 1541. Later, in 1642, Trustees were appointed.

The earliest mention of endowments of land at the bottom of Salcombe Hill (which was sold in 1920) occurs in a document of 1414. The locality was called Holways, and lay in the road between Salcombe and Sidmouth. This land recorded in connection with Sidmouth Charities is mentioned in 1543, when certain persons are described as Feoffees.

Gifts to the charities of more recent date include those of Mr. Oliver Cawley and Miss Sarah Sanders. The former by his will dated 10th February, 1779, gave the sum of £50 to Trustees upon trust to pay the yearly income of ten poor housekeepers in Sidmouth, to be selected by ten Trustees.

Miss Sanders (grand-daughter of Mr. Cawley) by her will dated 24th December, 1852, bequeathed a legacy of £100 and a share of her residuary estate of £88. 4s. 5d., with directions that the income should be applied towards the general purposes of the National Schools in connection with the old Parish Church of Sidmouth.

Among other gifts was the gift of John Conant, who gave £50 by will (date unknown). The Rev. John Courtice (a former vicar) by will dated 20th October, 1764, gave £10 as an addition to Conant's Charity. Many other gifts follow which space will not permit one to mention.

The land and house property now belong to the Charity lands under orders of the Charity Commission made in 1862 and 1881.

11

The remaining Trusts are invested in the name of The Official Trustees of Charitable Funds.

In the case of John Minshull's, also Miss Sanders' will, part of the income was directed to be applied in paying for the schooling of poor children of the Church Schools. That part applicable to educational purposes—The Sidmouth Educational Foundation— was constituted by orders of the Charity Commission dated 9th May, 1905, and 17th February, 1928. The sum of £42 annually is paid towards the cost of upkeep and maintenance of The Vicarage School, the remaining income to be used for Education other than elementary; under this latter provision, grants have been made usefully to enable students to take University Courses.

In the twenty-sixth year of Queen Elizabeth, John Arthur gave a house designed for the use of three poor persons of this parish. It was repaired or rebuilt in 1640. In this house meetings for the transactions of parish business used to be held. This house and the garden at the back lay between High Street on the east and Church Lane on the west. The house on the north belonged to Mr. Cawley and stood on the site now Lloyds Bank.

The premises had become dilapidated, and the then Feoffees finding that Mr. Cawley was willing to give a piece of land near the river seven times as large, felt that a benfit would accrue to the charity if such a change was effected. In an indenture of 1744 relating to this new piece of land which was proposed to be taken, was named "Radway and Hakesland" (also known as "Cock" or "Cock's") and from this it is presumed that the ancient Manor of Radway extended eastwards and southward to this part of the town.

"The Indenture of June 12th, 1744, relating to the land by the river (exchanged by Samuel Cawley the elder), was between John Courtice, of the Parish of Sydmouth, in the County of Devon, Clerk; Henry Carslake, Thos: Lyde, Samuel Cawley the elder, William Carter, and Thos: Channon, all of the said parish of Sydmouth, gentlemen, of the one part, and Samuel Cawley, of the said parish of Sydmouth, the younger, net maker, of the other part."

The present Alms Houses were built on this land about 1802 and the school adjoining about 1811. The master's salary during the early period was £6 per annum. In 1819 it was £10 and later rose to £40. The sum for building was raised partly by subscription and partly by poor-rate.

On the other side of the Alms Houses near the Mill there still stands an old building. This was the "Clink" or "Lock-up". Stocks were fixed in an open space in front. A door now stands at the entrance, but the cell with its high barred window can still be seen.

The last man submitted to be put into the stocks was named Franklyn and his offence was habitual drunkenness. This was about 1804. The stocks were placed outside the Market House in 1869. They are now in the Museum.

The following is copied from the Parish Book:—

"In 1730 May ye 9th Laid out for the Lord of the Manor for a pair of stocks 0.19.4."

NOTES OF INTEREST ON OLD SIDMOUTH DOCUMENTS

IT would be of some interest to quote parts of the Will of the Rev. John Minshull, who became Vicar of Sidmouth in 1635 and died in 1663.

Copied from the history of The Feoffees, under the date 26th November, 1663:—

"I, John Minshull of Sydmouth in the countee of Devon, Clerk, being very weak in bodie, but (God be thanked) of perfect memory, etc., etc." As Executors he appoints Christopher Isacke of Manstone and Nicholas Haydon of Ottery St. Mary.

1. To his wife Mary, he gives all the goods in his possession, and all his goods and chattels in Somerset and Dorset.

2. To Nicholas Isacke of Exon, Merchant, his grey mare, and Isake's daughter Elizabeth, his "Selver sugar boxe".

3. About £3 in Edward shillings and mill'd money in equal portions to Lady Rolle, Mrs. Margaret Rolle, Mrs. Deborah Huyshe, Mrs. Isacke, wife of Nicholas aforesaid and Miss Mary ffowler Harlowyn.

4. His little silver cuppe to the eldest daugher of Henry ffry.

5. To John Hill of Sidmouth, his Welsh mare, and the "castor" hat he had lately bought; and remits to him the remainder of the debt he owes.

6. He remits £5 out of £10 which Philip Drake of Dunscombe owes him.

7. To his servant Philip Godfrey, he gives £20, also such apparel as may be fit for his wearing, the rest to go to poor ministers. Also to P. Godfrey the bed, bedding and appurtenances which Godfrey had been used to lie on and 2 pairs of canvas sheets, the little chest and his worst hat and his great Bible.

8. He remits 40/– which William Godfrey owes him and gives him £3 more.

9. He gives to Grace Clarke 20/–: to Mary the wife of Thomas Cawley 10/– and to his servant Agnes Smeath 5/–.

10. To Thomas Lee, Parish Clarke £5.

11. To the wife of John Saunders and to the wife of John Hill his "handkerchers" to be divided equally.

12. To Mrs. Isacke of Manstone 5 yards of holland or thereabouts, lying by him.

To his Executors £10 a piece and to N. Haydon, his beavor hat, etc., etc.

All the rest of his goods and chattels to be sold and "remayne in stock for the use of the poor of Sidmouth for ever, as shall be fit."

An entry in the parish register records "1663 John Minshull, gent, clerke, vicar of ye pish, buryed Dec 4th. The goods and chattels fetched £360."

An interesting book in connection with Sidmouth Charities is the Overseer's account book, which contains particulars of the disbursements from the year 1840 to 1881. The heading of the first page is very explicit as to the source of the money:—"Mr. Isaacke's Gift and part of Mr. Minshull's Charity was distributed in Vestry in Feb: 1840", whilst the heading of another page refers to the payment of 5/– each to ten housekeepers, not receiving weekly pay, that amount being interest of £50 at 5 per cent, a legacy from Mr. Oliver Cawley.

Until the year 1862 it was the custom to distribute much of the charity in bread as well as cash, giving the Vestry the appearance of a baker's shop and frequently causing dissatisfaction either from the quality of the bread, or its not being required by elderly persons. So the gift of bread was discontinued and money given. With few exceptions 5/– has been the maximum.

INTERESTING EXTRACTS FROM BOOKS AND JOURNALS

Sidmouth in the 15th century

There is a small folio paper book without cover now in the parish chest. It gives an account of moneys received for schooling and those distributed to the poor. The book begins thus:—

"November ye 9th 1681: Then paid Robert fforward for schooling three pounds ffor half a yeare ended at michelmas last and distributed to ye poore."

In a long folio book bound in parchment and bearing dates ranging from 1697 to 1777, we have accounts kept by officers of the parish called the Waywarden and Boxwarden. I extract some of the entries of some of the names still known in the town:—

1681. Paid Pasker Cornish	01.00
the widow derby	02.00
Mr. Henry Carslake for 180 rede for ye forte	01.12.00
bear [beer] to the waymenders	00.13.00

1698.	for carrying soulders to Chudley	00.12.06
	paid Ellis [Elias] Cawley for keeping bills	01.00.00
	to Goyle [jail] and hospital	00.13.00
	Masters fee	00.01.06
	Salcombe Church	00.01.03
	Thos. Westcott for a tree to mak a gatt [gate]	00.01.06
1706.	to ringing ye good news of ye duke of Marlborows victory in flanders	00.01.00
	supplied Henry Potbury's wife her children having small-pox	01.00.00
	She promised it again att ye return of her husband at sea.	
	Pay Will Carpenter the sixon	00.01.04
	Thos. Curtis for a letter a turnye	00.01.00
	George Cawley the out sett of the ffort	00.18.03
	Elias Cawley for clerkship	03.00.00
	to ye doctor for a sick soljer and quarters	00.02.00

NOTE.—Copied from an old manuscript of Otterton Cartulary, Folio 28:—
"Walt Calle v. ix (C.A.V.I.–x)." The name Calli is not unlike Calley or Cawley, a name which has existed in this parish down to the present time.
("History of Sidmouth." P. O. Hutchinson).

PARISH BOOKS & WARDENS [*sic*] ACCOUNTS.

Copied from P. O. Hutchinson.

The old Parish Chest is of oak, but in 1860 a secondhand iron chest was bought and they are both there now. It is said that the iron chest belonged to Powderham Castle. The oldest volume is of paper. The earliest date is 7th April, 1586. The book is imperfect, at both ends: the first page is torn but the following is discernable:—

Thomas the sonne of . . . baptised the XXIV d . . .

At the back of the first leaf (page 2) there is a glimmer of 1587, but on page 3 the figures 1588 are plain.

In size the book measures 8 by 11 inches and is three-fourths of an inch thick. I begin with the baptisms and extract some whose names are still in existence in Sidmouth:—

"1593 Marye, the Daughter of John Calleye (Cawley) west in the corner was baptized the VI day of June 1593.

"Annya[1] (or Anna) the Daughter of Edward Callaye in the corner was baptised the XVI day of July."

Hutchinson adds a note:—

"In the corner" and "west in the corner" are expressions which occur several times, which I am unable to explain.

[1] The Cawleys are my maternal ancestors, and I was thrilled to find the origin of my own name "Anna", which has come through a member of the family ever since, my mother, self, my daughter, grand-daughter, and great-grand-daughter. (A. S.)

1800

Graham Sutton
Feb 1953

CHAPTER IV

SEA FRONT

IN the year 1800 Sidmouth was a small fishing village. In a water-colour of Sidmouth sea front looking south-west no houses can be seen, just a small thatched building at the eastern end, probably the Preventive station, and one or two old buildings scattered in the background, the old Brewery and Malt House[1] and the Dissenting Chapel (later to become the National School). There was a greensward outside where The Bedford Hotel now stands. In a map of 1796 building foundations can be seen opposite the entrance to the town by Marlborough Place, showing how much the sea has encroached.

Fisherman Bartlett declared that about 1790, a merchant and ship owner used to winnow corn on the beach inside these founda-tions and that grass grew where the esplanade now stands. He also said there was a wall in front of the old building, with an arched entrance through it, opposite the sea. Between this and the esplanade

[1] When passing the old Malt House recently, I enquired from a man who lived near, what use they made of the building; he replied:—"Gaw misses, you only got to cock yer nawse round thickee door, and the stink what comes down they stairs will zoon tull ee; they m-a-akes this yur stuff what yu putts on yer v-a-a-ce! (cosmetics !)."

16

was a strong square wall around what was then St. Peter's Chapel. Not long ago the esplanade caved in at this spot, and remains of a tunnel were found leading to St. Peter's.

St. Peter's Chapel stood behind Marlborough Place, and was used by the monks of Otterton as their Chapel-of-ease. A Market Cross mentioned in a deed of 1322 stood in the Market Square, outside St. Peter's. This cross was taken down in 1795.

Portions of St. Peter's can still be seen with thick stone walls, firm cement and arched doorway. (The Marlborough Cafe occupies the site of St. Peter's.)

About 1864, when a trench was being dug in the lane behind, a large deposit of human bones was found buried at a depth of 6 or 7 feet, and brought up in a state of perfect preservation. It must be conjectured that this was the site of a pre-Reformation burial ground.

Before the Chapel became so ruinous and had to be demolished in 1805, it had been used as an Inn known as "The Sign of the Anchor".

At the corner of *Prospect Place* sea-water baths were opened about 1805. (The lower part of the building and the middle house of Prospect Place is occupied by the Mocha Cafe.) After being patronised by H.R.H. the late Duke of Kent, they were later named "The Royal Baths".

Copied Oct 1951
by Anna Sutton

1826. PROSPECT PLACE AND BATH HOUSE

Around the corner stands Beach House, first known as "Blossom House". Remembered by me as the home of the King family, now a hotel, it remains preserved with its beautiful pillared porch, balcony and stained glass windows.

York Hotel and Terrace. In 1885 we read:—"Thomas Heiffer, an old sailor of Heiffer's Row, once told Mr. Hutchinson that he could remember when there was no York Terrace. Speaking of the latter years of the last century, he said the ground was occupied by dockyards and he had seen two vessels on the stocks at the same time.

They generally launched there in fine weather over or through the ridges, now the esplanade, and completed their rigging and fitting out in the shelter of Exmouth harbour, preparatory to their sailing to America".

York Terrace and Hotel were built in 1811. We first hear of Mr. Stone as proprietor of the hotel in 1824, when he suffered great loss of wines and liquors through his cellars being flooded in the great storm of that date. Mr. Hooke was owner in 1849.

Mr. Rogers in 1888 on the occasion of Queen Victoria's Jubilee, had a placard posted stating:—"To all fishermen, Mr. Rogers of The Royal York Hotel, will have much pleasure, at the Vaults to-morrow between the hours of 10 and 1 o'clock in giving each man one pint of beer and refreshments in commemoration of Her most Gracious Majesty Queen Victoria." What days they must have been ! The names of Huxtable, Barnard, Wright, and last of all Mitchell, will be remembered as proprietors of the hotel before it became a limited company. We read of hot and cold water baths being at 5 York Terrace in 1866, also a Miss Rose using one house as a Library. The others were lodging houses. A yard at the end of the Terrace was used for storing coal by Mr. John Potbury, before the Railway was built, and the coal was brought in by barges. Later it was owned by Miller & Lilley.

At the end of the yard stood the old Life-boat House (now a Garage). What excitement there was when the rockets were fired announcing the fact that the Life-boat was being launched, and one saw it passing down the slip-way filled with red-capped men, wearing cork jackets. Dick Solman was coxswain.

In 1909 Mr. James Pepperell bought a part of the yard and built two houses, completed in 1911, occupying "Shenstone" until he died in 1933. The next house built as a Manse for the Congregational Chapel was sold and is now the Strathmore Hotel.

In 1923 my husband, Ernest Sutton, bought the remaining piece of the yard and built Carlton Mansions, the first flats to be built in Sidmouth, retaining the fine old wall behind, which encloses a

CARLTON MANSIONS. SIDMOUTH'S FIRST FLATS

garden and tennis court. The flats were completed in 1925. Our example was followed, and the next flats to be built were those above the "Radway Cinema".

I have been told that rubbish used to be tipped out on the Life-boat slip-way to be washed away by the waves.

In "Sidmouth Murmurs, 1914" we read:—

> "It is a common sight on a windy day to see a truck load of waste paper tipped on to the beach to blow all over the town."

A coastguard "Look-out" was built at the corner of the site of the old Preventive Station, after the coastguards were disbanded. It was the excise office and is now headquarters of the Sailing club.

The old gas building and offices have been demolished and seats occupy a sheltered spot between the site and the Drill Hall. In 1918 the eastern end of the esplanade was completed. Mr. St. Leger Whitford, Surveyor and Sanitary Inspector, and Mr. W. Dingwall, M.A.S., gave valuable voluntary assistance.

Returning to the western end we see well-preserved houses, built about 1824, overlooking the shore. First comes Clifton cottage, a delightful old thatched bungalow. Next come the Beacon and Rock cottage, two lovely old detached houses, standing out facing the eastern bay, and appearing above Clifton Place, which was first known as "Heiffers Row" having been built by a fisherman of that name, all lodging houses with the exception of Rock cottage which belonged to my great-uncle Thomas Cawley, who in the early 70's used it as a summer residence.

Round the corner to the left a private carriage drive led to the Woolbrook Glen, "now the Royal Glen", truly a gem in a beautiful setting. Mr. Butcher writes in his book of 1810 that it was then known as "the King's house", built by a Mr. King of Bath. How far this is true I do not know. I have an idea (entirely my own) that this might have been the small Manor of Woolbrook, since it has the appearance of the other small manors, and nowhere in the vicinity of Woolbrook has there been a house anything like a Manor.

1815. CLIFTON PLACE AND THE FORT FIELD

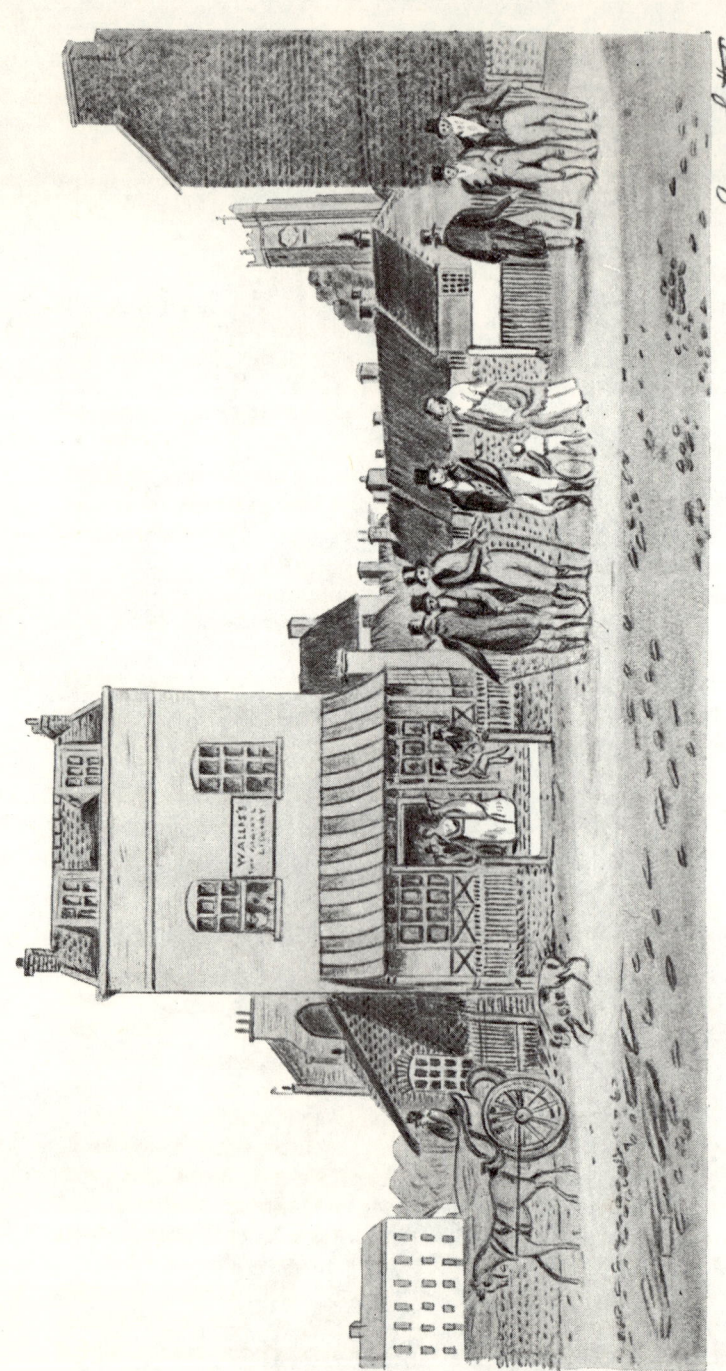

Anna Luther
August 1951

1815. Wallis's Library (now The Bedford Hotel)

Belmont was built as a private residence by Major Barnes in 1817 on land adjoining the Fortfield. It became the home of many good families including the Thorntons, Hine-Haycocks and lastly Mr. and Mrs. Stanley Wood, all great benefactors to Sidmouth.

The Fort Field (now the Cricket field) was unenclosed, with a beaten track or thoroughfare leading up from the sea front and passing out through where now stand numbers 7 and 8 Fortfield Terrace.

When Sidmouth was threatened with invasion from the French, a Fort was built with an ammunition store and four guns. After the battle of Waterloo the fort was demolished.

The field was a common playground where sheep occasionally grazed and children played cricket and football.

In 1827 application was made to the County Magistrate for leave to enclose the Fort Field and to stop up the beaten track. As it was Manor land, the work of building the wall pierced by embrasures parallel with the esplanade must have been carried out by the parties interested. When the surrounding rails were put up the road was filled in and levelled over. The three-cornered plot (now the triangle) then became the common playground.

Next came two small cottages with a garden and potato patch known as Fortfield Cottages. I remember it as Fort Cottage, a delightful old house surrounded by a lovely old garden.

A café and flats were built around the old house.

A car-park covers the spot which was once the "lovely Bedford Lawn", where tennis courts and garden beds delighted the eye.

SIDMOUTH BECOMES A FASHIONABLE WATERING PLACE

Fortfield Terrace was built between 1790–94. A letter in the possession of Mrs. Crabb-Watt, dated July, 1795, from Paton to Henry Halland, a London architect, states that Jenkins Lord of the Manor of Sidmouth, was very upset because Novoselski the architect had died before the completion of his new Crescent. This could hardly be anything but Fortfield Terrace, which was intended to be a grand crescent extending to Belmont, with No. 8 as the centre. Fortunately for Sidmouth this was not completed, thereby leaving us our wonderful Cricket Ground. Novoselski was a Pole born in Rome in 1760. He was a theatrical designer and speculating builder. This gracious old terrace still stands out, preserved in all its Regency beauty.

At this period the excellency of climate and natural beauties became known and attracted "the people of quality". Noted people chose Fortfield Terrace as their temporary residences, whilst they built houses for themselves, and Sidmouth became a fashionable watering place.

One of the first houses to appear on the sea front was built in 1805. It was opened as "The Shed" and in 1809 known as Wallis's Library. An old Sidmouth journal states: "The romantic watering place of Sidmouth at length boasted of what it long desired; a lounging place in a pleasant conspicuous situation, where articles of fancy as well as information and utility may be met with. It is under the most favourable patronage, among whom we have the honour to boast Lord Gwyder and Lady Willoughby, Lord and Lady le Despenser, and the principal nobility of the town and neighbourhood."

Lodging houses were built to accommodate visitors. We read in a journal of 1809:—"Taking the first turning to the left from Bedford House are two genteel lodging houses and three large handsome houses convenient for respectable families, named Denby Row. On the sea front other lodging houses were built, known as Marine, Portland, Marlborough, and Prospect Place."

CHAPTER V

OLD HOUSES

IN 1796 Mr. Baruh Lousada, a Spanish Jew, came from London and bought a house and fields known as Pick's Tenement. The house was enlarged and other fields known as Blower's Park were added. A nephew of the same name inherited the estate and sold it to the Manor Trustees in 1869, who bought it with the intention of making large-scale developments. The scheme did not materialize. (Many people were sad when Peak House was demolished and rebuilt by Sir Thomas Dewey.)

THE WESTERN FIELDS

BEFORE the Manor Road was developed sheep and cattle grazed in pasture land, covering the whole area bounded by "Peak House", "Whitheby" and "Cotmaton", known as the Western Fields, Fort Fields and Sea Fields. Woolbrook Cottage (The Royal Glen) was entered by a private carriage drive, the only entrance to the

Copied Oct 1952
by Anna Sutton

THE CRICKET FIELD AND THE RED HOUSE

25

fields was by little pathways, leading from Peak Hill and Cunning-hams Lane, crossing Glen Goyle by a little iron bridge. There were two paths; on the left, one through "The Little Glen" led to the Sea Fields; and on the right, through the Fort Fields to the town and sea.

The Manor Road was developed in 1881 when "Redlands", "Redcliffe", "Holme" (now the Vicarage), and "Westbourne", "Fairleigh", "Glen View" were built. Fortfield Place was built at the same time. Other houses in the Manor Road were built much later. The Manor Hall was built in 1891, followed by "The Kraal" and "Kenandy". At about the same time Sir Joseph Leese built The Red House (now The Fortfield). "Montague House" (Grey Turrets), and "The Bungalow" (Brinkburn) were built a few years later.

At the top of Seafield Road stands "Eaglehurst", the first home of the much respected Hawker family, who later moved to the house known as "Didworthy", where the present Mrs. Hawker lives.

The next building, "High Bank" (Littlecourt) and "Eglantine" all have retained their old-world dignity.

On the opposite side modern buildings, "Hylton", "Manor Garth", "Crossways", "Wychwood", "Glencoe", and "Pent-lands" were built on pasture land known as "Seafields", with "Meadhurst", "The Close" and "Regency House" behind. Bramley Cottage has been built recently on ground once attached to Cotmaton House.

At the bottom of the road stands "Pebble Stone Cottage".

A pleasant walk may be taken by way of Foxes Corner, a roadway behind Peak House. Passing Peak Farm and the entrance to the Golf Course and Club House and the Moorcourt Estate (developed in recent years), we arrive at "Sidmouth House", built about 1820. It is a gracious old building standing high in spacious grounds with a beautiful panoramic view of sea and coast. For some years it was re-named The Lodge and a large wing was added. In recent years both house and grounds have been beautified and it has happily reverted to its original name of "Sidmouth House". It is now owned by Mr. and Mrs. Silverman. Peak Lodge remains unaltered.

"St. Helen's" was built by the Rev. E. Butcher (the author of our first Sidmouth Guide), happily remembered by many as the home of Mr. Guy Shorrock and family and Mrs. Sheldon Withers, J.P. It is now a Hotel.

Captain Carslake built "Cotlands", for many years the home of Mr. and Mrs. Kennet-Were. Both were great benefactors of

Sidmouth. Mrs. Kennet-Were contributed much to the music of Sidmouth, providing an orchestra of outstanding merit. In her concert room adjoining the house, she gave delightful concerts to the townspeople.

"Witheby", built by Mrs. Powys Floyd, was sold to Major Cunningham, whose name appeared in the Sidmouth Directory of 1851. It was later sold to Mr. Stephen Cave, father of the late Sir Stephen Cave, M.P.

COTLANDS ESTATE

MODERN houses and bungalows have recently been built on "Cotlands"; they are well planned and gardens, terraces and lawns have developed very quickly. I must confess to feeling saddened at the loss of the fine old house and the lovely old trees over 100 years old. So many people have come to reside in Sidmouth and they have been able to build their homes in this lovely vicinity, and we are glad to welcome them.

COTMATON

IN my sketch of 1816 the only entrance into Cotmaton is shewn by way of a small bridge crossing the Woolbrook stream. The paths lead to the town by way of Mill Lane and into High Street, and to the church and sea by way of Seafield path. The two cottages on the left have been converted into "The White Cottage", now

COTMATON IN 1816, BEFORE ROADWAY

owned by Mr. and Mrs. Clifford Brown. Mills' cottage facing remains unaltered. Polwhele states: "Asherton, in the parish of Sidmouth, is a very pleasant and healthy habitation, upon a dry and sandy soil, seated in the open fields upon a small advanced ground, and commanding a full prospect of the sea. Nicholas de Asherton gave Asherton to Richard de Knightstone in frand-marriage with Isobell his daughter about the beginning of Henry III's reign. His daughter Margaret was wife of John Upton."

My first memory is of Mr. Morrit occupying the present "Asherton". He probably demolished the old house, as the present structure was built in the early eighties. (It is now flats.)

A small path to the left (Cheese Lane) led into Five Fields. No houses were there until after the Convent was built in 1883 and a roadway made. The old stone wall remains at the entrance.

"Cotmaton House" is best remembered by us as the home of Mr. Tindall, whose books and paintings will be a lasting memorial of a lovable, unassuming but great man. It is now a fine hotel, with all its old-world amenities preserved.

"Cotmaton Hall" was very old, but there are no records to show its age. For many years it was the home of General and Mrs. Elton and their daughter Violet. Unfortunately it was burnt down.

1826. COTTINGTON

The oldest house in Sidmouth, quoting Polwhele:—" 'Cotmaton', 'Cottington', an ancient seat commanding a pleasant view of the Bay, was sold by Mr. Duke of Otterton to William Harlewin. Sir John Harlewin (who was knighted for his valour in the reign of Edward IV) lived there; his relations resided there until the time of Charles II." It was marked in old maps of 1794 as Liberty Hall, but reverted to its former name "Cottington". It later became the home of Captain Carslake, who sold it to Dr. Cawley, a relative of his (and mine). In 1813 Dr. Cawley sold it to Mr. Bernard.

In 1883 it served as a temporary home for a few French Nuns, under the name of "The Convent of the Assumption". Major Berkeley Levett, Equerry to the Duke of Connaught, was the last to live there before it became flats.[1]

[1] 1958. The fine old house "Cottington" was recently demolished. Standing high, this lovely old house (seen in my sketch), once the home of my ancestors, had fallen into disrepair. Some very attractive houses and bungalows have been built on the estate. Old and young Sidmothians are very sad to see large blocks of red-brick flats imposing themselves on our otherwise lovely landscape. Fortunately, some of the fine old trees surround them; we must hope they will remain.

1821. WOODLANDS COTTAGE

Passing down Mill Lane to the left we reach "Woodlands", first known as "Old Hayes". Lysons says:—"The Manor of Old Hayes in this parish belonging partly to the family of Pole and partly to Crosse and Trelawney". First a farmhouse, it was converted from a barn by the Rev. J. Copleston. Lord Gwyder greatly improved it and changed its name. Mr. Shirley Newdick improved it and laid out the lovely gardens, formerly an orchard, leaving the stream to trickle through (the stream is still there).

About 1850 Mr. Johnson bought the place and covered the house with slates cut in hexagons. These can still be seen. "Woodlands" is now an Hotel.

Built by The Marquess of Exeter, "Spring Gardens" happily remains as a stately Regency house now occupied by Dr. and Mrs. Fison. In 1813 it was the home of Rear-Admiral Macnamara, who was praised, and also denounced, as an accomplished duellist.

Sidmothians will like to remember it as the home of Mrs. Caroline Brembridge, who lived to be 105. On her 103rd birthday she acknowledged in her own writing, a present sent to her by Queen Alexandra. She died in 1906.

"Powys", built by Mrs. Powys Floyd about 1800 as a low thatched house of one storey, about 120 feet in length, surrounded by lovely shrubberies, walks and gardens. My first memory of it is when my godmother, Miss Dawson, lived there with her sister. I was very small at the time. Happily there is no fear of this lovely place becoming an hotel, as it now belongs to Mrs. Campbell Watson, in whose hands it will be preserved in all its beauty. During the years that the late Colonel and Mrs. Campbell Watson have lived there, they have done much to benefit our town by handsome subscriptions to our hospitals, charities and sports. They throw open their gardens to the public, and lend their grounds for our Garden Club, of which they are keen supporters.

Opposite "Powys", "Audley Cottage" (formerly the home of the Dowager Lady Audley) was enlarged and converted from a thatched cottage by the Misses Dawson, who made it into an elegant building. Stone pillars removed from the Parish Church gates support the entrance gates. The beauty of the house and grounds, with lovely old trees and rare shrubs, has been further improved by its present owners, Doctor and Mrs. Macleod.

"Knowle Cottage", built by Lord le Despenser in 1805, after being occupied by the Marquis of Bute, was sold in 1811 to Mr. Foker or Farquier, who sold it to Mr. Fish, who created great interest by making it a show place for over forty years. It housed many exotic plants and in its grounds and deer park were many foreign birds and animals.

In 1887 there was a sale of land in the Knowle grounds to form a new road and a building site leading into Bickwell. "Knowle Grange" and other more recent buildings were built on the site.

Opposite Knowle Park is "Claremont", built about 1887. In my childhood days it was known as "Hampden Lodge", the home of the Lady Charlotte and Louisa Hobart-Hampden, daughters of the Earl of Buckingham.

"Sidmount", built by Mr. Mackie in 1825, was the home of Mr. G. J. Radford, a Solicitor, who lived there with his two daughters. Sidmouth is much indebted to him for the gift of the Ham as an open space and Recreation Ground for ever, and to Miss Radford for the gift of "Hope Cottage" to house our County Library and Reading Room.

"Hope Cottage" was opened as a solicitor's offices. The firm began as Messrs. Darke & Leicester, Leicester & Williams, Williams & Radford, Radford & Orchard, Orchard & Michelmore, and now is Michelmore, Davies & Bellamy.

The Local Magistrates attended to judicial business of an urgent character at these offices (removed some years ago to Honiton).

In 1863 the L. & S.W. Bank opened there, until they removed to Temple House in 1876.

Returning to Mill Lane, on the left we arrive at a lovely old residence which, then known as "Belle Vue", was occupied by Elizabeth Barrett Browning, for three years from 1832 to 1835. I knew it as "Oaklands", occupied by Miss Toller. It is now Cedar Shade Hotel. In its beautiful setting of gardens and wonderful cedar trees, the house surrounded by a verandah and conservatories remains unspoilt, to gladden the eyes of passers-by.

The premises, once known as "The Royal Dairy", were occupied by Mr. Harris, known to Sidmothians as "The Shah". He was rather a "tetchy" old man, unlike his daughter Eliza, a happy smiling soul, who married "Cap'n." Elliott. The "Shah" was a member of the Local Board when the Duke and Duchess of Edinburgh visited Sidmouth; he presented them with a cream cheese, after which he named his shop "Royal".

In my sketch of "The White Hart" Inn can be seen a brick wall. This enclosed a garden and two houses, one of them occupied by the Colwill family. Mr. Charles and the late Mr. Ernest Colwill have helped me by giving information for this book.

Jubilee Terrace was built on this site by the late Mr. John Skinner, for many years a much respected member of our Council.

"The White Hart" Inn stood at the bottom right-hand corner, and was built about 1710, and demolished between 1870–80, the last Licensee being "Billy Sweet". The Unitarian Old Meeting House was built on the site. The picturesque old thatched building, "May Cottage", still stands at the entrance to Blackmore Fields, with wicket gate, and passion flower covering the walls. It was the first Cottage Hospital, details of which appear elsewhere.

(I first remember it as the home of the late Mr. T. H. Sisterton and family. As Clerk of the Works for the Sidmouth Manor for over twenty years Mr. Sisterton not only studied the interests and welfare of many tenants but took an interest in the town's advancement.)

[*Copied by Anna Sutton*, 1951]

Overlooking the Triangle stands the "Church House". Built about 1812 as "Fortfield House" by a Mr. Phillips, it later passed into the hands of Sir John Kennaway, Bart., with houses adjoining, "Aurora", "Barton House" and "Barton Cottage". Miss Cash, who was a cripple, lived at Barton Cottage in the early 80's and occupied her time in embroidering names and monograms on linen in pink cotton. This was the origin of Cash's name tapes.

1870. The White Hart Inn and Sidlands Cottage at Mill Cross Looking up Mill Lane (All Saints' Road)

"Belgrave", now the Council Offices, described as a roomy lodging house, was built about the same time, by a French pastry cook; also the charming old house, "Villa Verdi" (now Harston). It was at one time Lady Claridge's school for genteel young ladies !

Mr. Amyatt, a relative of Sir John's, built Amyatt's Terrace in 1815 in order, it is said, to shut out the view of the Churchyard.

Coburg Terrace was built at the same time. A clump of trees and a large white gate stood at the entrance. "Coburg Cottage" was built ten years later by Sir John Kennaway for his groom. Horn's Coalyard comes next and then "The Bays". "Jubilee Cottage", built about 1810 to celebrate the Jubilee of George IV, remains unspoilt. At the corner of Haydon's Lane is "Swiss Cottage". I knew it as *Noah's Ark* when occupied by Mr. Noah Miller.

The old thatched cob building and cottages in Haydon's Lane remain intact.

The charming rose-covered "Alma Cottage" with trellised porch still stands at the corner of Alma Terrace, with "Rose Cottage" opposite. Mrs. Edinborough (who lives in Alma Terrace) tells me that her grandfather, Mr. Newman, lived in "Rose Cottage" and had a shop where now stands "Grasmere". He was building Alma Terrace at the time when the battle of Alma was won—hence the name. An old advertisement states:—"Newman, Stonemason, Lapidary and Jeweller, Established 1800." Mr. Newman was the first to be granted a licence to sell jewellery in Sidmouth.

Across the road in an old-world garden, with magnolia tree and other rare shrubs, stands unchanged a lovely old house named "Roselands", for many years the home of Mr. and Mrs. Berwick.

Many new detached houses known as the Roselands Estate have been built behind, on ground once the Nurseries. A charming residence named "Rosemount" lies on the left. In 1663 Walter Harlewyn made the pleasant grant of a lease of "Rosemount" for 3,000 years at a rent of two nutmegs a year if asked for.

Baroness de-Rosen lived there in the eighties. Next came "Elm Cottage", followed by the lovely old garden-fronted "Florence Cottage" (now "Milestones"), "Cypress Place", "Cypress Cottage" and the little thatched "Pages Cottage", now "Larbi Cote".

ARCOT HOUSE

HIGH up amid old trees and sloping lawns Arcot House was built by General Rumley in 1820, with a view of the sea and surrounding hills. I remember it as the home of Mr. Moulton-Barratt and his two daughters. A gentleman of the old school, both in manners and appearance, he was a fitting occupant for this gracious old

MAY COTTAGE, 1826

copied by
Anne Sutton
Oct 1951

BELGRAVE, 1826—NOW COUNCIL OFFICES

copied by 1951
Anne Sutton

mansion. (Miss Moulton-Barratt did much for the welfare of Sidmouth. She formed the Girls' Club, etc.) On entering one could sense the old-world atmosphere and visualize ladies in crinolines dancing the minuet, or ascending the old staircase, wandering through the conservatories into the rose garden. On one of the panes of glass are initials scratched by the rings of "Young bloods" whilst waiting to help ladies mount their horses from the mounting block outside.

Arcot House has been recently acquired by the Council as an "Eventide" Home; it has been converted into suitable apartments. May the peaceful atmosphere descend upon its occupants.

I visited the "Eventide" Home, which received its first residents on 1st February, 1953. Adapted with central heating and every modern convenience, the old-world atmosphere and lovely old staircase remain.

LIVONIA

IN letters written to Sir Howard Elphinstone by his sister Rosalie after his family came to live at Livonia in Sidmouth from Russia, we read that Livonia Cottage has its charms. Standing half-way between Sidmouth and Sidbury, with a few acres falling to the river Sid; it was not isolated. Nearby was a group of Georgian villas, houses built for gentlefolk, with fine cedars and lawns, a copse or two tucked into a fold of sloping field, each having a varied air of dignity and comfort. The days of giant crinolines were at hand, but the letters of Rosalie Elphinstone breathe more of the spirit of Pride and Prejudice. Balls at The Assembly Rooms in the nearby town of Sidmouth were great events. Rosalie shews us clearly the characters of all those who wandered in and out of the quiet rooms and through the open doors of the painted iron verandah into the garden. Livonia Cottage, less pretentious perhaps than some of its neighbours, was a low white house of Regency period.

Though we hear of a governess, a carriage, half a dozen servants and plenty of travelling, the family yet considered that the life they were leading was one of poverty. Things had evidently been more luxurious in Russia.

Sir Howard Elphinstone, the son of Captain Elphinstone, was tutor to H.R.H. the late Duke of Connaught. This may have been why the Duke did us the honour of coming to spend several winters in Sidmouth at the latter part of his life.

The Currys were the occupants in my young days. Lieutenant-Colonel Curry, familiarly known as "Monty", was made

1826. LIVONIA COTTAGE

Commandant at Ladysmith during the Boer War. He married Miss Moulton-Barratt of Arcot House.

The lovely old-world building and grounds with the Woolbrook stream running through the Goyle are being well preserved by its present owners, Commander and Mrs. Kettlewell.

CHAPTER VI

THE SEA-SHORE

In 1824 there were cottages on the sea-shore beneath Clifton Cottage. Dame Partington (who was supposed to have tried to sweep out the ocean with her mop) lived in one, and a fisherman named Bolt with his family in the other. It is said that he kept a pig and a cow there and visitors were supplied with milk and junket. There was a pig-sty and patch of sward.

COTTAGES ON THE SHORE AT CHIT ABOUT 1815
(BEFORE CLIFTON PLACE)

From time to time Sidmouth has been subjected to some great storms. In 1743 there occurred a very severe storm. In old parish books there occur two entries, 1743 and 1748:—"To John Potbury helping in the storm 0.0.6." "To help about the Church in the storm 0.0.6." At 4 o'clock in the morning of 23rd November, 1824, a storm of such violence occurred that the family of Bolt, occupying one of the cottages on the shore, had to seek shelter in the house above. Very shortly after, the cottages were swept away.

As the day dawned, an appalling sight presented itself. The gardens in front of the houses were laid bare and covered with shingle. The fury of the waves broke in the doors and windows of Wallis's Library and other houses, and people were lowered into boats by knotted blankets from upper windows. In the "Taunton Courier" of 1st December, 1824, we read:—"We regret that Mr. Stone of The York Hotel, having a numerous family to support, has suffered very considerable damage, not only as regards his house but in the loss of wines and liquors. Mrs. Street of the London Inn, a widow with 3 children has also been deprived of considerable property. Mr. Gale, Linen Draper and Mr. Longman, Druggist, in the Market Place were great sufferers. Mr. Edmonson of Bond St. [later Barrett's] had his shop of goods completely swept away. We are happy to report that everything will be renewed this season." So ends the report.

Mr. John Pile, Ironmonger, Fore Street, and Mr. Stone's Grocery Store in New Street were flooded, and they received £30 from the subscription hat.

The Esplanade was then only an earth bank. Not very long before this storm some London tradesmen opened a shop for the sale of silks, and other costly goods (where the house of The Marine Hotel now stands). This exposed place received the full fury of the storm. The waves rushed through the building carrying the drapery before them and the next day silks of all colours rolled and unrolled were found strewn about different parts of the town.

In this same storm the Chit rock crumbled and fell. For some reason or other it was an object of veneration to the seafaring folk, and on a certain day in the year there was a procession to the Chit rock at low tide, when one of their number was chosen to be "King of Chit" and was duly crowned and enthroned on the rock. The last King of Chit, called Bolt, survived his kingdom for thirty years.

The sea wall was commenced in 1835 and completed in 1838 at the cost of more than £2,000. Previous to this there existed only a bank of earth which was a very precarious safeguard between the sea and the houses, and during storms these houses were flooded.

The whole aspect of the shore was changed with the disappearance of the shingle and the disastrous breaking up of the sea wall. Holes appearing on the Esplanade from time to time were ignored by the Local Board of the seventies and eighties. They repaired the surface instead of paying attention to the foundations. Mr. Tindall states:—"From on or about December 16th, 1921, the finishing touch was given to an important sea defence scheme which has cost upwards of £30,000. Stout oak planking was added to the framework of the iron groin at the end of the west pier.

In 1922 the shingle beach was well supplied with solid terraces. At the York steps shingle covered three or four of the ten steps.

During a storm about this time the lowest steps of Jacob's Ladder were carried way."

On 22nd November, 1923, a large hole developed in the Parade. This was stopped up and barricaded internally. Three weeks later another hole appeared by the Shelter. On that day the town was flooded, the water reaching to Culverwell's.

On 19th December holes were filled up. A week later the mended holes again were broken and the town flooded. This time floods engulfed the gas and electricity works.

In 1924, just 100 years after the other great storm, the terrible thing happened ! From our windows we watched the sea pounding and carrying away huge blocks of pavement and in some places the roadway. I remember seeing a shelter swallowed up in a chasm. Had the wind not changed its direction at the critical moment, some of the houses on the sea-front would probably have been destroyed.

The Beacon lamp was swallowed up, also a block of stone at the head of small stone steps opposite York Terrace. In my child-hood days a flagstaff was attached to this stone and each Sunday a flag was hoisted bearing the name "Bethel".

The repair of the damage cost the town £80,000.

There were great rejoicings when the Minister of Transport reopened the sea-front in 1926.

A dwarf wall and drains beneath the road and pavements now enable the water to flow back into the sea. Groins have been placed on the beach.

My father, Mr. James Pepperell, drew plans for the Esplanade to be extended and carried round to Jacob's Ladder. (1959—This scheme is now being carried out). The cliff at the Battery field was to be sloped back, and a chineway made reaching to the shore on the same principle as the Hangar. The apron at the foot of Jacob's Ladder was the only part to be carried out and this has been much used for bathing tents and deck chairs.

On the face of the old sea wall opposite Kingswood, about 3 ft. below the Esplanade, there was a tablet erected at the expense of

E. H. B. Hughes Esq.,
Lord of the Manor, and of
many Voluntary Contributors,
In the year 1835.
George H. Julian, Architect,
James Clarke, Builder.

This stone was restored by John Skinner, 1914. In 1891 there was a dispute between the Local Board and the Lord of the Manor, Colonel J. H. Balfour, both claiming the Sea-shore; how it was decided I do not know, but the above tablet will be interesting. This tablet disappeared when the sea wall was destroyed.

HARBOUR

THAT there was once an open Harbour at Sidmouth into which vessels could enter from the sea, is a question of little doubt. In some writs of Edward II and III a deed of 1322 may be looked upon as proof of the fact. It is probable that the whole of the Ham formed an estuary where ships could lie in still waters. At that time, we learn, Sidmouth was a borough of no inconsiderable size and had to furnish 3 ships and 62 mariners at 40 days' warning. This it had to do annually.

The Rev. James Evans, M.A., states that the land west of the town formerly projected far beyond its present boundary, and probably formed a light or natural pier, alongside which vessels could shelter in stormy weather. In 1811 the sum of £15,252. 2s. 11d. was subscribed, but an opposition party raised obstacles, as they desired one to be built at Chit, so the project fell through. Again in 1825 we read of an estimate of £19,140 for a harbour to be built at the Western end, of which sum £15,320 was subscribed, but this project also came to nought.

However, the Sidmouth people, undaunted, in 1836 attacked with courage a scheme for enclosing an area of 10 acres on Chit Rock by running out two piers. A tunnel was carried for more than half a mile through the base of Salcombe Hill, and a railway laid all the distance. I have been told that when the engine arrived, it was too big to go into the tunnel: how far this is true I cannot say. The foundation-stone was laid with great ceremony, on the Chit Rock, where it still can be seen at low tide. Nearly £12,000 was spent and wasted. The Freemasons attended wearing full dress and regalia.

In 1831 a sea wall was built from the Salcombe end to Fort Cottage, marked midway by a round turret. A further portion extending to Clifton Place was built by the harbour committee; this wall would have been carried to the harbour.

In 1862 when the project for the railway was proposed, a harbour was included in the scheme, and yet another £7,200 was obtained and lost ! And only the railway was proceeded with.

In 1875 Mr. John Dunning, having purchased the Ham, erected Gas Works and prepared to make a harbour on a private plan of his own, but his plans also came to nought. In a big storm of

1877 the huge blocks were carried away one by one and the crane went with them.

In 1913 a councillor constantly urged that a harbour be built at the eastern end, where at that time the Esplanade ended at the Drill Hall. On 5th February, 1919, the same councillor produced a letter from the Board of Agriculture and Fisheries containing a proposal to send an Engineer to prepare plans for the scheme, as a "Peace Memorial", but other Councillors decided against it. And the scheme was dropped.

CHAPTER VII
THE TOWN

ALTHOUGH I intended to write mainly about Sidmouth from the "eighties" onwards, I must touch on some of its earliest happenings inspired partly by old prints, which I have gleaned from various inhabitants, and so enjoyed copying. These (with the various tit-bits gladly related to me by old friends who lived before my time) will, I hope, interest the reader as much as the gleaning of them has delighted me. In 1849 the delightful thatched houses in Church Street and the Market Place were all occupied by people whose families are still in Sidmouth.

Anna Sutton
Copied Feb.
1951

On the left of my sketch can be seen the drapery shop (now Fields). With the exception of plate glass windows replacing the small panes, the entire outside building is unchanged today.

The first draper, named Gale, suffered loss in the great storm of 1824. Mr. Hall (whose name appears in the sketch) followed.

The other two shops were Mackenzie, hairdressers (later Orman), with the Post Office in the middle.

An amusing article appears in a journal dated 1887, entitled "Progress Backwards", when the Post Office was removed to Fore Street (now Timothy Whites). It was freely asserted that pecuniary aid was offered by one or two Fore Street tradespeople, who clubbed together and agreed to pay the rent of the new offices. The removal was to make Fore Street the main street. I have been told that they paid once and no more !

In my sketch of 1884 the picturesque thatched buildings appear in a dilapidated condition, and in 1886 they were bought for

CHURCH STREET, SHOWING OLD MARKET, 1849

demolition (with the White Hart Inn) by the Local Board, who were severely reprimanded when a Government enquiry was held, because they bought the property before applying for powers to borrow the money to do so. The price paid was £700. A journal of 1886 states that the walls were over 4 ft. thick and needed strong efforts by horses and men for their demolition. In an old chimney in the centre of the block were found large slabs of dun-coloured stone and other indications which showed that the buildings were built between 1574 and 1587.

In a sketch looking down Church Street in 1849, note the old pebbled paths with lamp standard and socket for holding oil lamp. Also the donkey and cart then used for scavenging. On the right of sketch, the upper parts of the buildings are unchanged today.

Most of the shops in Church Street were general stores. I have been told many amusing tales by old folk, who remember those days. A Mrs. Frost, famous for her "Viggy Pudden" (Figgy pudding), which she sold at a "happeny" a slice. One man told me that he once asked for a "penneth", and she exclaimed:— "Lawks a messy yu c-a-a-nt ait a penneth t'would m-a-a-k-e ee zick !"

Another tale is of children, who went to buy nuts and were allowed to help themselves to a handful for a halfpenny, but they were never allowed a second "try". Just picture their fingers stretched to their utmost before plunging !

One rather "tall tale" is of an old woman biting a raisin in half to make weight.

A disastrous fire in 1927 completely altered the face of Church Street, destroying the quaint old thatched houses and a grape vine seen in old prints of 150 years ago. (This was said to have been brought from Hampton Court.) Many old names have gone. Hayman's have for many years replaced old Sam Wheaton, whom I just remember as butchers. Happily the good old names of Collier and Gliddon remain and Hope Cottage still stands sentinel at the top, as it appears in our oldest prints.

In Ebdon's Court, off Church Street, stood the old thatched Primrose Cottage, once the home of "Happy Churchill" and his "chirpy" little father and mother. It was demolished recently.

I have been told that in very early days the Market Place was outside the Church gates. In an old print donkeys carrying goods in panniers can be seen, also stocks for four persons. Another thing which points to the site of the Market being here is that the street leading into Western Town, now known as Chapel Street, was once known as Silver (or Silva) Street, a name associated with the proximity of a market. The delightful old houses in this street are well preserved. The tall building, Canister House, I am told, was once "Pearcey's Boarding House", which had a stretch of garden leading to the sea. Next to this on the corner stood the Inn, "The Jolly Sailor", a fitting name, as it led into Bedford Square, where lived the good old fisherfolk, the Woollies and the Wares and Conants.

Garages now stand on this site, also on the site of Silver Court, where I remember the families of Pinn, Pike, Cockburn, Cooper, Cordey and old Granny "Wopple" Tyrrell, and Virgie Merrifield. At the corner lived Charley Merrifield. Charley loved the sea and it is said that he built a capstan inside his cottage, and there it had to stay because he couldn't get it out !

An old "pound" stands intact next to Burgoynes Garage.

THE MARKET PLACE

THE first market we read of was held about 1200, at the time of Richard, the second Vicar of Sidmouth, where "sheds, stalls or shops" are spoken of in "In Marcato de Sidemuie". The first Market House was a low structure, having a painted weathercock.

Another house was built in 1839 (seen in my sketch of 1849). It was purchased from the Manor by the S.U.D.C. in 1903, together with the market tolls, for £2,000. This building was demolished in 1929 and another was then built.

In 1883 a conservatory was built at the corner of Old Fore Street and New Street. This building was erected for Mr. W. Hine-Haycock. It had an octagonal dome at one end (seen in my sketch of Old Fore Street, 1884), built of glass and iron, fitted up for the display of shrubs, plants and fruit, etc. It was occupied by Mr. Berwick. Everyone was pleased, as it substituted a ground floor building for a dirty brick wall enclosing a rubbish yard.

In 1888 Mr. James Pepperell purchased the building at an Auction Sale for £410 and revolutionized the Market Place by erecting the fine building known as the Belle Vue Dairy. Mr. Albert Maeer built the premises now Messrs. Drewe & Sons; Mr. Gliddon built a good solid block about the same time.

Although MacFisheries have replaced Lethaby's bookseller's shop, the upper part of the premises, also "May Smith's", remain intact (seen in my sketch of 1884), the latter I remember being Week's boot shop.

Sidmouth owes much gratitude to the late Mr. Lethaby, whose monthly journal and guide have delighted many present-day readers, and has been a source of great help to me whilst writing this book. I only remember his two elderly daughters, from whom I used to buy 1d. hanks of wool to make my dolls' clothes.

NEW STREET

A BIG fire in New Street destroyed Mrs. Casson's Grocery Stores and Opie's Outfitting Shop (now Mountstephens); fortunately "The London Tap", the London Hotel and old Assembly Rooms were saved. Opposite, at the corner was Mrs. Hutching's china shop (The Midland Bank). A quaint little pork butcher's shop kept by old Mr. Warren came next. I can just remember mounting three steps and hearing the tinkle of a bell which was attached to the door. Then came Finch's, saddlers, Bridgeman's (later Buxton) shoe shop, and last but by no means least, Mrs. Caroline Russell's bakery and sweet shop (now Palks). What thrills we had gazing in at a window full of sweets, before spending our Saturday penny. This would buy a $\frac{1}{4}$d. "Hanky-Panky", a $\frac{1}{4}$d. strip of liquorice, a $\frac{1}{4}$d. "Everlasting stick", and a $\frac{1}{4}$d. stick of rock, and no sweets have tasted so good since !

OLD FORE STREET

IN spite of two Inns, "The Anchor" and "The Ship", being at the bottom and top of the street, Old Fore Street always impressed me by its old-world air of decorum, probably because, in my earliest memory, several of the shopkeepers were women, and the premises were dignified old buildings.

Mrs. Barnard (whose lace shop Miss Barnard still carries on), Mrs. Mitchell and Mr. Bray (antiques), Miss Dare, famed throughout England for her sausages, and Mrs. Bolt, home-made provisions (especially toffees !). The structure of her shop and also the next shop (then Mr. Joe Mortimore, tailor) remain unchanged. There was also Wood's basket shop, followed by Godfrey and Lake and Sons, plumbers, whose family still carry on.

Across the road good modern shops now occupy the site of four old houses that have been demolished. I am told that Ben Smith lived in one and the three quaint shops with small windows, in the first of which Mr. Prout sold tobacco, snuff and fancy articles, with Mr. Sanders, cabinet maker, in the middle, and Mr. Moore, jeweller, on the corner. Trump's and Drewe's premises were built on the site of cottages occupied by Spencers and Stretchley Churchill.

FORE STREET

APART from new shop fronts, the fine old structures of most of the buildings in Fore Street remain unchanged.

Entering from the Esplanade on the left corner stood Temple House, first known by me as the L. & S.W. Bank. This bank was started in 1868 at Mr. Radford's office, Hope Cottage, and moved to Temple House in 1876. Later it became Barclays Bank, and is now the Savings Bank.

OLD FORE STREET, 1884

[Copied by Anna Sutton, 1951

Mr. Denby, a Honiton lace manufacturer, built High Hall; the late Mr. E. G. Trump bought the premises and converted them into an up-to-date café (now Tedbury's), with the Winter Gardens in the rear.

Next come The Dove Inn. This building with its old rounded window remains unspoilt. It was always a favourite meeting place for fishermen. I first remember Mrs. Guppy as licensee. Although a little lady, she held perfect control. I have heard that at any sign of disturbance she only had to point her finger to the door and the transgressor left !

Amongst her regular customers were "Scissors" Merrifield, who usually called for "Two penneth of Tiverton Middling" or a "Penneth of beer and ha'peth of Ale". "Too Wake Fiddy" or "Fiddy Smith", another "regular", so named because he boasted that he was too wide awake to be found napping. He was a fish hawker living in Dove Lane. In spite of his dark beetle brows and whiskers and piercing blue eyes, he was a popular, friendly character, and so was his wife, dear old Lizzie !

The well-respected family of Salter lived in Dove Lane for many years.

The old family of Prideaux took over the Dove Inn from Mrs. Guppy and are still there.

Premises, now Knights, were bought by Mr. James Pepperell and converted into a Restaurant (which was carried on by Mr. Darke). The same owner later converted them into Sidmouth's first Cinema, more details of which appear elsewhere.

I dimly remember an old-world garden with a summer house enclosed by a low wire fence in the space between Irish's and The Coffee Tavern (now Trump's and Frisby's). Mr. Turner, barber to the late H.R.H. the Duke of Kent in 1819 during his stay in Sidmouth, lived in the house now Irish's hairdressing establishment. The old thatched roof and upper structure remain, as also do the old Apothecary's premises, first known to me as "Chessals".

My first and happiest memory of The London Inn is of old John Lake and his popular son "Lew" standing outside those doors. They were owners of the fine Livery establishment and coaches and buses had their starting place there for many generations, amongst which were the famous coaches "Defiance" & "Telegraph". I can only remember a coach used on special occasions to convey parties to "The Meet", Football Matches and School Treats. What a thrill it was to hear the horn sounding, as the coach and four emerged from the stables opposite, with always a Channing on the box, flourishing his whip. I can only remember the Channings and Freemans as coachmen for Lake. Happily the families of both remain with us.

FORE STREET, 1884

In those days the tradesmen of Sidmouth were gentlemen in the true sense of the word. In the early histories, the name of Stone & Gove appear as Grocers. The business established by Miss Sarah Gove in 1813, later taken over by her husband, Mr. John Trump, retains the name but has recently changed hands, the fine old building externally unchanged. I like to recall Mr. William Trump, a fine genial man, with side whiskers, appearing in his doorway with gold watch chain stretched across his imposing figure. Also Jeweller Uglow in grey frock coat and silk hat in his shop (now Boots), old Mr. and Mrs. Culverwell, grandparents of the present stationers, Mrs. Bond, a tall handsome woman whose shoe shop was next to Hook's (later Hawkins) and "John-John" Ebdon standing in the doorway of the Commercial Inn laughing and rubbing his hands as he exchanged witticisms with "Banty" Hook in his fish shop across the road. The sound of their voices would quickly bring Fred Whitton and Danny Tedbury to their doors to join in the fun, and then from the grocer's shop at the corner out would come Jim and Chris Coulson to shout across their "Titbits of fun", and laughter rang out loud and long. Those convivial folk would hop into the Bar, which was tucked discreetly away in Trump's Lane, to be served and entertained by the popular and humorous attendant, "Freddy Winter". The Bar has been closed for many years.

It must be remembered that in those days there were no motor cars to drown their voices, or endanger children, who trundled their hoops along the streets, whipped their tops, played at marbles or hop-scotch on the pavements in safety. Those were indeed the days ! Before leaving Fore Street, I have been told that a Tailor named "Monkey" Holwill could be seen sitting in his shop (now Hinton & Lake's). He was rather unpopular, and the possessor of a red, bulbous, protuberant nose.

A verse was written of him:—"Old Holly's nose was red, Old Holly's nose was strong, T'would be no disgrace to old Holly's face if half of his nose was gone."

HIGH STREET

I was fortunate in being able to copy a very comprehensive sketch of High Street, 1870, extending to the cottages now the Wesleyan Chapel. Apart from modern shop fronts, most of the old buildings remain unchanged. Four Banks have replaced old buildings—Woolworth's stand on the site of the lovely old Regency building once occupied by Doctors Hodge, Macindoe, Bird and Grant Wilson. The little pony stands outside a butcher's shop, and Hayes Cottage, which was then Bolt's (now Holmes). Happily the family

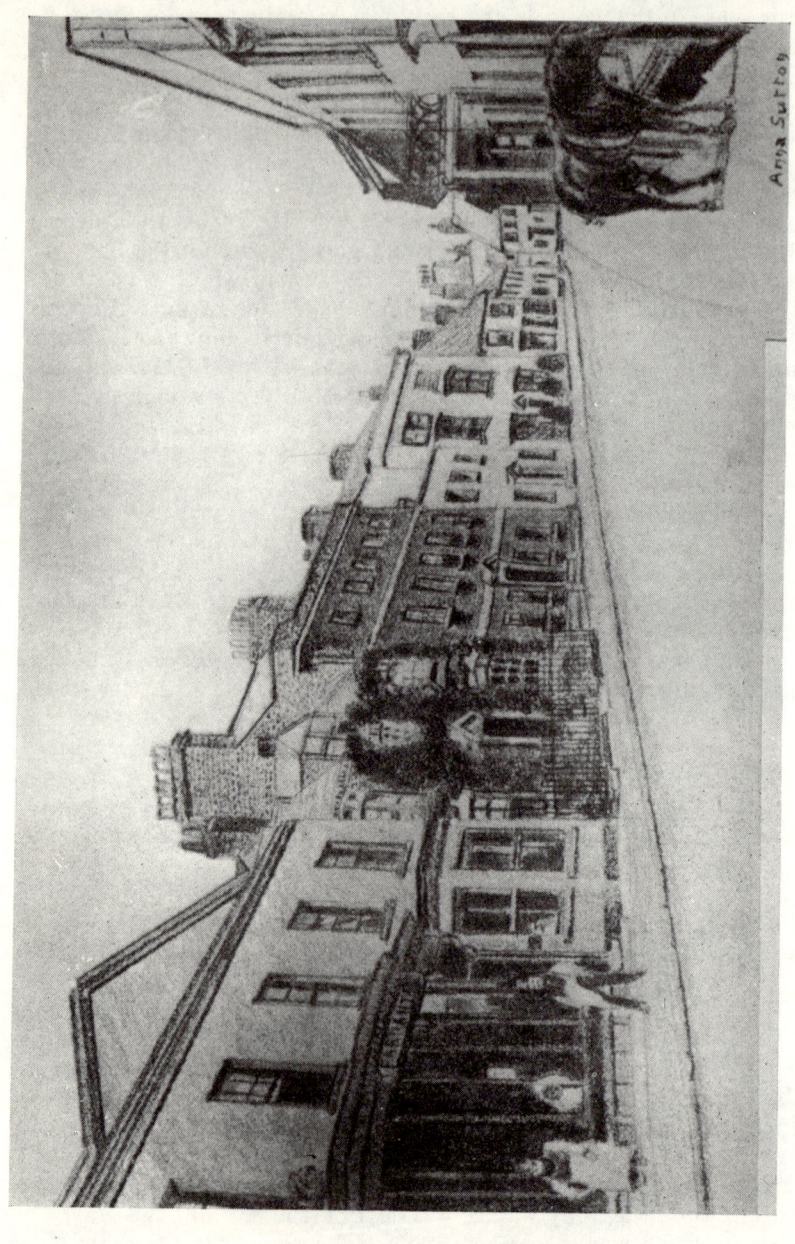

Anna Sutton

[Copied 1951

OLD HIGH STREET, ABOUT 1870

known as S. E. Sellick, Ironmongers, still occupy the house in which generations of their family were born. The upper part of the lovely old building (minus the creeper) remains the same as in my sketch of 1870. Although the structure remains unchanged, the name of Potbury has replaced "Farrant", which appears in my sketch. Mr. Charles Farrant built the furnishing shop (now Messrs. Potbury) in 1849; when he died Mrs. Ann Farrant took over on 1st December, 1861. Mr. James Hussey acted as Auctioneer and Valuer.

The Govier family, who lived in the unspoilt old Tudor House, have crossed the road into the China shop, which Mr. Govier tells me is over 300 years old. He covered the thatched roof with slates and filled in a stream which flowed past his door.

Note the lovely little "Clovelly House" tucked in between Barclay's and Skinner's. Albion House, Clode's (Broughton's, bakers) and the little thatched building remain. Wesley House with its garden perched high on land (once the river bank) is there, but the Grand Cinema which was recently burnt down was built on the site of Union Court, a quaint little place ascended by steps passing beneath an arch.

It delights me to go down a short passage and have a peep at the old wrought-iron gate opening on to a patch of green, behind "Connies".

In a quaint little shop (now Carter's Furnishing shop) I remember two prim maiden ladies named Ware, keeping a small haberdashery shop. A cob wall enclosed Myrtle Hall, Upper High Street, built by General Grenfield, with gardens covering the whole site of Myrtle Terrace, and the Masonic Hall. I dimly remember being carried past and seeing flowering shrubs and trees above the wall. Although red brick modern houses were built there, it is very pleasing to see charming gardens in the front. Next to the entrance to Blackmore Hall, Hillsdon still stands (minus the old Regency Porch). Hillsdon housed many doctors, and part of the premises is still a surgery. It will be best remembered as the home of the popular Dr. Leonard Williams, whom I have heard spoken of as a benefactor and lover of Sidmouth; he was followed by Doctors Leon, Colclough, Cohen and Fison (now James, Chemist). I am glad to have remembered Pike's Cottages. In the first cottage lived Miss Batten, well remembered by older inhabitants, especially boys (some now grandfathers), who tell me how they teased her. Her assorted goods were displayed in the cottage window, which was lighted by a candle; through a small hole boys would blow out this candle and shoot peas; it is not to be wondered that she became cross when, as a small child, I once went to buy a "Judy-come-

Anna Sutton
Copied Feb
1951

PIKE'S COTTAGES, HIGH STREET

tickle-me", which was the name given by our Dadda to wooden
dutch dolls. She thought I was making fun of her! Jimmie Jones
and George Hall, scissors grinders and umbrella repairers, lived in
one cottage, whilst Mr. May, shoemaker, lived in a cottage in the
court. The last cottage (occupied, we thought, by Father Christmas)
was our greatest thrill. Mr. and Mrs. Perry lived there. He was a
fine upstanding man with very blue eyes and white beard, and was
a model for many artists, and I remember him sitting patiently
and cheery; his son Roger inherited that cheeriness.

Newbery's have replaced Prince & Vincent's Bakery, and The
Irish Linen Shop replaces the little creeper-covered cottages occupied
by the Butters family. Opposite, a Garage covers the site of Burgoyne's Smithy. An up-to-date Milk Bar is a welcome addition to
Maeer's Dairy, which happily remains in the hands of this respected
old Sidmouth family. Curtis's, Ironmongers (now Ford's), built in
1799, was built on the site of the Old Mills (details are found elsewhere).

We now reach Upper High Street.

UPPER HIGH STREET

PURCELL'S little shop held a great fascination for us. We never
tired of watching Mrs. Purcell "chop off" the treacle which issued
from a hole in the side of a large canister into a jam jar. Joey Patch,

a blind man, displayed his basketwork in one of the small windows. The name can be seen on the little shop in my sketch of The White Hart Inn.

Shops replace the houses occupied by the families of Illsley and Drewe.

The road leading into Newtown comes next.

Newtown was a rather exciting and awe-inspiring vicinity to a small child, awesome, because the Police Station with P.C. Ford was at the bottom. Exciting because Billy Hunt lived there! Billy couldn't pronounce his "Rs" and he blinked; I never saw him wearing anything but a frock coat, green with age, a chimney-pot hat, and a royal blue tie. He was a popular, simple, though lovable character, vamped on the piano for parties or dances, but best of all, he showed the magic lantern at all our parties, always ending with the first moving picture shewn in Sidmouth, a snoring sleeping man, with a stream of mice entering his open mouth. "Chippy" Charles, a stonemason, who worked for Mr. Newman, also lived in Newtown. With flashing eyes and waxed moustache, Chippy exchanged jokes with everyone.

The upper storeys of the next block of buildings, now Schofields, etc., and The Radway Inn, remain unchanged, also Radway House and Enfield Villas across the road.

Vicarage Road, Temple Street, Landpart

Radway Lodge, enclosed by an old cob wall, was a charming, low, old-world house, surrounded by lawn, flower beds, and old shady trees. Once the home of the Jenkins family, Mrs. James Jenkins sold it in 1880 to Mr. Moisey who, on becoming Vicar, added part of it to the Vicarage, paying £5 a year for the addition to his lawn. I first remember it as the home of the Misses Walker.

In fancy I close my eyes and look back. It is a summer afternoon and cows stroll in a leisurely manner up the Salcombe Road, on the way to be milked at dairies in the town. A pony and trap stands outside Radway Lodge, with a groom at its head. The Misses Walker appear, step up and take the reins. The groom jumps up behind and sits with folded arms. The only sound to be heard is the "clip-clop" of the pony as it trots up the Vicarage Road. Cattle are grazing in a field of buttercups, which occupies the area between Enfield Villas and "The Grove".

Across the road a wall, reaching half way, encloses the old Vicarage and lawns, whilst fields known as Culver Park cover the remaining space to "The Hermitage".

The original vicarage was a small house of great age, enlarged about 1863 and still further enlarged in 1884. This vicarage was

copied by
anna Sutton
1951

THE OLD VICARAGE, 1826

demolished in 1928, at the same time as Radway Lodge. The
Radway Estate and Theatre, also the General Post Office, houses
in Connaught Road, and Victoria Road, were built on the site.
A new vicarage was built in Culver Park, but became Culver Guest
House, when the present vicarage was removed to the Manor
Road.

The old stone walls and many of the trees remain on both sides
of the Vicarage Road.

A modern school has been built below "The Grove". This
lovely old house, once the home of Miss Acraman, a great worker
for the temperance cause, has recently been acquired by the
Wesleyan community.

"The Hermitage", "The Balsters" and "The Shrubbery" remain
preserved in their old-world beauty.

Turning into the Elysian Fields, a name suitably descriptive of
a cluster of lovely old houses. They were built in 1826–27, all
private houses with the exception of Sidholme. First known as
Richmond House, occupied by the Earl and Countess of Buckinghamshire, later the home of the Lindemanns, the late Lord Cherwell

(Professor Lindemann) was born there; now known as Sidholme Guest House.

I remember it as a house filled with beautiful furnishings, and rare treasures, having a fine music room and organ.

Below stands Temple Cottage, now Fairlawn, the home of Dr. and Mrs. Gibbens.

Across the road a modern house, "Curraheen", and Elysian Villas have replaced old thatched buildings.

Temple Street and Landpart, as described to me by older people (much of which I remember) might have been a delightful village on its own, with its Manor and small farms, until the aspect was changed by the advent of the speculating builder.

Entering Temple Street, on the left, Jago's Grammar School is now a Warehouse. On the right Clarke's Smithy, followed by Goss, stood behind. Dunn's the plumber, Hooke, tea merchant, and Cload, pork butcher, were the only shops. The Volunteer Inn stands unchanged, where many generations of Newtons have been "Mine Hosts".

Why was the Constabulary not built on the site of the old Gas works instead of *in front* of an old house and garden?

On the left, the Brewery, built in 1832. The name of Searle preceded Harvey and Vallance. In the late Victorian period "Ribbon" building was a sign of the times where utility was considered before beauty. The builder certainly did good in providing homes for many, in a healthy position, when he built Peaslands Estate on pasture land known as Knappy Peaslands and the Brewery field. Lime Park, Yoruba and Florence Villas probably preceded Peaslands, as I am told that the two latter terraces were built on farm land and the farmer, known as "Gentleman Farrant", lived in Eaton Place (now Pope and Bailey). Dean's Bakery was built at the entrance to farm buildings and the pasture land adjoining was procured for the Cemetery, which was consecrated on 16th December, 1878.

Water Lane conjures up the names of Mansfield, Luxton, Selley and Holmes, etc. It is refreshing to feel that some of these dear people are still there to greet one, and occupy the cottages in which they were born. Miss Holmes, now 90, tells me that her grandfather, who built the cottages, once lived in, and added the wing to Woolcombe House, a very old building which was sold to Miss Leigh Browne, and is now the Museum, details of which appear elsewhere.

Three Holmes brothers, still living, are active members of the Sid Vale Association.

The charming old house of Ascerton, stands on an eminence overlooking the lands which were once the Manor of that name, which in old maps appears to cover the area from here to Woolcombe Lane, reaching to the river. The name of Richard de Ascerton is first mentioned in 1260.

Across the road from Ascerton House stand two charming old cottages, Fern Cottage (for many years the home of the Beacon family) and Ye Olde House. The late Mr. Ernest Selley lived in this house in which he and many generations of his family were born. I make special mention of him as being the creator of many beautiful landscape gardens around Sidmouth. Princes Row, Fuchsia Cottages and Knapp Cottages are still there, with old Sam Rowland's small farm buildings (now Potbury's). An old "Pound" at the entrance brings us to Turnpike Cottages, which happily all remain. I like to remember the delightful rural atmosphere when these were dotted between pasture lands and market gardens. The families of Mutters and Bill and John Irish can still be found in Turnpike Cottages.

Although I do not remember the old Turnpike or Toll House, I remember the lovely old Devonshire lane, known as Turnpike Lane, with pasture land and cornfields dotted with poppies on the site of the houses in Winslade Road.

Turnpikes are first mentioned in 1869 in a statement that the Salcombe Turnpike had been moved a mile further out towards Trow Hill. I have not found any mention of the Turnpike at the bottom of Salcombe Road where the old Toll House remains.

The Act for repairing the road from the great East and West thoroughfare known as the Lyme Turnpike on Gittisham Hill to Sidmouth bears the date 21st May, 1816.

Honiton and Sidmouth Turnpikes or Toll Houses were sold at The York Hotel on 18th November, 1878.

The decision to purchase Salter's meadows for Council houses was made on 2nd March, 1914. Miss Leigh Browne's offer to lay out the land was gratefully accepted. There are two fine rows of 48 buildings, with a good wide road known as Sid Park Road. Mr. Dingwall was appointed as "Clerk of the Works". and Mr. J. A. Carter, of Exmouth, obtained the contract to build them.

Arcot Park was bought by the Council, who erected 90 houses; the Arcot Housing Estate is quite in keeping with its surroundings. The late Mr. R. W. Sampson, assisted by Mr. Dingwall, was the Architect, and these houses were opened by the late Mr. Neville Chamberlain on 24th May, 1927.

Lime Park or Sidbrooke was built by General Walker about 1828. It is an old Regency House standing in spacious grounds. The last occupant was Mrs. Lindsay-Cropper, before it was purchased by the Council. The house has been divided into suitable apartments for elderly folk, and attractive houses and bungalows built on these and adjoining lands extending to "Livonia".

CHAPTER VIII

PLACES OF WORSHIP

ALL SAINTS' CHURCH

ALL SAINTS' CHURCH was erected in 1837, and consecrated in 1840, The land on which it was built was given by Sir John Kennaway. Bart., of Escot. The Rev. Joseph Bradney, who then resided in Sidmouth, subscribed £1,000 and invested £500 in Stock. The building cost about £3,000.

The living was a perpetual curacy. The parsonage, a large Victorian building, adjoins the Church grounds. The Organ was erected in 1855 at a cost of £150. The Church was restored in 1871 and the organ was then removed to the south gallery. In 1881 Mrs. Hine-Haycock of Belmont purchased the Parish Church organ and presented it to All Saints'. The original organ was sold to the Congregational Chapel, where it still remains. The Mission Hall attached to the Church was built in 1884 and has accommodation for 230.

The Rev. B. Baring Gould was the Vicar from 1869 to 1878. The Rev. John Leathley Nightingale was Incumbent from 1895 to 1904.

In April, 1901, the infant son of the Rev. J. L. Nightingale was baptized in All Saints' Church. This is believed to be the first baptism. All Saints' became a Parish in 1918. The present Vicar, the Rev. H. Kitchen, was inducted in 1954. The church was first licensed for the solemnization of marriages in 1920.

THE CONGREGATIONAL CHURCH

IN June, 1811, a Protestant dissenting Chapel was opened in "The Marsh", having been erected by public subscription. The present Church is a fine old building in Western Town.

The first Pastor whom I remember was the Rev. Charles Rhodes. He came with his wife to Sidmouth to become Pastor in 1891 and remained until 1911. His much-loved wife predeceased him. During his ministry the Church was in a prosperous state and well attended. The Rev. Ernest Bernstein, and later the Rev. E. J. Hawkins, B.A., came to assist Mr. Rhodes and were ordained here. The latter left for the Southernhay Church in Exeter. The Rev. Humphrey Davies followed Mr. Rhodes. Many ministers have come and gone, the present being the Rev. Francis Gibbons. The late Mr. H. F. Selleck,

Mr. H. J. Price, Mr. Foyle, Mr. Thompson and Mr. Hawkins, who served for 35 years, were all Deacons and did much good work. Alas, all have gone. Mr. H. J. Price served for over 40 years and has only recently died, and the Church has thus sustained a great loss. Many old faces remain and they are a very happy community.

Another church was built at Primley to serve the growing population of that district.

On Sunday, 9th August, 1953, the Congregationalists celebrated their 107th Anniversary. Sermons were preached morning and evening by the Rev. Dr. J. S. Whale, M.A.

The Wesleyan Methodist Chapel

The first Wesleyan Chapel was the room now the Y.M.C.A. The stone was laid for the present Chapel on 10th July, 1884, and opened on 11th April, 1885. It is a well-fitted commodious building. The first sermon was preached there by the Rev. Mark Guy Pearce. The Church was enlarged and a fine organ and gallery installed in 1903. This friendly community has prospered and done much for its cause by acquiring Sidholme as a Methodist Guest House, and quite recently has acquired "The Grove". Large congregations fill the Chapel to its utmost capacity. Therefore it is probable that "The Grove" might be opened as a sister Chapel.

The Sidmouth Old Meeting or Unitarian Chapel

The Sidmouth Old Meeting was founded in 1710. An old Deed of Trust was dated 14th December, 1813.

The Chapel was part of an old thatched building with entrance from the High Street, the other part being the White Hart Inn with entrance from Mill Lane. The first minister, the Rev. Bennett-Stevenson, was followed by the Rev. William Palk in 1719. This building was demolished about 1884 and the present Chapel erected on the site.

The Schoolroom was completed in 1886 and enlarged in 1897.

The Leigh Browne Hall was built in 1938.

In 1939 a new Schoolroom was erected by Lady Lockyer and Miss Kilgour in memory of Miss Leigh Browne.

The Plymouth Brethren have for some years gathered in a hall at Holmdale.

The Convent

When the Jesuits came to Sidmouth in 1881 to find refuge, having been driven out of France, there were only four Roman Catholics in Sidmouth. "Sidmouth Journal" stated:—"Quite a stir was created among the inhabitants when it was learned that Peak House had been let by the Trustees of the Manor to four French Jesuits. It horrified some people, scandalized others, and astonished everybody !"

These men, who were students for the priesthood, proved themselves to be a peaceful community, interfering with no one, and rarely seen in the town. The feeling of apprehension proved to be unwarranted, when, after three years, they departed as quietly as they came.

A Convent was built (the foundation stone laid on 7th June, 1883) on land adjoining Bickwell Lane and Jenny Pine's Corner; also a nunnery and private dwelling house.

A few French Nuns, members of a Belgian Community, had resided temporarily at Cottington, under the name of The Convent of the Assumption.

An extract from a Journal of 1883 runs:—"On Thursday, June 7th, though it was in one sense a public ceremony, there were not more than two or three score persons present at the laying of the foundation stone of a Romish Chapel, besides those engaged in the transactions. The outer walls having been carried up to the first floor, planks covering the joists led across to a small altar-like table, bearing nosegays of flowers and surmounted by a Cross which was placed in the centre of what will be the Chapel.

"From the elevated position, on this genial summer's day, the prospect was a charming one, embracing the hill sides of Salcombe and Peak and the mouth of the valley with the Knowle Hotel and Sidmouth in the front bounded by the sea.

"The time appointed for the ceremony was 4 o'clock, and within a few minutes of that hour there was heard the sound of chanting voices in the distance, as a procession took its way through fields and orchards from Cottington, where the Nuns have for two or three years been located, to a gate at the side of the ground on which the Chapel is being built.

"The procession was led by a cross-bearer, carrying the emblem loftily upwards, having on each side an attendant with a massive candlestick and candle several feet high. Then followed about half a dozen choristers, with their service books, twice that number of children, a few ladies and gentlemen, six nuns, in their severe costume, and two others, presumably priests, and the chief ecclesiastic for the day, 'Father Collins' of Plymouth, a tall and venerable man with a pleasant manner and a clear distinctive voice. From twenty to thirty of the French Jesuit students from Peak House formed the rear guard. All who took any official part in the ceremony wore their characteristic surplices and robes. Two little boys in red frocks or tunics, the priestly Father being especially noticeable. The pamphlets distributed were in Latin and consisted of numerous prayers and chantings, of which the most noticeable was the melodious intoned 'Ora Pro nobis' (pray for us) sung a few score times. An address in English by Father Collins was listened to with much attention; reference was made to the devotions of the nuns, and the liberality of a donor to the building fund. Strange to tell, that donor is said to be a Presbyterian.

"The laying of the stone was performed with due ceremony, the engraved Cross on each of its sides being carefully traced over with the crowd by the Priest, who concluded by making two or three processional walkings round the platform and sprinkling walls and stones with Holy water which had been brought for the purpose.

"The Benediction was pronounced and Priests and Nuns with other helpers in the ceremony returned to Cottington chanting, as when they came."

The Convent buildings were enlarged in 1905. Another Chapel was built on the Radway Estate in 1936.

Matthew Bridges, the writer of that well-known hymn, "Crown Him with many crowns", lived and died in Sidmouth. Born in Essex in 1800, was brought up an Anglican, became a Roman Catholic in 1848. He lived as a tenant at Convent Villa, died on 6th October, 1894, and was buried in the Convent Cemetery.

Matthew Bridges published several volumes of poetry and history and was quite a noted man.

Miss Rose Trevor, another writer of delightful poems, is still living in Sidmouth.

CHAPTER IX

SCHOOLS

THE Rev. John Minshull, who died in 1663, founded the first National School in this parish, and the Schoolmaster's salary was £5 a year.

Built in 1811 as the first Dissenting Chapel, the building known as "The Marsh School", was established on 22nd June, 1821, and was a school "for the infant poor", kept by voluntary subscriptions. The old building remains and is now used for religious services. The old stone building, now known as the Parish Hall, was built about the same time as a school for boys. In "the seventies" Mr. James Burgoyne was Headmaster, and he was followed by Mr. Drewe. This school was closed down when the new school was built at Woolbrook. The lovely old Master's house remains in a good state of preservation.

All Saints' School, built for boys and girls in 1848 at the cost of £700, was enlarged in 1864 and again in 1906. I first remember Miss Edwards as Headmistress. Many hundreds of Sidmothians are grateful for the solid foundation they received under her tuition. Familiarly known as "Dolly Edwards", perhaps because she was so "petite", with dark beady eyes and Roman nose, she was like a little bird, small in stature, very just, feared, but honoured. The names of the teachers who were with her for many years are Miss Gertie Drewe, Miss Minnie Drewe (later Mrs. Potbury), Mrs. Wheeler (*née* Wattley) and Mrs. Morrell.

Special mention must be made of Miss Purchase, the one survivor, who was in charge of the infants. It was a pleasing sight to see her standing outside the door on the steps, facing the road, ringing a little tinkling bell to call the "tinies" to school. Her placid face and sweet welcoming smile shewed how she loved her wee charges, and I am sure they must have loved her. One can still meet her in Sidmouth looking little changed. Many of her children, now mothers and grandmothers, will be wishing that their children could be in her care. Later, the school, owing to reorganization by the County educational authority, became simply a girls' school, and when the new school in the Vicarage Road was opened it became the infant school for the district.

We read of many small private schools in our early history. In 1849 Lady Claridge is mentioned in Sidmouth Directory as a professional teacher, having a school for select young ladies at Villa Verdi (now Harston). We read later of Miss Harding's in High Street (now Eveleigh's) and Miss Tighe at 5 Cambridge Terrace. My mother went to school at "The Bays".

Many grandparents will remember Mrs. Copleston's Dame School at Newtown; she taught their parents, including my father, and after retiring for some years, "obliged" by relieving them of their infants !

I remember her as a little old lady wearing a black silk frock and lace cap. She grounded the children well in reading, writing and "sewing a seam". I was impatient, when told that I was "making Dadda's shirt", by drawing the cotton without a knot through a strip of flannel!

Our first school was kept by the Misses Gertrude and Lilian White at No. 1 Cambridge Terrace. (Miss Lilian died in 1958 in Sidmouth, aged 98.) We later attended a school for older children known as Radway School, kept by Miss MacDonald on the opposite side of the road. Later came Miss Le-Ray, whose school was taken over by the Misses Wheeler and Greene and our children attended this school, which was at Arcot House (now The Eventide Homes). Robin and Connaught schools followed. The Convent is a good and popular boarding school.

Miss Bellamy and Mrs. Halse have Kindergarten Schools. Cox's Grammar School was at 1 Fortfield Place, until it moved to Ottery St. Mary, where I believe it became merged into King's School. Mr. Jago's Grammar School was held at Temple House (now a Furniture Repository). St. Martin's Preparatory School, with the late Rev. W. S. Airy as Headmaster, was a fine school, and much sadness was felt when it had to be closed owing to Mr. Airy's ill-health. It has recently been reopened as a Kindergarten School. The National School in Vicarage Road and Woolbrook School are both excellent modern schools.

New Schools

WEST BANK SCHOOL for girls, opened in September, 1954, is a very fine school at the Manor House, situated in lovely grounds.

Situated in spacious grounds in Sid Road, Clevedon School for boys has recently been opened at the fine old house, once known as "Greenmount".

CHAPTER X

HOTELS AND INNS

SIDMOUTH is provided with some of the finest Hotels in the County. The first hotel to be opened was "The Bedford", built in 1805 as "The Shed". This fine old building stands in the centre of the sea-front and continues to be one of Sidmouth's most popular hotels. "The York" at the eastern end of the sea-front, built in 1811, has from time to time been much enlarged and modernized. "The London", situated in Fore Street, was in the early days an old coaching Inn. It is still a popular rendezvous of the Friendly Societies.

Built in 1805 as Knowle Cottage, the Knowle was opened as an hotel in 1882. Within ten minutes' walk of the sea, this fine up-to-date building stands in beautiful grounds, the only sign of its antiquity being the lovely old trees and shrubs surrounding it. Some years later Mr. Michael Healy bought the "Red House" and converted it into "The Fortfield Hotel". Overlooking the Cricket Field this fine building was honoured when H.R.H. the late Duke of Connaught took up residence there whilst wintering in Sidmouth.

In 1903 Colonel Balfour built "The Victoria" at the western end of the sea-front.

THE ROYAL GLEN

In 1920 Mr. Fitzgerald bought and enlarged "Belmont" adjoining the Cricket Field, and converted it into a luxurious hotel retaining its old-world beauty.

Known as Woolbrook Cottage when His Royal Highness The Duke of Kent resided there in 1819, "The Royal Glen" Hotel has been enlarged and beautified by its owner, Mrs. Martin. Whilst every modern convenience is supplied, this lovely old building retains its old-world atmosphere.

A spacious courtyard replaces the gardens of Marine Place. "The Riviera" Hotel was built by Miss Ratcliffe on the site. "The Torbay", facing the Cricket Field, was converted from a block of buildings known as Denby Place.

"The Westcliffe" and "Redlands" are modern hotels, charmingly situated overlooking the eastern bay, and near the Connaught Gardens.

Many other hotels have been developed from large private apartment houses. These include the "Woodlands", "Cedar Shade", "Littlecourt", "Meadhurst", "Eaglehurst", "Waterpark", "Cotmaton House", "Brinkburn", "Meadhurst", "St. Helen's", and on the sea-front, "The Faulkner", "Devoran", "Kingswood", "Elizabeth House", "Shenstone", "Wyndham", "The Sussex", etc. All the latter have emerged since the first world war, when apartment houses became non-existent.

In the early days the only accommodation for travellers was to be found at inns.

Among the non-residential inns are fine old houses: "The Dove", "Commercial", "Radway", "Volunteer", "The Mason's Arms", "Horse and Groom", "Swan", and "Balfour Arms", built recently at Woolbrook.

The Ship Inn. At the top of Old Fore Street stands "The Old Ship Inn" in a wonderful state of preservation. Said to be 600 years old, it is a substantial building with cob walls nearly three feet thick and was said to be once a Monastery. It then became an inn, and as Sidmouth was one of the chief centres of smuggling in East Devon, the premises were a rendezvous for smugglers.

A passage at the back led into Church Path, which in turn leads to the Parish Church, and from this may be deduced the close connection between church and contraband in the past. There is said to be an underground passage reaching to Blackmore Hall.

The extensive stables at the side and rear of the building, part of which are now a shop, show that farmers riding into Sidmouth market used the inn as a meeting place many years ago.

When licensing laws were imposed, the old passage to Church Path was bricked up because it was thought it was being used as

MARINE AND PORTLAND PLACE, 1815

Anne Sutton
Copied 1951

a private entrance. Up to comparatively recent times "The Old Ship Inn" was a notorious doss-house. In one room on the ground floor vagrants used to cook their own meals, and a large room on the first floor was their dormitory.

"Dappy Pinn" said that he remembered the property changing hands for 20 guineas, the money being handed over the bar in a quick deal during a typical rowdy scene, when Hubert Selley was the Licensee. The Ship Inn has been completely metamorphosed and is now a very nice Guest House.

CHAPTER XI

HOSPITALS AND NURSING

THE COTTAGE HOSPITAL

IN 1884 at a meeting held at Barton Cottage called by Mrs. Trepplin, it was decided to open May Cottage for use as a Hospital. Miss Leigh Browne offered to pay the rent for three years. In spite of opposition from a medical quarter, a hospital was opened on 14th March, 1885.

At Michaelmas, 1889, an anonymous donor offered a sum of £500 towards a building, and Colonel Balfour gave a site, which, with other subscriptions, enabled the Hospital to be erected to the plans of Mr. Cave. It cost £1,200 and accommodated eight to ten patients. Queen Victoria granted permission for her name to be given to the new building. Hence the name "The Victoria Cottage Hospital".

With the growing population it was apparent that a larger building was needed. Colonel Balfour presented a plot of ground doubling the site area which made extension possible, and plans were approved in 1928.

Private donations and subscriptions resulted in a fine Hospital being completed in 1930.

Pleasantly situated, this hospital has been (and still is) one of the best equipped and happiest hospitals in the County. Plans are being prepared for further extensions.

NURSING SERVICES

SIDMOUTH is well served in her Nursing Services—by The Red Cross and St. John Ambulance Brigade. A branch of V.A.D., Devon 28, was formed in Sidmouth many years ago.

During the 1914–1918 War Mr. T. D. Dewey opened Peak House as a Hospital, and many a service man who was nursed back to health there will remember with gratitude the care bestowed upon him by the late Miss G. Collins, O.B.E., Commandant; Dr. Cohen, Medical Officer, and the efficient band of Nurses.

The detachment was disbanded after the 1939–1945 War, but has since been re-formed and is now a thriving division. A new hall at Manstone was opened in December, 1952, with Mrs. O. Hepple as Commandant; Mrs. Pym, Assistant Commandant; Mrs. Fison, Nursery Superintendent; and Dr. Fison, Medical Officer. A junior branch of Cadets has been formed, with Miss Cohen in command.

St. John Ambulance Brigade

On 6th April, 1927, a meeting was held at the Manor Hall to promote a branch of St. John Ambulance Brigade.

Supt. A. W. Irish, Ambulance Officer H. Turner and Transport Officer E. Breach were appointed. Mrs. B. Lake undertook command of the Nursing Services. Miss Sheldon now holds that position.

On 10th January, 1936, a new Ambulance was dedicated on the Bedford Lawn. The dedication prayer was read by the late Rev. J. G. Cornish.

The Brigade has grown into a training institution with full-time attendants at their headquarters in Fore Street. It is good to see Sergt. Quaintance and Corporal Chick still at their posts, having served since 1934 and 1939.

In December, 1952, the Brigade paraded under the direction of Supt. A. W. Irish, Ambulance Officer H. Turner and Transport Officer Cyril Irish, when Dr. Richard Gray, Area Commissioner, with County Officer W. Wood, carried out an Inspection and expressed his pleasure with the turn-out of members and first-aid work.

On 18th April Sidmouth were being asked to stage the Annual County Competition for 1953. Much gratitude is owed to Divisional Surgeon Dr. H. R. A. Michelmore, whose help and enthusiasm have been outstanding; also to Mr. G. W. Hodges, who has been a keen supporter for many years.

For many years Divisional Officer and Secretary of Sidmouth St. John Ambulance, Miss Daisy Benham, of Beatlands Drive, who died on 10th June, 1958, in her 76th year, worked during the war at Sidmouth Civil Defence First-Aid Post. An active worker in the Nursing Division, she was responsible for collecting 100 guineas for the Hospital Comforts Fund.

The Queen's Nurse

Miss E. Salaman came to Sidmouth as the Queen's Nurse in 1930 and continues her service among us. Her wonderful skill and care in visiting and ministering to the sick have brought relief and healing to many thousand homes. Sidmouth is also fortunate in having a qualified Maternity Nurse and Infant Welfare Centre, where mothers can take their babies and receive expert advice.

CHAPTER XII

TRADE AND INDUSTRIES

POLWHELE describes Sidmouth as "A little fischar town". In 1630 Risdon writes in "Survey of Devon":—"Since the surrender to the Crown, Sidmouth is one of the chiefest fischar towns of this shire, and sendeth much provision to the eastern parts, but in some time past it was a Port of some account." Fish were plentiful in those days and we read of trading with Newfoundland. Men would be employed in ship-building in the docks, occupying the site on which York Terrace now stands.

Sir William Pole describes it in 1630 as a small market town famous for its fishing, and "Fairs are holden in the market-place on Easter Mon. & Tues.—the 3rd Mon. in Sept. for cattle".

In 1790 Sidmouth was a little straggling village with a few scattered cottages, surrounded by farms. Dairy farming and fishing were the main industries. Some dairies housed their cattle behind their shop premises. They were driven in from pastures in Vicarage Road, The Lawn and Salcombe Road (now Milford Road). Sidmouth was celebrated for her dairy produce, the richness of the soil and pasture-land providing milk, butter and cream of outstanding quality. Devonshire clotted (or clouted) cream, was renowned. Mrs. Bray, writing in 1836, remarks:—"The custom of preparing clouted cream is no doubt of great antiquity. I once told a woman that she little thought how ancient the custom of preparing it was. 'Ancient', she exclaimed, 'I'se warrant he's as old as Adam, for all the best things were to be had in Paradise, and our cream might certainly claim a place there!'" Right up to the 1939-1945 War, tons of cream were despatched weekly to all parts of Britain. The ban on its production was a great loss to the farmers and dairies.

Blacksmiths, Wheelwrights, Saddlers and Thatchers have practically disappeared, although some skilled thatching is still found on old houses.

In the decade between 1811 and 1822, when the beauties and soft climate became known, extracts from a journal state: "As a watering place Sidmouth deserves attention. It is much frequented by people of fashion and many high families."

Lodging houses were built and furnished, when visitors flocked into the town during the Summer. The fishermen were busy with pleasure boats and their wives tended bathing machines.

LACE

MANY women were employed in lace-making, which was in much demand; their children, too, attended lace-schools from the age of five and became experts, enjoying it too.

Much of the lace was taken to two Sidmouth lace-traders, Denby in Fore Street and Chick in High Street. These men paid for the lace from a store of groceries kept on the premises, thereby gaining much profit.

JOURNAL of 18th June, 1874, states:—

"SIDMOUTH LACE

We think, judging from the prize list of the lace show at the Exhibition of the Bath & West of England Society at Bristol, that the above name is more applicable than 'Honiton Lace', for the principal laurels for design and execution have fallen on our towns-folk."

Miss K. P. Radford of Sidmouth won the ladies' 1st prize for her beautiful designs for Banner Linen and 1st for trimming lace; Mrs. C. Hayman also took a prize for a coiffure.

Miss Barnard (grand-daughter of Mrs. Hayman) still carries on the lace-shop in Old Fore Street, where I remember her mother working. Her great-grandmother, Mrs. Nicholls, made a special pattern for H.R.H. The Duchess of Kent and H.R.H. Princess

Victoria. In 1830 Mrs. Hayman made the wedding lace for H.R.H. Princess Christian and a pocket handkerchief for H.R.H. Princess Louise. In 1934 Miss Barnard made a set of lace table mats for the Duchess of Kent, and in 1953 ruffles for the Duke of Wellington to wear at the Coronation.

Families with small-holdings in the outlying districts brought their produce into the town by pony and donkey carts and sold from house to house. The Churchills and Ebdons from Woolbrook and the Battens from Bowd, with their fruit and vegetables, etc. Although Sid Churchill has passed away, it delights me to see his son still selling from the same old two-wheeled covered pony-cart (1959). Now large motor vans bring goods and produce to the town, mostly descendants of the old families. Our shops are well provisioned and up to date, and are second to none.

"All-a-blowing and a-glowing" was a very welcome "cry" when each Saturday a barrow was wheeled into the Market Place filled with mignonette, wallflowers, stocks, pansies, musk, roses, etc., etc., all the old-fashioned sweet-scented flowers sold at a 1d. a bunch. I cannot remember the name of the vendor, or if he sold any other produce, as he was always known as "All-a-blowing". I never remember any particular Market Day, as the Market was rarely used.

In later years Baker's had a vegetable and fruit stall there, following Mrs. Wellaway.

Stalls of fruit, vegetables, meat and fancy goods now occupy the Market.

SLEEP'S FACTORY

THERE was much head shaking and doleful prophesying when it was reported that a Glove factory was to be built on land bought by Mr. Sleep of Knightsbridge in September, 1884, for £365, and there were visions of a great red block (like Ottery St. Mary). These forebodings turned to pleasure when people learned that the buildings would be of only two storeys, with no engine power, and therefore no factory chimneys, as the gloves would be hand made. Mr. Sleep proved to be a great benefactor to the town, not only by giving work to many without taking from the existing industries, at the same time making what could be termed as "Slum clearance". Stocker's Court, the site on which Holmdale is now built, was built in 1842 as five houses, but some years later the number was doubled by means of a wall along the centre of the row which thus cut them in half and thereby excluded light and air. This meant that five of the abodes fronted the street and five looked upon a yard in the rear surrounded by old sheds. Mr. Sleep also bought The Dolphin Inn, a beer house situated at the lower corner (below the Labour Exchange). This he converted into two houses for persons engaged at the works. At the same time he bought the Old Brewery and Malt House (the latter is still in existence) situated opposite the old Marsh School. The Dolphin Inn, which stood on the corner, was demolished and Merrifield House built, probably to house the factory manager. The factory did not survive many years and was withdrawn to London.

CHAPTER XIII

MEANS OF TRANSPORT

THE SIDMOUTH RAILWAY

WHAT a week of rejoicings welcomed the opening of the Sidmouth Railway on Monday, 6th July, 1874. The Church bells rang out merrily, bunting decorated the town, fir trees lined the esplanade, and ornamental arches outside the York and Bedford Hotels, bearing the words "Welcome" and "Peace and Prosperity". On the first day over 1,000 children from Sidmouth, Sidbury and Salcombe Regis, headed by the Band, marched to the Station, where they saw the arrival of the 1.45 train and the departure of the 2.40; after which they marched to a field in Landpart (the "tinies" being conveyed in waggons), where a sumptuous tea was served and games and sports continued until 8 o'clock.

Steamers brought a large number of people from Exmouth and Teignmouth to the Regatta. On the last day about 400 old people were given an excellent dinner and tea in the Knowle Grounds and were taken for a trip over the new line, after which they were given a silver coin direct from the Mint.

About 50 shareholders "partook of a dinner of the most 'recherché' description in the Town Hall".

Trustees of the Manor bought Peak House and estate with the intention of making large-scale developments. These included a scheme to carry the railway through the Golf Course, over Peak Hill to Budleigh Salterton and Exmouth; fortunately for Sidmouth these plans came to naught.

OTHER MEANS OF TRANSPORT

WHEN I was young the principal means of transport was the Railway. A horse-drawn "Station Bus" used to convey passengers to and from the station, with Nobby Hamson on the step. Those needing the bus left a message at the Office, as is done now when taxis are needed. For a charge of 6d. passengers would be called for (or returned from the trains); luggage was hoisted to the top of the bus, reached by a ladder fixed at the back. Sometimes passengers had a long ride if calls were made on the outskirts.

Messrs. John Lake were proprietors of The London Hotel Livery Stables, their stables being in East Street, also on the site which is now the St. John Ambulance Headquarters. They hired out horses and conveyances of every description. There were several owner-drivers, who could be found waiting for hire on cab stands along the Sea Front; Messrs. Hiscox, Dagworthy, Alf Dean and J. Dean, Harry Spencer, W. Parratt, "Hockety" Spencer, two Smith brothers, etc. It was a delight to see the well-drawn carriages and pairs of private families (and there were many in those days) with cockaded coachmen and footmen. (Most of the big houses are now Hotels.) This brings to my memory an oft-told tale. A light Barouche, drawn by a pony, belonged to the Rev. G. Baugh, Vicar of Salcombe. One day their old coachman, named Raffell, was taking Mrs. Baugh to pay a call in Sidford. The pony stopped outside "The Blue Ball" and was only persuaded with difficulty to proceed. On Mrs. Baugh enquiring the reason, Raffell replied:—"Aw 'tis a gait he got Mum !"

A brand new Brake appeared at the time of King Edward's Coronation, with a double row of seats for two (as today); this was a big stride from the waggonettes. At the time of these horse-drawn conveyances, passengers got out and walked up the hills. There were always donkeys at Spencers and Dagworthys ready for hire, with a donkey boy, and as we grew older ponies. Then came bicycles. I do not remember the "Penny-farthings". I have been told that Mr. Trick had a cycle shop, where Hook's Fish Shop is now.

Later, Mr. Ted Mitchell opened the first Ladies' cycle shop in High Street between Lloyds and The Westminster Banks. There were shocked exclamations and head-shakings at the boldness of females who rode bicycles, and very full-divided skirts were worn. (Fortunately we were children, so hadn't to wear long skirts.) Bicycles were hired out at 6d. an hour. At first we had one bicycle of our own to be shared by four of us, and so had to hire three. That we are alive to tell the tale is a wonder ! There was no free-wheel, just two foot rests, attached below handle-bars. Oh, the thrill of sticking our feet up on the foot rests, just outside Rock Cottage and "coasting" down to the Esplanade ! Oh, the tumbles we had when brakes had to be applied suddenly, but we were careful to hide our bruises from our parents.

Mr. Dagworthy came to the fore, with the advent of the motor car about 1908–9.

Mr. J. A. Orchard had the first car, and I remember Mr. Ernest Bonner buying one of the earliest ones, a 1906 model, in which he took us for a ride. Enveloped in heavy coats and thick veils tied around our hats, we set out with mixed feelings of thrill and fear, at the vibration and noise of the engine. In the Sidford Road the car stopped dead. I cannot remember how we got out of the difficulty!

On 11th June, 1911, came Mr. Hodges with the first Taxi-cab for hire, a very welcome innovation; he built up a thriving business. From then onwards things moved apace and garages sprang up all around. When Messrs. Lake gave up their Offices, they were taken over by "The Sidmouth Motor Company" with Mr. Griffen as manager. Later the company amalgamated with Dagworthy's (I might add in more ways than one, for Mr. Griffen later married Miss Dagworthy.)

With the opening up of the "Devon General" and other omnibus services, Sidmouth is now well served, and country is traversed that was never seen before. Messrs. Greenslade, who have taken over coaches from Burgoyne & Dagworthy, provide motor coaches to convey passengers to visit all surrounding "Beauty Spots" in the greatest of comfort.

Special mention must be made of "The Toast Racks", two useful conveyances taking and fetching to Peak and Salcombe Hills every half-hour during the summer months.

We sadly miss the familiar figure of "Lawyer Dunn" sitting in the driving seat of his "State Coach" (the Toast Rack).

Happily we still greet several old friends around at the garage. "Nobby" Hamson, Joe Freeman, Follett, Mitchell, Slade, etc.

On the Esplanade Greenslade's Coaches stand ready to convey passengers to the southernmost resorts of Cornwall on the West, and Weymouth and Bournemouth on the East; there is also a good coach service extending to Scotland. What more transport facilities could we wish to have?

The nearest air port is at Exeter. Fortunately there is nowhere in the neighbourhood suitable for an aerodrome.

PLEASURE STEAMERS

WE first read of *The Duchess of Devonshire* calling at Sidmouth in 1894. There were three Pleasure Steamers calling at Sidmouth, the *Victoria* dropping and picking up passengers for Torquay and sometimes Dartmouth. Although there was no pier, there was plenty of shingle and a small bridge used to be thrown out from the boat to the shore. The *Duke of Devonshire* conveyed passengers to Bournemouth and Weymouth, calling at Seaton and Lyme Regis. The "Duchess" plied mainly between Exmouth, Budleigh Salterton and Lyme Regis. The Town Crier announced the time of arrival and departure. In the 1914–18 War these steamers served in the Bristol Channel Ferry Service, but only the "Duchess" returned for pleasure trips. It was a sad day when she was wrecked off Sidmouth in 1934. My husband and I were sitting in our window at Carlton Mansions. There was rather a "swell" but not very rough sea; suddenly we saw she was in difficulties and could not be righted and she came in "broadside"! All the passengers were taken off and no one hurt. She was dismantled where she lay and pieces of metal wreckage can still be seen embedded at low tide.

CARRIERS

THE first carriers that I remember were the Hollands; they lived in Mill Street and ran their waggons to and from Exeter, picking up goods and passengers, mainly the farmers' wives and their produce. Mr. Holland had not only sons to help him, but a daughter, Mary Patience, who told me that, at the age of 7 she used to take two horses to White Cross (riding one) to meet and be attached to the waggon in order to draw it up the hill. The mother of several sons (one the well-known "Bunny Palmer"), with a daughter and grand-children, in 1951 at the age of 75 Mary Patience enjoyed a sea-bathe! Many felt sad when she died suddenly in 1952.

She gave me this poem:—

> "Glorious, sunny Sidmouth
> Place of peace and calm.
> Nestled in embrace of hills,
> A perfect chain of charms.
> Each must see to comprehend
> Each must gaze and wonder
> All who fail to see the sight,
> Make an awful blunder.
> Peak and Salcombe Hill top,
> Core and Salter's Cross
> Indescribable by pen,
> Speech is at a loss.
> If you don't feel like walking
> The pilgrimage to make
> Just you take a trip
> And go by Holland's brake.
> For Dick Holland is as jolly a chap
> As on the road you'll "vind"
> "Vor if ee 'a-a-n-t got room in 'vrint'
> 'Ee'll let 'ee jump 'op' be-hind!"

CHAPTER XIV

IN THE GOOD OLD DAYS

EXTRACT from the Rev. E. Butcher's "Beauties of Devon", 1836.

GENERAL INFORMATION

Pleasure Boats. Attended by expert and careful seamen are always ready; the principal are kept by J. & R. Bartlett, Thomas Heiffer, John Taylor, Henry Conant, R. Boult, W. Radford, T. Selley, and T. Sanders, etc.

A twohour sail is charged		5s.	0d.
To Exmouth and home	£1.	1s.	0d.
To Dawlish or Teignmouth	£1.	5s.	0d.
To Seaton	£1.	1s.	0d.
To Lyme	£1.	5s.	0d.

Bathing Machines kept by Marmaduke Taylor, and Thomas Heiffer for Gentlemen.

Terms of bathing one shilling first time and sixpence each time after.

By Mrs. Barrett & Co. for Ladies. One shilling and sixpence first time and 1s. each time after.

Sea Baths (*Warm*) fitted up in an extremely convenient and comfortable style have been established both by Mr. Hodge, and Messrs. Stocker & Longmore; they embrace every mode of bathing.

Horses may be hired of B. Butter, Painter, William Gove, Grocer, William Gale, Linen Draper, Dunsford and Hill, Saddlers; H. Smith have quiet and manageable donkeys with proper saddles for invalids. The latter supplies *Asses' Milk*.

A Coach to and from Exeter is established in a most respectable manner by Mr. William Street of The London Inn. As it is well horsed, and in every way deserving encouragement, the proprietor confidently hopes for the patronage of the Public.

Fare to Exeter and *back*, 10s. inside; 7s. outside.

A Caravan with a strong powerful horse, and driven by an experienced coachman, runs three times a week to Taunton and returns to Sidmouth the alternate days; carries four passengers.

Sidmouth to Honiton 4s. 6d., ditto to Taunton 12s. Taunton to Honiton 8s.

Carriers. John Way and William Cockram convey goods to and from Exeter every Monday, Wednesday and Friday.

J. Govier conveys goods to and from Honiton every Saturday.

Sedan Chairs and Bath Chairs are kept by William Rugg, R. Puddicombe, J. & R. Bartlett, W. Radford and T. Selley, etc.

A Violin, etc. Parties desirous of making a dance at a short notice, will be waited upon by James Barnard near the Post Office.

THE MAIL CART

Feb., 1822. "The Mail Cart left Sidmouth for Awliscombe (Near Honiton, 10 miles), returning in the morning; inhabitants could hear his return along down Old Fore Street to the Post Office in the Market Place. His lively whistle could be heard."

(March, 1919. Mr. Henry Banks, Mail Cart driver, resigned after 34½ years. He was presented with a wallet of Treasury Notes.)

The Post arrives from Exeter every morning about 9 o'clock, which conveys the letters from London put in two days previous. Letters for London or elsewhere must be put in the office by 6; but, by paying one penny with each letter, they are received from that time till half an hour after, when the bag is closed. A requisition to F. Frieling, Esq., has received upwards of 200 signatories in favour of the Mail passing to Exeter through Sidford. Letters would be received from London which were put in the day before, and might be replied to by return of the Mail.

TOWN CRIER

MR. THOMAS PAUL was the first Town Crier that we hear of, and a journal of 1886 states that he was appointed because he had a "good round voice and was able to read well". Also having previously been a postman, he "was acquainted with all town matters", and residing at Prospect Cottage (now Rickwoods) could easily be found.

A Mr. Newton was the first Crier that I remember; his voice and accent shewed that he was not a Devonshire man. He was followed by "Theof" Mortimore, whose accent or brogue shewed that he was truly one of us.

Born in Sidmouth, with a fine burly figure, dark eyes, hair and side whiskers, his stentorian voice rang out, "Oyez, Oyez", and when, in later years, he was presented with a uniform of gold-braided hat, scarlet coat and velvet knee breeches, white stockings and buckled shoes, he caused much interest to all visitors. He was succeeded by his son Charley, since whose death Sidmouth has had no "Town Crier", and mourns the loss of two popular Sidmouth characters.

HEARSE

February, 1884:—"A Hearse such as has never before been seen in Sidmouth, a handsome article, with ornamented plate glass sides and ends, was used to the funeral of a Mrs. Woodfall. In further contrasts to funerals of the wealthy, there were neither mules at the door, plumes on the hearse, trappings on the horses or hatbands or scarves for mourners", etc.

THE SIDMOUTH VOLUNTEERS

ON 11th December, 1883, a meeting was held to aid in the formation of a Rifle Volunteer Company in the town. Sir John Kennaway presided. Mr. W. Hine-Haycock moved the opening of a subscription list for the purpose of raising £250. About £5 was subscribed at the meeting.

This Company, known as the 3rd Devons, developed into a "live" Corps, as will be seen from an article appearing on 17th June, 1891:—"The 3rd Devon Company of Volunteers assembled in the Market Place for Parade inspection. Capt. Orchard was in command and Lieut. Vallance was also present. Headed by the band, the Company marched to the Cricket Field where skirmishing took place. The men paraded through the town by way of Station Road, to headquarters in the Market Place where they were dismissed." I well remember being taken to the Cricket Field to watch their drilling to the accompaniment of the Band. It was one of our Saturday treats.

In 1895 Mr. G. J. Radford gave land on The Ham for a Drill Hall to be built. The Hall was opened by Mrs. Kennet-Were in 1895. Subscriptions did not cover the cost of the building, and money was advanced by Mr. R. H. Wood, of Belmont. On the retirement of Major Orchard, Mr. Wood presented the deeds of the building to the Corps, wiping off the £600 debt.

18th August, 1891. The Royal Horse Artillery, consisting of 4 officers and 86 men and 79 horses, arrived here under the command of Major Wallace and were billeted in the town.

Much excitement was caused when it was learned that a regiment of soldiers were expected, and the streets were lined by expectant crowds. The officers were billeted at the Hotels and soldiers in various parts of the town.

In November, 1914, a local Volunteer Force was formed, with General Gwynne in command and Mr. F. C. Purcell as Honorary Secretary. Drilling took place on the Blackmore Field.

LIGHTING—CANDLES, OIL LAMPS, GAS, ELECTRICITY

SEVERAL old Sidmothians have told me they remember when a little shop in Church Street was lit by *tallow candles* stuck in the tops of cottage loaves of bread. This shop was a general store, kept by a little old woman who sold oil, kettles, pots and pans, lollipops, shoe-laces, etc. Salt-fish, tallow candles and bread were kept all together in one barrel.

In my Church Street sketch of 1849 can be seen the lamp-standard with socket for *oil lamp*. One of these sockets attached to a wall in Western Town was removed in 1953.

Gas was introduced in 1837, with Works at Landpart. These were removed to The Ham by Mr. Dunning in 1875.

1880. In 1880 at their monthly meeting, the Local Board were unable to come to an agreement with Mr. Dunning for gas to supply the Town Lighting, and so a decision to use oil lamps again was decided upon. A petition was sent by numerous ratepayers, asking them to revert to gas lighting, but the request was not granted.

The Gas Undertaking was bought by the town in 1911 and the works later removed to a site beyond the Station.

We first hear of *Electric Lighting* when a Seal was affixed giving the Council powers to acquire Gas and Electricity on 1st July, 1912. Owing to the Council having heavy commitments, the Electricity Scheme was shelved until October, 1922. Works were built on land near the Gas Works, and were later acquired by the East Devon Electricity Co.

In the summer of 1952 Electric Lamp Standards were erected along the Esplanade. They were built of special wood from the Gold Coast named Inoke, which is hard enough to resist pen-knives and does not need painting. The scheme cost £3,000. There are mixed feelings about these new standards; although at night the effect is pleasing, one received a shock to see them obtruding on the landscape owing partly to their height.

Coombe Lane becomes Alexandria Road

July, 1882.   "Rough and Ready

'Rough and Ready', a suitable inscription this, to place each end of a new road, recently opened up from the railway station to the Woolbrook road, from whence it turns off a little beyond Mr. Mogridge's Arcot House. It has been a long time in course of formation, and now that it is formed, the traffic comes not, nor is likely to do so while the intolerable roughness remains. For pedestrians it is quite unavailable, for as it is laid with a thick coating of sharp flint stones, those who have corns on their feet or who do not desire unduly to patronise the shoemaker will go any distance round about, rather than perform the feat of helping to press down a mass of loose material. In its olden state and condition, known as Coombe Lane, it was a delightful pleasant Devonshire lane, being narrow and bounded throughout nearly its entire length with thick hedges and large and lofty trees, whilst in the spring and summer wild flowers were in abundance. Its new name has not yet been stated; it can no longer be Coombe *lane*." (The name is now Alexandria Road.)

The project was urged principally by the Sidford and Sidbury inhabitants, by whom the route was much used after the opening of the railway. But it was contended that Sidmouth ought not to bear the whole or even half of the expense of making the road or its upkeep, as it was little used by the inhabitants.

The Roads and "The Steam Roller" 40 years ago

The cry of Rob Wilton, "Ee-wot-a-todo ! !" would best describe the controversy and correspondence which passed between The Manor Agent and the Council agent regarding the use of the Steam Roller on the roads. It was claimed that damage was caused to gas and water mains by its use, whilst from all sides complaints of the state and upkeep of the roads poured in. In a journal of March, 1914, we read:—"We do not profess to have a knowledge of road making, but a road, which in dry weather is a mass of oozing mud cannot be regarded as satisfactory."

I gather that the roads were composed of rough flints from a quarry in Woolbrook (which I remember seeing lying in heaps at the roadside, where a man, wearing goggles, sat and cracked these stones with a hammer). A "thick" coating of clay was laid on the top. One complaint was that after a heavy shower the clay was washed down the sewer, leaving the rough flints exposed. Therefore the use of the horse-roller was of little use and the advent of a steam-roller was welcomed. However, as such damage to mains was caused, a suggestion was made that it should only be used on the outskirts of the town. A letter in the press suggested that several deserving women be hired to use flat irons on these roads !

Fore Street was christened "Duck-pond-lane".

Later, in 1914, I find that 1,000 tons of granite and also a steam-roller were bought for the town, and from then onwards things improved.

If the people of these days could have witnessed (as I did) the wonderful efficiency of road making in 1952, when the road along the sea front was laid by mechanical devices and only a few men, taking only two days, with excellent results, they would think it was all a dream !

REDUCTION OF M.O.H.'S SALARY

October, 1883.

In the early days the people of Sidmouth seemed averse to ventilation, which caused worry to the Medical Officer of Health, and when one reads in the old journals of the many deaths at an early age, at times whole families being wiped out, one does not wonder at his anxiety. The M.O.H. therefore advocated ventilators to be provided for the town. When a meeting of the Local Board was held in October, 1883, after they had spent hundreds of pounds on these "pet objects", the question of the doctor's salary came up for discussion, and it was proposed and seconded that his salary of £35 per annum should remain the same as before. But an amendment was moved proposing that only £20 should be given, and 6 voted for and 3 against. As the Government paid half the salary, the gain to the town was £7.10s. 0d. The doctor might well have exclaimed as he thought of those whose cause he advocated, "Save me from my friends !"

1880—COFFEE TAVERN

THE Coffee Tavern was situated in Fore Street. In March, 1880, we read :—"The first proposal for a Coffee Tavern was made in November, 1879, by the Rev. G. McArthur. He spoke of the desirability of having a place where refreshment might be had without intoxicating drinks; there were two hundred members of the Church of England Temperance Society for whose sake, as well as others, the place was needed."

Although Lord Willoughby de Osborne offered £20 and Mr. Hine-Haycock £10 towards the undertaking, the project broke down because of differences of opinion as to a suitable site. When it was finally decided in January, 1881, to rent the Reading Room

(Mr. and Mrs. Kenneth Balfour having promised to pay the rent for three years, and the Manor Trustees bearing the cost of £30 upon repairs to the front of the building) the Coffee Tavern was opened on 10th January and was open daily from 6.0 a.m. to 10 p.m. At the appointed time there was a large gathering of ladies, gentlemen, tradesmen, and merchants, etc., who with much glee and hilarity drank tea and coffee, such a miscellaneous company as had never previously been associated together in a "tea drinking house". There was a discussion as to who should supply provisions, and it was decided that the committee should hold an important testing for quality. Mr. Bunce (draper), Mr. Chessal (chemist) and Mr. Lethaby (bookseller) were invited to meet. Four numbered samples were left with them, and no other person allowed to be present. First, the samples were tested by the nose, and decision taken as to the aroma, then a quarter oz. was carefully weighed by the chemist and placed in a tea cup, 6 oz. boiling water added and again the noses made their report. Then the tasting process was gone through and then a thin biscuit eaten between the sippings. Twice or three times the tasting was repeated, and all agreed on the superior sample, both as to aroma and flavour. Capt. Toup Nicholas and Mr. Radford with Mr. Harding then entered the room, and on the envelope being opened it was found that Mr. T. Channon, grocer of High Street (now Santer) was the successful competitor. This Coffee Tavern is still in existence.

EARLY CLOSING

IN July, 1891, at a meeting, Sidmouth tradesmen décided to close their shops at 5 o'clock on Thursdays instead of 8 o'clock. In those days all shops were kept open until 8 p.m. on weekdays and 10 p.m. on Saturdays.

1914. 14th October.

Extract from a local journal states:—"The early closing movement is having its drawbacks in regard to Saturday nights. Some of the shops are unable to close punctually at 9 o'clock owing to the people from the surrounding villages being unable to complete their shopping so early, and other shop-keepers are complaining of this."

1918. October.

A meeting of tradesmen decided against Saturday early closing.

CHAPTER XV
ROYAL AND DISTINGUISHED VISITORS
THE VISIT OF KING GEORGE III TO ESCOT

IN a journal or diary, Miss Burney (better known as Madam d'Arbley), writing on 9th August, 1791, speaks of lodging with a Mrs. Dare:—"She is a baker, a poor woman whose husband died of fright, after seeing a ghost just after her Mother was drowned." The lodgings were not desirable, but were near the sea and the town was full. She told how she and her daughter rode double-horse to Sir George Young's to join in rejoicings in the park, on the occasion of the visit of King George III to Escot.

In Sidmouth a bullock was roasted, cut up and handed round. In the midst of the rejoicings:—"We had such a fine sermon that made us all cry. They had the King all 'drawed' and dressed up, all in gold laurels, and they put 'un in a coach and 8 horses, and carried 'un about. All the grand gentlemen in the town and round abouts come in their own carriages to join, and we had the finest band of music in England, and we all singed 'God Save the King'".

In 1819 Their Royal Highnesses the late Duke and Duchess of Kent came to reside at the Woolbrook Glen, bringing with them their infant daughter, Princess Victoria (later to become our beloved Queen).

During their stay some lads were shooting at birds in the Western Fields when a stone from their catapult penetrated the window of the room where the little Princess lay. Fortunately she escaped injury.

An amusing story was told in connection with the arrival of their Royal Highnesses. Most of the principal inhabitants paid their respects to them, and one of the gentlemen, though holding a good position in the town, does not seem to have had any clear idea about Royalty and the Peerage; but desiring to be very civil he is alleged to have said, "I hope your Lordship and Mrs. Kent are well".

Princess Victoria's first shoes were made in Sidmouth by Mr. John Taylor.

In 1831 the Russian Eagle was placed over Nos. 7 and 8 Fortfield Terrace, when occupied for three months by the Grand Duchess

Helena of Russia, wife of the Grand Duke Michael, brother to the then Empress. Some of her suite were lodged at No. 1. She held a reception at No. 8, and later enjoyed moving freely about the town and chatting with the people. When the original eagle fell into disrepair, Mr. G. Sisterson, at the age of 16, carved the existing one.

On the occasion of a visit of the Duke and Duchess of Edinburgh on 23rd May, 1881, who came in their yacht, the sea was so choppy that the lifeboat was launched. The Secretary of the Lifeboat, who sat on the gunwale, through the lurching of the boat, fainted and fell into the sea. Two of the crew, George Horn and Henry Conant plunged in and rescued him.

The Fife and Drum Band and the Brass Band were playing on the Front. Dr. Pullen presented a photo of "The Royal Glen".

How proud the people of Sidmouth were, when they learned that H.R.H. The Duke of Connaught had decided to winter in Sidmouth. It was during a time of national crisis, when it was desirous to keep money in this country, that H.R.H. set the good example of wintering in England. The Duke first arrived on 28th October, 1931, and spent several winters here.

It was a great pleasure to see this handsome dignified gentleman living amongst us, chatting to his friends and entering into, and evidently enjoying, the life and entertainments of the Sidmouth people, without interference. Accompanied by his Equerry, Major Berkeley Levett, his first walk, on his arrival, would take him along to the eastern end of the Esplanade for a chat with the fishermen. Taking up residence at the Fortfield Hotel, he was visited from time to time by his relatives, Princess Louise, Duchess of Argyle; Prince and Princess Arthur of Connaught and their son, the Earl of Macduff; his daughter, Lady Patricia Ramsay; Prince Gustav Adolf of Sweden, Ex-Queen Ena of Spain, and the Queen of Denmark (then Princess Ingrid). They all seemed to enjoy the freedom of our town and must have sensed the pleasure it gave its people to have such a gracious gentleman amongst them. His passing was sadly felt by all, but Sidmouth is glad to have the Connaught Gardens, which he opened, and also a road named after him, which will go down into posterity.

Among other distinguished visitors to Sidmouth were:—The Gaekwar of Baroda, who, during his three months' stay, enjoyed playing cricket and other sports; The Grand Duke of Hesse, the late Earl Jellicoe, Mr. and Mrs. Bernard Shaw, and Sir Henry and Lady Wood, all took up residence at the Victoria Hotel. The late Coleridge-Taylor, composer of "Hiawatha's Wedding Feast", etc., stayed at the York Hotel whilst staying in Sidmouth, when he may have received inspiration for some of his wonderful compositions. Who knows?

CHAPTER XVI

Distinguished Residents

The name of Peter Orlando Hutchinson stands out as being the first to be mentioned. Although not born here, he lived here as a young man with his parents. Not being robust (for he was lame with some infirmity of the hip-joint), but with a very active mind and no profession, he employed his time with local antiquarian and historical research. He spent two years in an architect's office, which accounts for his skill in craftsmanship and sketching.

He was author of the Sidmouth Guide, which he took 30 years to complete and 11 years to transcribe.

He was rather eccentric and often could be seen driving a donkey attached to a cannon while dressed in a sort of uniform of his own devising, and on one occasion when the Yeomanry were having a field day on Peak Hill, much indignation was caused to the Colonel and Officers when they found themselves on their return to Sidmouth, preceded all the way home by Mr. Hutchinson in this ludicrous semi-military equipage.

It was due to Mr. Hutchinson that the unique and beautiful glass which exists hidden away in the vestry was not destroyed when the church was restored in 1863. His house, "The Old Chancel", which he built from material left over after the restoration, is a memorial, and there are still a few who remember him, and his constant companions, a cat, a raven, and a crooked apple-stick. He must have have been as marked a feature as the vanished Chit Rock.

Mr. Hutchinson came to Sidmouth in 1824. Later a furious local quarrel ranged round the retention or removal of the organ in the Parish Church. "High and Low" wrestled for its destruction or preservation. The enemies of the gallery hit on an ingenious device for its removal.

The Duke of Kent had died at Sidmouth, so it was suggested that a window to be given by Queen Victoria to his memory should be put behind the gallery. The Queen, knowing nothing of the battle raging, agreed. Mr. Hutchinson, indignant at this unfair method, took council with himself and acted promptly. He wrote out a full history and petition, arranged himself in his Volunteer uniform, mounted the Exeter coach, and travelled to Osborne, where the Queen and Prince Consort were in residence. Alone and trusting to his uniform, he got past the sentry and penetrated to the drawing-room, before being questioned . . . . The Queen withdrew her offer of the window. Five years later the gallery came down, with the consent of all, and the Queen presented the window.

SIR AMBROSE FLEMING, KT., M.A., D.SC., F.R.S.

SIR AMBROSE FLEMING held the first professorship of electrical engineering at University College, London, a chair he occupied for 41 years. He was personally associated with the introduction into this country of three great electrical innovations which have become commonplace in our daily life—the telephone, electric lighting by incandescent lamps, and wireless telegraphy.

Sir Ambrose's most noteworthy service to wireless was the invention of the two-electrode thermionic valve which revolutionized the practice of wireless.

His many honours included the Hughes, the Gold Albert, the Faraday, the Duddell, and the Kelvin and Franklin medals. He was created a Knight Bachelor in 1929.

Sir Ambrose lived in Sidmouth from 1926 until his death in 1945. He married Miss Olive Franks, a well-known Singer.

A regular worshipper in Sidmouth Parish Church, he was happy in the absolute reconciliation of his science with his deep religious convictions. Armed with this unshakable faith, he lived and passed from among us with the most precious of human endowments—a mind that was always serene.

The richly-carved Litany Desk was given to Sidmouth Parish Church by Lady Fleming in memory of her husband.

SIR NORMAN LOCKYER, K.C.B., F.R.S. (1836–1920)

SIR NORMAN LOCKYER, the originator and part founder of the Norman Lockyer Observatory, was born at Rugby on 7th May, 1836. He was the son of Mr. Joseph Hooley Lockyer, a lecturer on scientific subjects at Rugby School. As a result of his discoveries in connection with the sun and his private astronomical work, in 1875, after holding many important posts, he was offered and accepted an appointment in the Science and Art Department at South Kensington by Mr. Disraeli. He erected an Observatory at his home at Hampstead.

The Observatory on Salcombe Hill was founded in 1912 through his energy and foresight, when he, with Lady Lockyer and a small band of enthusiasts, presented land, money, instruments and practical services. These early benefactors included Sir Francis McClean and his brother, Capt. McClean, who has acted as hon.

secretary since its foundation. The Observatory not only survived the two world wars, but developed with the help of generous donors, among them being Sir Robert Mond, who made considerable gifts of money and equipment; also Lady Lockyer, who bequeathed the whole of her residuary estate to the Observatory, bringing the capital to about £40,000, in addition to about 44 acres of freehold land and equipment.

Sir Norman died in 1920 and was succeeded by his son, the late Dr. W. J. L. Lockyer, and Mr. D. L. Edwards, A.R.C.S., D.I.C., F.R.A.S. The latter, after the death of Dr. Lockyer, was director until his sudden death in September, 1956. Sidmouth mourned the loss of this distinguished man. Assisted by Mr. D. R. Barber, B.SC., F.INST.P., F.R.A.S., the observatory has earned for itself an important place in British Astronomy.

The Norman Lockyer Observatory was transferred by Sir Richard Gregory to the University College of the South West and was accepted on behalf of the College by Sir William Munday on 1st May, 1948.

COLONEL JOHN EDMOND HEUGH BALFOUR

COLONEL JOHN EDMOND HEUGH BALFOUR, who died at The Manor House, Sidmouth, was a County Justice of the Peace, a former High Sheriff of Devon in 1922–23 and Deputy Lieutenant for the County. He had a distinguished career, joining the 4th Battalion Leinster Regiment in 1882, 11th Hussars in 1892, serving with the Devon Yeomanry until 1910, having been in command for four years and also becoming Hon. Colonel. He became A.D.C. to Sir Ian Hamilton in South Africa and gained the D.S.O. He was twice mentioned in despatches in the first World War and received the C.M.G. in 1918.

He married Evelyn, second daughter of the late Hon. R. J. Gerard Dicconson, in 1910, and there is one daughter.

Colonel Balfour died in October, 1952.

SIR ARCHIBALD BODKIN
"A Great Man and a Bonny Fighter"

SIR ARCHIBALD BODKIN was born in 1862 and called to the Bar in 1885. It was not long before his outstanding merits secured him a large practice in the Criminal and Licensing Courts. In due course he became Senior Treasury Counsel at the Central Criminal Courts in 1907, and in 1920 he was elevated to the high and responsible office of Director of Public Prosecutions. He retained this post until 1930, when he retired and came to live in Sidmouth, shortly afterwards to succeed Sir Francis Newbolt as chairman of Devon Quarter Sessions; he resigned his chairmanship after fifteen years.

For nearly twenty years he served on the Ottery St. Mary Bench of Magistrates, being chairman from 1946 to 1950, when he retired under the age limit at the age of 88.

Sir Archibald was a keen horticulturalist, and secured many prizes for his wonderful show of blooms, etc., at our Garden Club Shows. He died in January, 1958, aged 95.

THE LATE LORD CHERWELL

FIRST BARON, created 1941, of Oxford, Frederick Alexander Lindemann, P.C. 1943. F.R.S. Paymaster General 1942–45 and since 1951. Professor of Experimental Philosophy, Oxford. Fellow of Wadham College 1919; Student of Christ Church 1921; son of the late A. F. Lindemann, Sidholme, Sidmouth. Educated Blair Lodge; Darmstadt; Berlin University (Ph.D.); Paris. Served in European War 1914–18; Experimental Pilot; Director of the Physical Laboratory of R.A.F., Farnborough; Personal Assistant to the Prime Minister 1940.

MR. JOHN TINDALL, M.A.

MR. JOHN TINDALL came to live in Sidmouth in "the nineties". The all-consuming passion of his life was his art, and though a skilled instrumentalist, his great love was for drawing and painting in water-colour.

In 1907 he published a book, "Sketching Notes". Another little book, "The Sidmouth Volunteers 1914–1918", a record of the activities of the "Town Guard", is the only compact history of Sidmouth during those war years.

Mr. Tindall joined the Volunteers when he was nearly 70, and became Sergt. Signaller. When General Gwynn and Major Hastings called for volunteers at a meeting in the Manor Hall, Mr. Tindall was sitting next to old Mr. George Woolley, who remarked:— "Us be too old I think, sir". However, Mr. Tindall got up. Mr. Purcell asked his age: "Sixty-eight", "Shilling please". It was paid and the thing was done.

He compiled several volumes of "The Foreshore", and his last paper on this subject was read at The Devonshire Association at Dartmouth on 29th July, 1929.

Mr. Tindall died 20th December, 1933, at the age of 87, and Sidmouth lost a fine type of English gentleman.

Miss Leigh-Browne

Miss Annie Leigh-Browne, born 14th March, 1851, took a very keen interest in the well-being of Sidmouth, was one of the founders of our Cottage Hospital and a warm supporter of the Sid Vale Association and any project to maintain the natural beauties of Sidmouth.

In conjunction with Lady Lockyer, she purchased and saw to the preservation of Woolcombe House (The Museum) and was interested in many other charitable societies.

Miss Leigh-Browne bequeathed "All her land over which the River Sid flows, from the south end of Lovers Walk to the northern boundary of Lymebourne meadow, together with land over which public foot-paths run, and property in Salcombe Regis and Bickwell Valley (both to be retained as pastures); also £500 for the upkeep of the banks of the River Sid".

Mrs. Christabel Withers

Mrs. Christabel Withers, wife of the late Dr. Sheldon Withers, for some years M.O.H. for Sidmouth, is the daughter of Captain and Mrs. Wake, and before her marriage lived with her mother at St. Helens. Mrs. Withers has occupied many official posts in Sidmouth, as School Governor, Guardian, and for many years sitting as Magistrate on the Ottery St. Mary Bench. The following paragraph relating to her parents will be interesting.

"The Marriage of Miss St. Aubyn and Captain Wake on 19th February, 1860. A wedding took place at Sidmouth Parish Church, the bride being Miss St. Aubyn, daughter of Sir Edward and Lady St. Aubyn of St. Michael's Mount, and the bridegroom Captain Charles Wake. At the time the Parish Church was being restored and the roof was non-existent. Captain Wake being a sailor, the coastguards arranged for him and his bride to be married under a roof of flags. The happy couple had come to Sidmouth with parents and relations in order to be married by a favourite uncle, Canon Knolles, who was wintering here in York Terrace."

Mr. and Mrs. A. E. Chandler

On 22nd March, 1952, Mr. and Mrs. A. E. Chandler celebrated their Golden Wedding.

Since coming to Sidmouth they have done wonderful work. Mrs. Chandler is President of the Townswomen's Guild; Mr. Chandler, serving on the Council during the 1939 War, gave invaluable service to the evacuee cause.

A great worker for the Sid Vale Association and serving as Curator of the Museum, Mr. Chandler, until his death in 1958, devoted much time in the interests of "The Eventide Homes".

Mr. A. E. Piper, b.e.m.

Mr. "Bert" Piper, a member of an old and respected Sidmouth family, served with 1/4th Devons, 1914–1919, when he joined as "Gardener, Imperial War Graves Commission", became Foreman Gardener 1922. Loaned to New Zealand Government to supervise layout of Garden of Remembrance.

1922: Conducted the late H.M. King George V during his visit to War Cemeteries; 1923: Promoted Assistant Travelling Superintendent in Bapuame District; 1929: Cambrai, Ypres, Eastern Belgian Areas. Aided in getting most of staff and families evacuated from Dunkirk; 1945: Promoted Superintendent Horticulture of Belgium; 1946: Awarded, by the late King George VI, The British Empire Medal for services rendered at all times; from the officials a silver cigarette box; from the staff a canteen of cutlery, "Presented as a small token of esteem"; 1947: Joined the Sidmouth Urban District Council as Head Gardener and later promoted Parks Superintendent.

Well done, Bert Piper, we are proud of "One of Freddy Drewe's Boys"!

Old Sidmouth Names

A paper was read by P. O. Hutchinson at the Meeting of The Devonshire Association at Torrington in 1875, entitled "The Population of Sidmouth from 1260". It starts with a list of the people living in Sidmouth in 1260, the total number being 160. These include: Adam-de-Radweye, Nicholas de Ascerton, Richard Medicus (Dr. Calli, Culley, or Cawley) Walter Calli amongst them, to the total of 160 names. From this list Hutchinson estimates the total population as about 600.

In an old deed occurs the name Johannes Hibdon, probably the origin of John Ebdon, whose name appears over the shop in an old print of Church Street.

John Hake (Hakesland) married Janet, second daughter of Nicholas Radweye.

Levy by Henry VIII, 1523. A document gives particulars of the levy in Sidmouth. These names include Thomas Purchass, Edward Slade 1541, Thomas Calley (Cawley) 1523,Thomas Channon 1623, William Purchass, Walter Calley, John Channon, William Cawley 1623.

In 1628 Prideaux appears. In 1663 appear the names Haydon, Cawley, Drake, John Hill. 1639 John Searle. 1681 Carslake, Elias Cawley. 1760 Baker. 1764 Thos. Turner. 1770 Potbury, Baron. 1773 Robert Stone. 1775 Dr. Hodge. 1824 Bolt. 1836 John Curtis.

Pinn, Pim, Pinn Beacon, Pinney.

Henricus de Pinne appears as a witness to a deed in 1285. In the year following Thomas de Pinne, a Norman Baron, had a Castle at Pinn Farm in the Parish of Otterton. In the wall which is constructed of red-rock, squared and put together with the regularity of brickwork, is a stone tablet bearing the date 1587, with initial letters R.P. and J.P. Immediately behind the farm rises the point of a high hill known as Pinn Beacon, jutting out from the western side of Peak Hill. It is said that Thomas de-Penne was a Norman Baron who lived in a Castle at Pinn Beacon.

Otto the Dane held ground around Brixham before 1050 (was this where Otterton, Ottery, Otter derived its name ?).

The names Conant and Sanders appear on tablets in the Church at an early date. I remember Mr. George Conant as Sexton of our Parish Church, and his wife could be seen conducting parish-ioners to their seats in the Church dressed in black, a lovely face appearing beneath a close-fitting bonnet. After her husband's death in 1910, Mrs. G. Conant and her son carried on the duties of care-taker and sexton until her death on 21st October, 1920, aged 69.

Old Mrs. Selley was Sextoness of All Saints' Church, and her son Charley was organ-blower at the Parish Church. They lived at Pebblestone Cottage. Charley was a little "simple", always smiling, and could usually be seen chopping sticks in a little cubby hole facing the road. Although "simple", Charley was artful, and a story has been told of his being offered to choose a gift of a penny or a shilling; taking the shilling, he remarked, "I won't be greedy, sir, I'll take the small one !"

SIDMOUTH "WORTHIES"

JOHN SPARKS started his service as a local postman in 1879, as a "Sunday Sub" to Sidbury at a wage of 1/6 a week. In December of that year he went on the Branscombe round at a salary of 14/– per week, and in 1880 he commenced a morning round embracing the district from the Town Brewery on to Woolbrook and Core Hill at a wage of 7/– per week. The low rate of pay in those days explains why so many postmen occupied their spare time in boot-making, tailoring, etc. From 1882 to 1884 Postman Sparks did the double walking round to Sidbury, and in the last years he was transferred to the town. He was appointed head postman in 1906.

In connection with the Sid Vale Association the late Mr. Sparks, with Mr. Holmes, have been of great assistance in preserving By-Paths and Rights-of-way, traversing many miles in so doing.

I remember postman Sparks from my earliest childhood bringing our letters; he would always open the door and hand in the post, shouting "Yur-you-are . . . ." mentioning the name !

November, 1952. I heard more about John Sparks today, meeting his friend "Jimmy" Clarke, of Peaslands. He tells me that John was a keen botanist and they would walk for miles seeking out the earliest plants. Kneeling down on soaking ground, John would produce his microscope and say, "Gaw Jimmy, look-ee-zee this yur flower, did ee ever zee anything more 'bootiful'?"

They sought in vain for wild Lobelia, until one day, on looking over a hedge, Jimmy found it near Kilmington; he picked a piece of the flower (they wouldn't take a root), placed it reverently in his pocket to shew Jack. They worshipped it together, this huge and the small man. Jimmy, who worked for my father when I was a girl, is small in stature and, though 85 years old, worked until last year. During the first World War, though over 50, he insisted on joining up and put his age down as 38. The pluck of a true Briton !

24th January, 1920, appears the following: "A presentation to Postman Charles Pidgeon of a silver watch suitably inscribed, on his retirement as town postman. During his 39 years' service he had traversed a distance equal to eight times around the world."

This book would not be complete if the names of the following old friends were omitted and with whom it has been my pleasure to meet and have a "little chat" of old times. Foremost in my mind are the Holmes brothers, Mr. Tom Hazelock, Mr. Kennard, all for many years great workers in connection with Sidmouth flower shows; "Benjy" Weeks, Jack Townsend, "Bungay" Channing and "Doe" Carnell (usually found on the sea-front "looking out zay"); then comes George Cross, Fred Bond, Bert Wood, George Horn, Tom White, Bill Marks, Reg. Holland, etc., etc.

Copied Oct 21st 1951
Anna Sutton

A CORNER OF BEDFORD SQUARE

CHAPTER XVII

ENTERTAINMENT

THEATRE AND ASSEMBLY ROOMS

"IN 1805 a substantial building near the beach was fitted up as a small theatre; the scenery and the performers were both above mediocrity. When they performed in the Autumn of 1814, they were respectfully attended."

The theatre was on the north corner of East Street, which was then known as Theatre Lane. It did not survive long and dwelling houses replaced it.[1]

"Butcher's Guide" (1820) states:—

"The Assembly Rooms are at the London Inn. Large and well fitted up. Balls are frequently held there, and the floor has an excellent spring. Nearly 200 persons have been seen in this room, without the assistance of a master of ceremonies. Last season Mrs. Marshall of Bath undertook the duties of the situation. The rooms are open for cards every night. Except the billiard, card and assembly rooms, Sidmouth has no other place of public amusement."

We read of Mechanic's Hall next to the former Y.W.C.A. building and a Reading Room which later became "The Coffee Tavern", all used for "Penny Readings" and small entertainments.

The Literary Society held their meetings in a room now annexed to Potbury's. We also read of a downstair room at Canister House in Western Town being used for "Happy Gatherings". This was once "Pearcey's Boarding House" and next door to "The Jolly Sailor".

The upper floor of the Old Market or Town Hall was used by the Volunteers as Headquarters before the Drill Hall was built. It later became "The Conservative Club", Girls' Club and a room hired for Dancing classes.

Then came the Manor Hall, built by Major Balfour in 1891, with dressing-rooms and a Lecture Hall attached. This was a great acquisition for Sidmouth, and from then onwards we had every sort of Entertainment.

[1] I like to think the lovely old thatched house, now occupied by Mr. Stone, and the houses adjoining, so well preserved, might be these buildings.

ENTERTAINMENTS

I AM often asked how people amused themselves in the "old days". We read of Tea Meetings, Services of Song, "Penny Readings", etc. I do not remember the latter, but will quote from a Journal:—

> "In June 1866 'Penny Readings' were a great success and well attended. A typical programme lasted about 2 hours and these are some of the items:—'The Death of Nelson', by Rev. H. G. J. Clements, Recitation 'The Heart of Bruce', Dr. Mackenzie, 'The Jackdaw of Rheims', the Rev. J. B. Lloyd, followed by Glees, Duets, Comic Songs and the National Anthem'. A note reads:—'One word as to the Programme, for which small page a penny was charged—the same sum as for admission—measuring one charge with another, while the entertainment was 'dirt cheap' the programme was 'Plaguey dear' and 'meagre'!"

Most of those entertainments appear to have been held in the Assembly Rooms.

Mr. W. J. D. Tucker reminded me of Entertainments given 40 years ago for the Good Templars and Band of Hope, in which he and Mr. C. Colwill were the leading lights. There were conjurings, acting, part-songs and dancing. These entertainments were usually held in the Drill Hall and were very good.

Then there were "The Black Hawk Minstrels" (I can just remember them) with Lew Lake as Interlocutor, W. Bending, Till, Newton, "Artful" Wattley and Freddy Winter. The two latter were excellent comedians and tap-dancers.

It is a far cry from "Penny Readings" to "The Winter Chamber Concerts". These can be best described as "Real Musical Feasts"! Started by Miss Allen and her brother about 1918 or 19, and assisted by Miss Whittington and Miss Norton, with Miss W. Darnell as Hon. Secretary, they were always well-attended afternoon concerts. The season tickets were quickly sold and enabled us to engage many of the best Soloists and String Quartettes, and cover expenses. Among the many were Mark Hambourg, Solomon, Pouishnoff, Orloff, Lionel Tertis, Keith Faulkner, Isobel Baillie, May Mukely, The Griller String Quartette, etc. We always began the season with that wonderful violinist, Jelli d'Aranyi, sometimes accompanied by her sister, Madame Foucherie. The Concerts were attended by audiences from all the surrounding districts. It was a sad day when war broke out and it was decided to discontinue them.

Fortunately, we have keen musicians of a younger generation who are anxious to bring these wonderful concerts back to us, and we have had two series of these.

CELEBRITY CONCERTS

1958. After a world tour, on 12th June the Robert Masters Pianoforte Quartette delighted the audience by their masterly performance at the Manor Hall, and on 1st August Mr. John Hunt, the distinguished pianist, gave much enjoyment to a packed house.

On 18th September a Recital of Violin and Organ by father and daughter was held in the Parish Church. Rosemary Brown, Solo Violin. She is a pupil of Robert Masters and shews great promise for the future. Clifford A. Brown, Organ.

SIDMOUTH MUSICAL SOCIETIES

THE first musical society of any note was formed in 1856, but found little support.

On 16th October, 1862, Mr. J. G. Pinney was appointed Organist of the Parish Church at the age of 18; a Madrigal Society and a Band were formed with Mr. Pinney as Conductor.

In 1864 Mr. Pinney died and his brother, Mr. G. Pinney became, his successor. On his removal to Ramsgate in 1870, Dr. Haines Wood was appointed. In 1872 a Choral Society was formed. The subscriptions were 10/6 for a course of twenty lessons, for members of choirs, etc., 5/-. They met for weekly practices, but there is no record of any concerts being given.

In 1873 Mr. H. A. Harding (later Dr.), of Salisbury, was appointed and it was through his zeal the Choral Society obtained a sound footing. The first Concert was given at the Assembly Rooms in April, 1874. It was a miscellaneous programme with choir and orchestra of about forty performers. Amongst familiar names appear Mrs. Hine-Haycock and Mr. Charles Farrant as vocalists and Mr. P. O. Hutchinson (flute), Mr. Chick (violin), etc.

On 25th December, 1875, the first Oratorio, "The Creation", was performed and the first paid soloist, Mr. Cox (tenor) was employed.

In 1889, after four years, Dr. Harding was appointed Organist in Oxford. Mr. Macpherson succeeded him until in 1894 Mr. J. A. Bellamy was appointed Organist of the Parish Church.

In September, 1895, a meeting was called to reorganize the Society, and the Sidmouth Choral and Orchestral Society was formed. In January, 1896, the first concert, given by Mr. J. A. Bellamy, was a great success. There were nine rows of reserved seats and the Hall was densely packed, many standing. "Samson" was performed. Mr. J. A. Bellamy was a fine musician and a master in the art of conducting, his unruffled gentlemanly manner endeared him to all. After thirty-six years Mr. Bellamy retired through ill health. He died in 1936. Sidmouth mourned his loss.

Mr. J. Holden and Mr. Marcom became conductors for a short time until Mr. Clifford Brown was appointed in 1930. During the war years, whilst Mr. Brown was on military service, the Society was held together by the kind services of Mrs. Barrie and Mrs. C. A. Brown.

CHORAL SOCIETY

MR. CLIFFORD A. BROWN, A.R.C.M., is a fine musician and, assisted by his wife, with his keenness and enthusiasm he has brought the Choral Society through many vicissitudes. He has also formed a "Youth Choir", thus ensuring voices and members for the future. Members of this choir have already gained distinction as soloists in Broadcasting. The Society are fortunate in having an excellent and enthusiastic Orchestra, with Mr. Hugh Spottiswood as Leader and Mrs. Clifford Brown as Accompanist. The outstanding event of 1959 was the impressive performance of Bach's St. Matthew's Passion given in conjunction with Exmouth Choral Society at Exmouth and Sidmouth.

SIDMOUTH OPERATIC SOCIETY

THE Operatic Society was formed in 1896 when Mr. J. A. Bellamy, assisted by Mr. R. W. Sampson and Colonel Dunbar Huyshe, produced "The Mikado". This performance was a great success and many other successes followed. Mrs. Cissie Herbert and Mrs. J. A. Bellamy played leading roles in these performances.

We first hear of Mr. Sampson in 1894, when he appeared as a comedian at a concert. Though an architect by profession, he was a great actor and comedian, and one of the mainstays of the "Operatic Society" right up to the time of his death in 1951. During the first World War this Society temporarily ceased to exist.

THE ARTS CLUB

AT a Parish Church "Social" in 1922, some enthusiastic members produced a play, "The Fairies' Dilemma", written by our late Vicar, the Rev. C. K. Woolcombe, M.A.; this was so successful that a more ambitious choice was made, and in 1923 "The Rajah of Rajahpore" and in 1924 "The Rebel Maid" were produced. In the latter Miss Dorothy Hughes was the heroine and Mr. James P. Martin, the hero. This was a wonderful success, and so "The Arts Club" was born.

Among its earliest members were:—Messrs. H. Edinborough, Ronald Boyce, George Richards, Bob Smith, E. Whitton, J. W. D. Tucker, Fred and Frank Tedbury, H. Russell, J. P. Martin, W. L. P. Martin, Bert Foyle. All are still members excepting Bob Smith, with, of course, many additions. The ladies were Miss Symonds, Dorothy Hughes, M. Drewe, Mrs. Greaves and Mrs. Fitzgerald. The late Mr. Greaves was the excellent Conductor.

The Arts Club are lucky in having Mr. Gene Gerrard as their present Producer. This year, 1959, "The Arcadians" was a great success.

SIDMOUTH AMATEUR DRAMATIC SOCIETY
November, 1958.

A meeting of members interested in an Amateur Dramatic Club for Sidmouth was held in the small Manor Hall in January, 1923, and it was decided to form an Amateur Dramatic Society. The first Play produced was "Tilly of Bloomsbury", and it was decided to do two Plays a year, if possible.

During the war years, 1939–45, the Society closed down and re-formed in 1946, when the first Play was "Mr. Pym Passes By" in 1947.

Some very successful plays have been produced since then. This year (1958) "The Green Goddess" was very well produced and performed, and was well patronized each night from Monday until Saturday, with two Matinees. Produced by Mr. Gene Gerrard. President: Mrs. Hugh Davies.

BANDS

ALTHOUGH Sidmouth already had two Bands, the Volunteer, under Bandmaster Purchase, and the Fife and Drum Band (I read a paragraph from a local paper, of the eighties, asking that the Bandsmen of the Fife and Drum Band should not be offered intoxicating liquor, as they were teetotallers)—another Band was formed to be known as "The Town Band", under the conductorship of Mr. H. Russell. Mr. Harry Russell was a keen musician and a clever cornet player. His brothers, Messrs. John and James Russell, played 1st and 2nd cornet, and I have been told that the latter's small son, Reg., played 2nd cornet with his father and had to stand on the cornet case in order to reach the music stand—he is now a grandfather ! This Band performed select music while the Volunteer Band programme consisted of martial music. Even so, there was a strong competitive spirit between the Bands. In those days a portable bandstand was erected at various points of the Esplanade and in the town. This was very convenient for those who could not walk so far as (say) the Connaught Gardens. We miss those concerts on the Sea Front.

A journal states:—"September 9th, 1891, The Volunteer Band performed a selection of music at Coulson's Corner in High Street.

At the same time the Town Band discoursed a selection on the Esplanade, opposite The York Hotel."

I remember hearing that "messengers" would be sent from one band to the other to see which held the largest audience.

After the disbanding of the Volunteers, the bandsmen evidently amalgamated, and when Mr. Russell left the town, Mr. E. Barnard became Bandmaster, and under his excellent leadership the Band was successful in winning the County Championship in November, 1930, and is now known as the Silver Prize Band. A Silver Cup and £20 was won at a Band Contest in Bournemouth. Seven other bands competed. At the same contest a gold medal and many other individual prizes were won.

For many years Mr. Davey was a keen and popular musician. He died suddenly in 1951, and is much missed; his assistant has now taken over and many hundreds have enjoyed their twice-weekly concerts in the Connaught Gardens.

The Cinema

Our first Cinematograph was introduced into Sidmouth by the late Mr. A. W. Ellis. In 1911 he started to show moving pictures at the Manor Hall at intervals. In those days the films were thrown on to the screen from the middle of the hall, quite unprotected and using only limelight. Then in 1912 Mr. Ellis hired the Drill Hall for a season and here a great advance was made on the old methods. Electric lighting was installed and safety appliances provided. Great progress was taking place in "The Movie" world and cinemas were being opened all over the country. Mr. Ellis, with the help of Mr. James Pepperell, converted "The Belle Vue Restaurant" into an up-to-date Picture House (now a Drapery Establishment).

In 1913 Mr. Ellis invited Mrs. Kennet-Were to open it formally. There for the first time, films 3,000 and 4,000 feet long were shown to the public.

In 1928 a Company was formed. The Grand Cinema was built and opened in 1929 by Mr. T. E. Fitzgerald, Chairman of the Council. Assisted by his son and Mr. Earland, Mr. Ellis also carried on a successful photography business.

Sidmouth lost a good man in every sense of the word when Mr. Ellis died at the age of 65 in 1939.

The Museum

The first mention of a Museum in Sidmouth was on the occasion of the Devonshire Association's visit in 1873. We read:—"A Museum of objects of local interest was held at the Town Hall.

The most striking object was a handsome display of arms arranged by the Coastguards, one of chief interest being the flag of the 40th Regiment, over 100 years old. There was a collection of pictures by renowned and also local artists. A quantity of antique lace was shewn by Mrs. Chick and some specimens by Mrs. Hayman. Also fossils and Sidmouth pebbles by Mr. Newman, mammoth teeth by Mr. P. O. Hutchinson, who also read a paper."

In 1914 a Naturalists' Club was formed by Mr. Ernest Bonner and opened at Woolcombe House. A pamphlet of that date reads:— "There is now an Exhibition of local and other fossils, shells, feathers, Crystals, Old Prints and curios. Open on Thursdays and Fridays from 3 to 5 and 7.30 to 8.30. Admission free. All interested are invited."

This Club consisted chiefly of juniors and lads of that day can recognize some of the Fossils they collected when accompanying Mr. Bonner on their rambles. Lady Lockyer shewed much interest and assisted by lending the room.

On the occasion of the visit of The Devonshire Association, an Exhibition was held at Hope Cottage.

On 29th July, 1950, the present Museum was opened at Woolcombe House by Miss Kilgour, aged 99 (Miss Kilgour visited the Museum on her 101st birthday). Mr. Bonner was amongst those present. Mr. E. Chandler was the Curator, and through his keenness and perseverence the Museum has reached its present state of perfection.

After a short illness, Mr. Chandler passed away on 8th May, 1958. He devoted most of his time to perfecting Sidmouth Museum. Shortly before his death Mr. Chandler gave an order for a case to house some of the gifts to the Museum to be placed in the ground floor extension; this was almost completed when he died. In his memory members of The Sid Vale Association and friends gave this case as their tribute to this great-hearted gentleman. Mrs. Gibben has succeeded Mr. Chandler as Curator.

SIDMOUTH SOCIETY OF ARTISTS

IN 1952 an Art Class, under Gilain Glover, was started at Wool-brook School Evening Classes. After three years it was decided to form "A Society of Artists", and to hold an Exhibition for one week in August, at Hope Cottage.

Each year the number of students and standard of Exhibits had so greatly improved that in 1958 the Exhibition was extended to two weeks. Students now come from Exeter, Lyme Regis, Colaton Raleigh, Newton Poppleford, Exmouth and Ottery St. Mary.

A Studio has been set up in the town where students meet and sketch from models.

RECREATION GROUNDS

IN the old days, apart from the Cricket Field, there were no public playing fields. The children played their games of cricket or football on the "Three-cornered plot", which was then an unenclosed patch of grass, or on The Ham, where there was always the danger of the river, or else in the streets. For the adults there was nowhere, unless they had private tennis courts.

This need must have been felt, when in 1884 a suggestion was made that the Coburg field (then known as "Little Blackmore") should be secured for pleasure grounds. In a journal we read:— "Is there public spirit enough to prevent this field being sold as a building site?" (This had been suggested in 1880.) Another motion suggested "purchase for pleasure grounds to form thereon a pleasure garden open to all, where inhabitants and visitors, invalids or the aged, might sit or walk in summer or winter". Nothing was done, however, but, happily, Coburg Field remained as pasture for grazing.

In 1896 Mr. J. G. Radford conveyed to the U.D.C. "The Ham", to be enjoyed for the use of the inhabitants and visitors to Sidmouth, as a place of recreation.

A sheltered lower walk was laid out with shrubs and plants and seats placed along the riverside. At the northern end is a fine shelter overlooking a shallow pool where children sail their boats.

On many occasions the ground is used for various displays or gatherings.

In 1899 Major J. E. Balfour presented (as a gift for the free use of the public) unenclosed land popularly known as the "Three-cornered plot" to the S.U.D.C. for the parish of Sidmouth, the land to be preserved always as an open space for the use and benefit of the inhabitants and others.

On the 4th June, 1902, Major J. E. H. Balfour desired, as a thankoffering for his safe return from active service in South

Africa, to grant to the parish of Sidmouth land known as Manstone Meadow, to be used only as a public recreation ground under the control of the District Council.

This recreation ground has been a great asset for dwellers in that district, also to the town, and is used for Cricket and Association Football.

In 1939 the Council decided to enlarge the Recreation Ground by purchasing an adjoining orchard for a sum of £300, thereby giving greater accommodation for the games. At the same time they decided to erect a Pavilion.

A few years later "Long Park" at Exeter Cross was secured as pleasure grounds for children living in that district, thus preserving the Recreation Ground for Cricket and Football.

There were still no Tennis courts for the public nearer than Sidford, where good courts were laid out at the end of "The Byes". In 1918, through the generosity of Miss Leigh Browne, the Woolcombe tennis courts were opened and much patronized. Miss Leigh Browne's kindness was probably inspired by the hopeless struggle, carried on by a few public-spirited men to secure Blackmore Hall and Coburg Field for pleasure grounds. And what a struggle it was ! The people who enjoy their games little know how these men persevered and, in face of strong opposition, secured the Blackmore Hall.

How Blackmore Hall was acquired for Sidmouth

Blackmore Hall was built by Mrs. Storey about 1815. In 1905 Mrs. Scott bought Coburg Field and added it to the estate, to prevent it being built upon.

The first proposal to buy Blackmore Hall estate for the town was made on 25th November, 1913. A Local Government Inspector held an enquiry regarding the application of the Council for sanction to borrow £4,400 for the purchase of Blackmore Hall for the purpose of a public pleasure ground. On 24th March, 1914, on the proposal of Mr. Budd, seconded by Mr. Pepperell, the Seal of the Council was affixed to the contract.

Shortly after, fears were expressed as to the desirability of retaining the property, and suggestions were made that it should be offered for sale. A councillor (who strongly favoured a Harbour Scheme) was most emphatic against retaining it—"It meant a 1d. rate and would be no more attraction to visitors than the Gas Works, etc.,etc., and by selling it they would get another ratepayer."

A resolution was moved that, provided the Council obtained an offer of a certain sum for Blackmore Hall or grounds, the property be sold. Mr. J. Pepperell strongly objected to selling, suggesting an alternative that it might be let for three or even more years. "Look ahead", said Mr. Pepperell, "and think of the future. The estate was bought with the view of keeping Coburg Field for the town as a pleasure ground, and that it should become a valuable asset." He pointed out that an offer had been made by Mr. C. E. Roberts, the Rev. J. Hutchinson, and Mrs. Bartelott to give £800, as soon as a covenant was made and handed over that Coburg Field should be kept an open space. Mr. Pepperell was supported by Mr. J. G. Halse, who moved that the question be referred back. This was seconded. Mr. Pepperell, Mr. Skinner, Mr. Albert Maeer, Mr. Halse and Mr. Lake voted for and three against.

These are the facts showing how, through the efforts of those public-spirited men, the Blackmore Hall Estate and Coburg Field were secured for the town. The 1914–18 war prevented the Coburg Field being developed at once, and it was let for grazing until such time as the money could be spared. An excellent arrangement regarding Blackmore Hall was also arrived at:—On 15th June, 1914, Col. Bouverie offered to purchase Blackmore Hall, provided he gave the Council option to re-purchase at the same price after the death of the survivor of himself or Mrs. Bouverie. This offer was accepted.

THE WAR MEMORIAL

THE following is an extract from a Sidmouth Journal, 18th December, 1918 :—

"Dear Sir,

Will you kindly allow me a space in your paper to offer my suggestion for a War Memorial. I note that a proposal has been made for indoor recreation and Free Library, but nothing for outdoor games, etc. . . . .

Blackmore Hall with Coburg Field now belongs to the town, and should be laid out for tennis, bowls, putting and croquet, etc., with a suitable Pavilion. The Coburg Road should be widened, the Church House wall taken down or lowered, and while the field in front may be included, the hedge leading from Heydon's Lane should be taken down, etc. This, in conjunction with Blackmore Hall (which will eventually come back to the town) would provide Public Gardens. Why not also a Library and Rest Rooms, etc. ? The whole of this scheme may not be carried out at present, but the Coburg Field should be laid out as soon as possible.

I claim to have been the means of this estate being bought for the town, and have been awaiting an opportunity to bring the above scheme forward, and feel it my duty to bring this before the public, as a suitable memorial for the friends of the fallen and the lads who are coming home.

Yours, etc.,

'Shenstone', Sidmouth.   JAMES PEPPERELL."

1920, 26th May:—

"The Surveyor was instructed to prepare a scheme to include as much of the Coburg field as it was considered possible to lay out during next winter."

1920, 6th October:—

"Mr. Fitzgerald proposed that four tennis courts and a croquet lawn be laid out on part of the Coburg field."

1922, 8th April:—

"A decision was made by the Council to open the Coburg tennis courts on April 8th."

All those men have passed on, but they lived to see Coburg Field laid out for Tennis, Bowls, and Putting, and I know how happy Mr. Pepperell was when, in 1922, the courts were opened and he gave Mrs. Butteris (who also worked hard for the scheme) her first lesson in Croquet.

(*Twenty-eight years later.*) A Sidmouth Journal states:—

"There is rather an unusual history attaching to the acquisition of this property, writes our Sidmouth representative. The whole area was originally purchased by the Council in 1914. The Coburg Field was retained and has since been laid out for bowls, tennis and putting green, but the remainder of the estate representing the property now being acquired was sold to two joint purchasers. It should revert to the Council at an agreed price. The Council will enter into occupation in about a month."

From "Express & Echo", 29th December, 1951:—

"COUNCIL BUYS BACK PROPERTY

The Blackmore Hall Estate, Sidmouth, including a large house, with outbuildings and 2 acres 29 perches of land is to be purchased by the Sidmouth Urban Council for £3,000, and vacant possession will be given on completion of the purchase on Jan. 25th, 1952.

This was announced by the Clerk to the Council (Mr. R. Pickard) to-day, in a statement in which he described the property as one of the most valuable acquisitions ever made by the Council.

The estate is entered from the High Street and a considerable part of it abuts on the footpath intersecting the Coburg Field pleasure ground.

Its central position affords great possibilities of development and for adding substantially to the amenities of the town."

1954. 15th July. BLACKMORE HALL, together with some adjoining land, was advertised to be sold without effect.

It had fallen into such a state of disrepair that the house was demolished.

The gardens have been beautified, seats placed on the site of the house, shelters built and seats placed beneath the beautiful old trees, creating a wonderful atmosphere of peace and now known as The Coronation Gardens.

How happy my father (James Pepperell) would be, and the other councillors who supported him in his hard-won fight, could he see the wonderful results, and the peaceful atmosphere for those who cannot walk far, to rest right in the heart of the town and listen to, and feed, the birds.

1956. February. BLACKMORE HALL HOUSE having been demolished, the site is cleared and the Council decided to retain its ownership. It was decided that any decision in respect of its development should remain for the time being.

CONNAUGHT GARDENS

ACROSS the road from Peak House, at the bottom of "Battery Field", ran a path, leading to Jacob's Ladder and the Chit Rocks. These latter conjure up memories of happy childhood days, spent in paddling, bathing and shrimping, and when older wandering over to Lade Foot. Never were there such prawns found elsewhere. When tide compelled us to go by way of Jacob's Ladder and the Cliff path we had mixed feelings of excitement and fear at having to pass (what we then imagined it to be) the home of an Ogre !

At that time "Sea-view" was inside grounds completely hidden from view by high hoardings placed on the top of the wall reaching far up the trees. A pseudo-castle with clock tower and a boat-house, complete with a boat hanging from its davits, and with stone steps descending the cliff to the shore lent itself to awesome enchantment. I do not remember, but we might have heard the murmur that smugglers used the house to store their contraband in cellars hidden beneath the Connaught Gardens.

Little did we think that, as at the touch of a fairy's wand, the

Ogre's Castle would be transformed into our beautiful Connaught Gardens.

In whose brain the idea was first conceived I do not know; but I *do know* that Mr. James Pepperell (who was for years a member of the Council, and was, I believe, at that time President of the Sidmouth Development Association) had something to do with it, for I have found his notes with sketches and plans for the laying out of the grounds, also the suggestion that at the death of the elderly owner, Mr. Jemmett, "Sea-view" should be acquired for the town and its grounds developed. Many misgivings were felt as to the wisdom of acquiring it, as the cost of its purchase and upkeep would be great, the house and grounds being more or less derelict.

On 28th May, 1930, the first negotiations to buy "Sea-view" were made and the purchase was confirmed on 4th June at a cost of £3,500.

Our gratitude will ever go out to our Council in their final decision; the result so justifies their "extravagances".

The late Mr. Macdermid was Chairman at the time. Once it was purchased, they sought and found experts in the practised arts of gardening, building and, above all, men with a love of nature.

The old house had to come down, but a large part of the rugged, weathered stone walls were preserved and fitted into the designs of the shelters, and covered walks.

Some of the trees and shrubs of great age and beauty were retained. The camellias still thrive after over twenty years, and a spacious lawn has given pleasure to hundreds of people when listening to our own and visiting bands, or watching the Folk Dancers and joining in the Old Time dances. In the coldest weather seats can be found, sheltered from the wind. One's eyes are gladdened by a beautiful miniature framed by the archways at every point. Seen through the west archway, the picture of cliffs, sky and sea, cannot be surpassed in Italy or the South of France.

The Gardens were opened on 3rd November, 1934, by H.R.H. the late Duke of Connaught, who gave his name to them. The late Mr. Saunders was then Chairman of the Council.

1955. 20th August. The massed Bands of the Arab Legion. The Army of the Hashemite Kingdom of Jordan, is known to the British as The Arab Legion.

During the war it fought side by side with the British Army in the Middle East under its British Commander, Lieut.-General J. B. Glubb, C.M.G., D.S.O., O.B.E., M.C. Its Bands were in this country on a goodwill visit "to show the Flag".

The establishment of the Arab Legion includes three military Bands, one of which visited the Connaught Gardens.

These Bands performed under their own Jordanian, trained at the Army School of Music, Kneller Hall.

The Bandsmen's uniform consists of white drill jackets and trousers, the latter being tucked into white spats. The head-dress is the famous red Smagh, which is secured by the black Ajal—the distinctive head-dress of the Arab Legion.

I listened to one of these concerts and much enjoyed them. The bandsmen were very proficient performers and their uniforms and dark complexions made an attractive spectacle in the picturesque surroundings of The Connaught Gardens.

A Miniature Peep

CHAPTER XVIII

SPORT

CRICKET

SIDMOUTH has the finest cricket ground in the county. Standing in an elevated position with an uninterrupted view of the Bay on the south, surrounded by fine buildings and beautiful scenery in the background, with well-kept tennis courts, it is unparalleled.

The first Cricket Club was established in Sidmouth in 1823, and played on the present cricket ground, which was unenclosed. I quote an extract from "Wootman's Exeter Gazette" of 21st August, 1824:—

"The return match between the Sidmouth and Exeter Clubs was played at Quicke's Ground on Monday. The day was favourable and more animated, and so equal a contest has seldom been witnessed. The first innings were gained by the Exeter Gentelmen, making 88 notches and their opponents 76; the second innings the Sidmouth Gentelmen ran 75 and Exeter 55, making upon both innings 8 notches in favour of Sidmouth.

A certain incident arose during the match which is referred to the President of the Mary-le-bone Club for his decision . . . .

Play lasted from 11 till 6, when the parties and their friends in all between 40 and 50 sat down to a handsome cold collation and spent the remainder of the evening in high glee."

In 1827 we hear of cricket being played here with great assiduity, and especially promoted by Capt. Clarke of Sid Abbey, and a Club house was erected. It was an oblong thatched building, containing a spacious room in which many a good dinner was served. After the death of Capt. Clarke and the removal of one or two leading members, the game languished and then became entirely neglected. The Club house fell into decay and was pulled down before 1840. The first Mr. Thornton took a 14-year lease from the Trustees of the Manor, sometime in 1872, and by mowing and rolling kept the ground in first-rate order. So cricket became popular again. On 3rd August, 1874, a match was played on the Fortfield between a party of gentlemen, styling themselves "Incogniti" v. "Gentlemen of Devon", resulting in a win for the Devon team by 211–159. Mr. R. N. Thornton gave a grand ball on the Friday evening, to which gentlemen of both teams were invited, and which was also attended by the "crème-de-la-crème" of Sidmouth Society.

In 1879 Mr. W. Hine-Haycock became lessee of the Cricket Field (then known as "The Fort Field") and another Pavilion was built. Sidmouth owes much gratitude to these keen sportsmen, who have enabled us to enjoy such excellent cricket up to the present day. Added to these names in my memory are the much-revered names of Clifford Wells, Marzetties, Mann, Carlos-Clarke, five members of the Leese family, Brutton, Brandt, Moore, Hunt, etc., etc. All had distinguished themselves at Winchester, Marlborough, Oxford or Cambridge.

Most of these families visited Sidmouth annually without cessation from boyhood; they grew up with us and were looked upon as Sidmothians (an honour granted only to those who have lived here over a number of years !).

The opposing teams included such names as Nondescripts, Incogniti, I Zingari, Old Tonbridgians, M.C.C., Old Marlburians, Crystal Palace, Old Alleynians, Sheffield Collegiates, Devonshire Dumplings, Old Tauntonians, etc. In the early days the matches began in April and ended the first week in September, when the Tennis Tournaments were held.

The season started when the Rev. J. H. Copleston brought a team from Honiton. What a keen old sportsman he was; his dear old eyes would twinkle and glisten as he described some of his triumphs. He was Rector of Offwell near Honiton. One Sunday, when preaching, he knocked his watch off the edge of the pulpit. Quickly catching it he exclaimed: "How's that, Umpire ?" !

Sidmouth had many good keen local players (as they still have) who played for Sidmouth during the early months of the season, giving way to the non-residents (whose names I have mentioned) in August. Amongst these were Freddie Orchard, Reg. Russell, several of the Mills family, etc.

Extract from a Journal:—

"A novel cricket match was played on the Cricket Field between Sidmouth Eleven and thirty of the local fishermen. The Eleven consisting of: W. H. Potbury, J. R. Potbury, Bingley Pullin, W. Guppy, George Clarke, H. Culverwell, Captained by J. P. Mullen of the Bedford Hotel, were dismissed for 95 whilst the fishermen, captained by Edward Connant compiled 35. A dinner followed in the evening at Host H. Bolt's London Hotel and an enjoyable evening was spent."

It was a great day when Hobbs and Woolley brought a team to Sidmouth on 16th and 17th September, 1926. People flocked into the town from all outlying districts. We breathlessly watched Hobbs make his century, after which he hit out getting one boundary after another, a sight not to have been missed.

Extract from an Exeter paper of 29th May, 1952:—

"Yesterday and today cricket enthusiasts from Devon packed their sandwiches and went to Taunton by rail and road to watch Somerset tilt the lance at the Indians.

"Not only Devonians will be there of course—but the Shire of the Sea Kings has a special, even a proprietary! interest in Somerset cricket. For was it not at Sidmouth, the fashionable Devon sea-side resort, that, in August, 1875, the decision was taken to form a County Cricket Club in Somerset."

1952

I looked in at the Pavilion this morning to refresh my memory by looking at old photographs. The following are a few of the names of old players:—Major Denys, Considene, H. Culverwell, F. H. Carrall, Prendergast, Fulcher, Tate, Clifford, Russell, E. E. Whitton, E. A. Sutton, J. Pepperell, E. P. Mills, A. G. Skinner, Capt. Horton, Capt. Moore; and later names: A. F. Irish, Carter, two Badcocks, J. Maeer, etc.

Cricket slowed down during the war years but was not allowed to lapse. Many improvements have been made. The Pavilion was enlarged and the Cricket Ground bought for the town in 1936, both by means of subscription. Deck chairs have replaced the hard seats and this year we have acquired a new, movable and mechanical scoring board and box. Dear old "Hoppy" has gone and so has Carrall, and they are much missed. Old faces go, but the game goes on.

A fitting end to this report took place on 4th and 5th August and I had the joy to watch the match !

Extract from "The Daily Telegraph", August, 1952:—

"A Surrey Memory. With Surrey heading for their first solo Championship victory since 1914 I note as a coincidence, that C. T. A. Wilkinson, who led them in that auspicious season is again in the news.

Playing this week in a two-day match at Sidmouth against the Nondescripts he followed up a first Innings of 53 by taking all 10 wickets in the visitors' second innings for 27 runs. Sidmouth won by 156. He is 67."

An extract from "The Cricketer", 23rd August, 1952:—

"August and Sidmouth are almost synonymous words. Until August Sidmouth rely on local talent and an indication of their strength is that six of their regular members have played for Devon. They are the Captain, T. V. Hollingsworth, A. F. Irish, who also had a turn with Somerset, Major V. T. Troman, C. S. Taylor, J. H. Stallibrass and G. Whittington. The doyen of the August visitors is of course C. T. A. Wilkinson who has a

Sidmouth record extending over thirty years. During that period he has taken almost countless wickets and scored a great many runs. And so has G. F. Summers, whose record for the last three seasons is over 1,500 runs at an average of virtually 45. But these figures are bettered by J. M. A. Marshall, the former Warwickshire Amateur, who, since the war has made 2,738 runs, average 57, and has taken 239 wickets, average 13. D. L. H. Mercer, the old Hornsey and Nondescript Wicket-keeper, has lived at Sidmouth since his retirement and has put in a tremendous amount of work for the Devon Club, who have another prominent Club cricketer, J. A. Macdonald, as Hon. Match Secretary."

We owe gratitude for the maintenance of Cricket through times of vicissitude, to too many names to be mentioned.

SID VALE CRICKET CLUB FORMED

13th April, 1921

A MEETING was held at The London Hotel on Friday under the Chairmanship of Mr. J. Pepperell, with the object of forming a cricket club to enter the Exeter & District Cricket League. The Chairman having explained the object of the meeting, it was decided to form a Club and name it "The Sid Vale Cricket Club", also to enter Division I of the League.

2nd August, 1933

"In an 'Old Timers' Cricket Match, Mr. J. Pepperell, aged 74, took three wickets for 24 runs and deserves to be congratulated for carrying his bat for 12 runs". (Extract from Journal.)

1957

Cricket success was scored by a Sidmouth player, Mr. H. L. Baker. In July, 1957, he completed his 1,000 runs.

CRICKET HISTORY MADE AT SIDMOUTH

13th September, 1958

Cricket has certainly been played at Sidmouth for the past 120 years or more. Local history was made on the ground on Saturday, when R. J. Palmer clean bowled D. S. C. Philips' hundredth wicket of the season—the first time as far as records of the Club show that 100 wickets have been taken by a Sidmouth amateur.

CRICKET SCORING BOARD

VISITING cricketers often admire the fine scoring board on the cricket field, but few realize that it is made from what is probably the last surviving bathing-machine.

Believed to be nearly a hundred years old and made of cedarwood, it was at one time a private family bathing-machine, belonging to Mr. F. A. Lindemann, who owned and lived at Sidholme. His son, the late Lord Cherwell (formerly Professor Lindemann), was Britain's Atomic Chief.

The machine was acquired by the late Mr. Dagworthy, and I remember seeing it for years on a piece of waste ground at the rear of "The Baths". Mr. Dagworthy gave it to the Cricket Club and other friends of the Club undertook to cover the cost of converting it to its present use.

FOOTBALL

FOOTBALL, started in 1884 and played on Coburg Field, has always been one of the most popular sports in Sidmouth, and there has always been a first-class team. My father never played, but was always a keen supporter, and so were his daughters. I can always remember Saturdays as red-letter days, when we took our seats in the stand and shouted our heads off, watching Tommy Fitzgerald dodging cleverly up the field with wonderful passing, and scoring the tries, which Sammy Skinner converted. Sammy was very artful, often off-side when getting the ball into the scrum and looking so innocent if challenged. "Neeby" Woolley, Frank and Harry Skinner (later Fred Skinner) were forwards with "Inky" Vallance, Reg. Russell, Freddy Orchard as halves, all clever players. There were also Bert Potbury, Bert Slade, Bill and Harry Skinner and Holland. Old John Newton was always there, a fine old gentleman whose stentorian voice would ring out across the field "Well played, b-hoys"!

Dear old Mrs. "Poll" Trick rarely missed a match. I remember once seeing her take off the hat of a stranger sitting in front and waving it. Mrs. Trick died in 1952, whilst dressing to go to a match at the age of 84. She had been made a life member. Sidmouth mourns the passing of a dear character. She could be seen every morning feeding the seagulls outside her house at 7 York Terrace; the "gulls" swarmed down directly she appeared.

People avoided sitting next to my father as, quite unconsciously, he gradually edged them along the seat as he followed the ball up the field with his eyes. He was so keen that if any of the team had a chill, he would take hot gruel and whiskey to their homes to get them fit to play.

Blind "Dappy" Pinn rarely missed a match, and shouted encouragement.

"Theof" Mortimore, our popular Town Crier, was also a keen supporter and so were his family. At a Cup match his daughter Milly (then a girl, now a granny) came dressed as a boy in complete

football togs ! Toff also organised the torch-light processions.
I shall never forget when Sidmouth won the Senior Cup in 1897.
Headed by the Band playing "See the Conquering Hero Comes",
the team with a member carrying the Cup, was drawn round the
town.

Although I cannot remember this, I copy a report from a
journal:—

"Sidmouth won the Junior Cup on Feb. 14th, 1891. A good
crowd of supporters. Coach for the players, brakes, landaus, and
pony carriages. Besides these, many were seen 'making tracks' by
'Shank's pony' and several by boats. The coach and brake by
way of Woolbrook and Newton Poppleford, although 2 miles
longer than by Peak Hill, it was easier for the horses. The journey
enlivened by means of music dispensed by means of a cornet
by Mr. J. Burgoyne and a violin by Mr. G. Turner. The Sidmouth
team were the winners, the score stood as follows:—Sidmouth
team 1 goal, 8 tries, 1 dead ball, 1 save; Budleigh Salterton, nil.
Sidmouth team were:—J. S. Potbury, back, E. S. Reynolds,
G. B. Lloyd, J. Clark ⅜s, W. Skinner and F. Whitton halfs,
G. Taylor, W. Pidsley, E. Tucker, H. H. Martin, C. Mills, T. R.
Potbury, H. Skinner, E. Weeks, F. Cockburn, forwards.

The scene after the match was a lively one. On reaching
Sidmouth a great welcome was ready, and the coach drove along
the Esplanade and through Fore Street. The musicians played
'The Conquering Hero' en route. The scene at the headquarters
of the Club was great and loud cheers greeted the visitors as
they drove up."

During the 1914–18 war the Football Field was ploughed up
for allotments, and after an interval of five years the game was
resumed and played on the Coburg Field.

November, 1952. I remember when on the occasion of a match
between our local team and Exmouth, scarcely anything else was
talked about for days previous to the event. A contemporary account
runs:—"Last week visiting Cranford (Exmouth), Sidmouth were
the better side throughout, their very strong forwards taking control,
and they had no difficulty in defeating Exmouth by one goal and two
tries (11 pts) to nil." This was the seventh successive game in which
Sidmouth had no points scored against them. Maurice Gooding
was the Captain.

1952. We find that Sidmouth footballers are again at the top of
form and have won many laurels.

Extract from "Express & Echo", December, 1952:—"Queens'
College, Cambridge, hitherto unbeaten this season, came to Sidmouth for the first time yesterday when, after a display of in-

vigorating football, they were defeated by 11 points (1 goal, 1 penalty goal and 1 drop goal) to 3 points (1 try)."

Passing over the years, Football is still the chief winter sport with a thriving Club, an excellent team with keen supporters.

OFFICIALS OF THE SIDMOUTH RUGBY FOOTBALL CLUB, 1953

Mr. T. S. Sanders	..	President
Mr. D. L. H. Mercer	..	Hon. Treasurer
Mr. G. T. Bolt	..	Hon. Secretary
Mr. A. G. Clapp	..	Hon. Team Secretary
Mr. J. A. MacDonald	..	Chairman of Committee
Mr. S. J. Hayman	..	Vice-Chairman
Mr. A. Irish	..	Trainer
G. Whittington	··	Captain
Derek Rees ..	..	Vice-Captain

At the Annual Dinner of Sidmouth Rugby Football Club, held at the Victoria Hotel in April, 1953, Mr. T. Sanders, President of Devon Rugby Football Union informed the company that Sidmouth Rugby Club had a wonderful season for the third year in succession and during that period had only lost 26 out of 127 matches played.

ASSOCIATION FOOTBALL

ALTHOUGH Rugby Football has always predominated in Sidmouth, there is also an Association Team. Their matches are played on the Recreation Field at Manstone.

"The Sidmouth Herald", December, 1952:—

"Willey's *v.* Sidmouth. First round tie for the East Devon Cup. Sidmouth beat Willey's by 8 goals to 6. Again Sidmouth B. *v.* Budleigh Salterton B. Sidmouth won by 7 goals to 3."

3rd May, 1958. "Sidmouth win East Devon Senior Cup. History was made at St. James's Park, Exeter, on Wednesday evening, when Sid-town, defying the gloomy forecasts of all the experts brought off a surprising, but deserved win by two goals to one to defeat Friernhay in the final of the East Devon Senior Cup. Victory did not come until two minutes from the end of extra time, when after a free-kick for Sidmouth, taken by Vincent, had been blocked by Friernhay defenders, the ball came back to Jack Matthews who slammed it into the back of the net. Sidmouth led 1—0 at half-time, David Rew having given them the lead, but Friernhay equalised in the second half through Atkins. This was a fine success for Sidmouth with every man playing his part in a match in which team spirit was predominant.

The Cup was presented to Capt. Gerald Bess by Mr. A. S. Line, chairman of Exeter City Football Club."

HOCKEY

(Extract from "Sidmouth Observer"):—

October, 1919. "Sidmouth Hockey Club was formed about 7 years ago, by Mr. Pepperell, who has worked indefatigably towards its organisation and the coaching of beginners.

In pre-war days there were a large number of members and some excellent and successful matches were played. It is proposed to revive this excellent game . . . . Practices take place in the Western Fields. Further particulars can be obtained from J. Pepperell, 'Shenstone', etc."

In December, 1952. Hockey is still going strong. An extract from the "Sidmouth Herald" reads:—"On Saturday last the men visited the Depot Devonshire Regiment and Wessex Brigade at Topsham Barracks and won by 4 goals to 3."

BOWLS

BOWLING was started on the Bedford Lawn in May, 1908, and the first match was on 22nd August with the City of Exeter Reserves at Sidmouth.

In May, 1922, a meeting was held at the Coburg Field in order to resuscitate the Bowling Club. It was decided:—"That a Town's Bowling Club be formed within the jurisdiction of the Council." Mr. Thorpe-Haddock was elected President, Mr. J. F. Vallance, Captain. On the death of Mr. Thorpe-Haddock, the late Mr. Gilbert Ford became President.

Bowling has become very popular and is keenly supported. Members have gained high honours in the county and at the Bowling Club's Annual Dinner at The Victoria Hotel on 15th January, 1953 (from a report):—"The Council's plans for the transfer of the Club's headquarters to the Blackmore Hall was made known."

A second green has been provided, and it is hoped that a Tournament can be arranged. The Club celebrated their Jubilee in May, 1958.

As Mrs. Butteris strongly supported the purchase of "The Coburg Field", we are happy to see her in 1952 still enjoying its amenities. Her family have been strong supporters of Bowling. The present President is her son-in-law.

The present Officers are Mr. Edgar Smith, President; Mr. F. J. Selley, Captain; Lt.-Col. Corner, Vice-Captain. The ladies have many honours: Mrs. L. Broughton has been appointed County President; Mrs. K. Selley, Captain; Mrs. Clarke, Hon. Secretary.

BOXING

BOXING also has a strong following in Sidmouth. Mr. J. O'Brien won many honours, and he now concentrates on training. Many of our

Sidmouth lads have gained honours at contests all over England.
Extract from Journal, 10th January, 1953 :—

"Big surprise in London Boxing Circles. On Wednesday evening
Peter Sellick travelled to London to meet Pte. R. Kelly (R.A.O.C.)
in a three-minute round contest. Kelly, an Army welterweight
champion, has represented the Army against Holland, Belgium,
Denmark and Wales in International Championships . . . . . .
It was a 'top-class' contest . . . . . . Sellick dropped his opponent
for a count of two and a count of five in the last round. Roger
Baldwin is also a first-class Boxer and has won many victories."

OTHER PASTIMES

AMONGST our many Societies are:—A Camera Club formed in
October, 1919. The Townswomen's Guild with Mrs. Chandler as
President, Mrs. Burgoyne Chairman, Miss Foster Hon. Treasurer,
and Miss Harris Hon. Secretary. A Garden Club founded in
1949. President Dr. Gerald Gibbens, Secretary Mrs. Roberts.
Monthly meetings and lectures are held and well attended by
enthusiastic members. The Garden Club holds two successful
Flower Shows each year.

CHAPTER XIX

I Remember

Born in May Cottage.

My first memory of anything was of sitting on a table having a blue bonnet tied on (the strings were too tight), sticking out my feet and seeing new blue shoes; then afterwards being carried out and placed in the lap of a lovely lady, who was sitting in a carriage with two horses.

The lovely lady was Mrs. Lindemann, the mother of the late Lord Cherwell (Professor Lindemann), who was born in Sidmouth, and I was being taken to have tea at Sidholme. Apart from driving into a beautiful garden, I can remember nothing more of that visit. Years later I was entertained in the lovely house filled with rare treasures, with its beautiful music room and organ. It is now Sidholme Guest House.

The 5th of November, known as "Bonfire Day", was to me a day of terror. When rough men carrying "guys" wearing ugly masks went from house to house and with rough voices recited or growled some doggerel of "please for a penny to burn the old Pope". Even the excitement of being taken on to the beach after dark to see a huge bonfire into which the guys were thrown did not allay my terror.

After the first war this "festivity" was dropped and later replaced by delightful carnival processions which are still carried on.

A red-letter day was August Bank Holiday, when the "Foresters" held a fête, preceded by a procession with wonderful tableaux on horse-drawn waggons, the same people taking part each year. Headed by the band, came in the first tableaux, Mr. Cload of Landpart, a big burly man with sandy side-whiskers, dressed as a shepherd, holding on to a sheep. Then came an elderly woman, "a widow" clad in long black dress and veil surrounded by small children, also clothed in black.

A happier note was struck by a trolley carrying a bevy of Maypole Dancers, in charge of Miss Slade (Mrs. Marks).

But the greatest thrill was of Annie Spencer dressed in white sitting on a kind of throne, with long fair tresses. Led by Robin Hood, the procession paraded the town and proceeded to Knowle Park, where the fête was held. In spite of our pleadings we were never allowed to go into the vicinity of the park.

123

I think the outstanding day of the year was "Show Day". Held a few days before Christmas, all shopkeepers vied to outdo one another in their window display. On the slab of the butcher's window, pink pigs lay with oranges in their mouths, whilst fairy lights twinkled in the holly-covered walls and ceiling. The entire front of Tedbury's was covered with turkeys and geese. In Coulson's window (Veale) a clockwork man smacked his lips and moved his head from side to side whilst he drank a bottle of wine. Across the road in Russell's (Boyce) confectioner's shop a donkey nodded his head amongst the iced cakes, etc.

The grocers presented their customers with a Christmas Box parcel filled with good things. Minstrels blacked their faces and with tambourines, etc., entertained on street corners and houses, collecting for "The Black Hawks".

Another grand procession took place when the circuses came to the town. Lovely be-spangled ladies rode on horseback. Bareback riders and clowns, headed by elephants, zebras and camels, led by a blaring brass band, completed the thrill.

I remember the German Bands playing at street corners, and the barrel-organs with either a monkey, or cages of love-birds on the top, who, for a penny, would pick out a paper telling your fortune. Sometimes a "bambino" would be in a cradle strapped to the organ. And there were the dancing bears, who stood on their hind legs and ambled around to the tuneless intoning of their keepers.

I like to recall the cosy feeling of looking from the window in winter and watching the lamplighter, a little man named Alsopp, and later Fox, Wattley, and "Stumper" Wood, carrying their poles to turn on the gas lamps—Alsopp used to give a little skip and hop as he hurried along.

(Extract from a journal, 21st September, 1891):—

"GREAT STATTY FAIR

As is usual on the third Monday in September, this 'Great Fair' was held, and the immensity of the Carnival will be recognised when we state that it consisted of no less than two stalls containing all kinds of sweetmeats and fancy articles, a whelk stall, also an ice-cream barrow, all of which were well patronised.

This fair is a great event in the eyes of the juvenile population who apparently found the delicacies too great to be resisted while the pocket money lasted.

The savoury whelk stall did a roaring trade.

Penny rides and donkey rides were very popular. Towards evening great excitement was reached while the old joke of taking the lantern to see the fair was acted upon."

We were given extra pennies on Fair days and the special sweets "comfits" tasted wonderful. There was dear old Mrs. "Fiddy" Smith at her winkle stall, and I remember the fascination of watching her wares being eaten with the fingers from tiny saucers, after being sprinkled with vinegar shaken from bottles with pierced corks. We saw carriages crammed with children being taken around Coulson's Corner by way of Old Fore Street for 1d. rides, and also donkey rides. There was a roaring trade in these. We could watch the skittling for a pig in the side street, also the Hoop-la and other competitions, but the biggest thrill was being taken after dark and seeing the stalls lit by naphtha flares. Yes ! Those were the days !

As we walked down the streets on Sundays there was delightful quietude, the only sound being those of our own feet and of the tinkling pianos playing hymns issuing from various houses. People all finely dressed in their "best", children with starched frocks walking in front of their parents. It all sounds too funny in these days, but they were such happy days. This might sound "priggish", but it was not so.

We often wish we could return to those days, especially when the cost of living was so cheap. When I was speaking to an old inhabitant, she mentioned the enjoyment they got after a long walk, gleaning a pram full of sticks and calling at the shops on the way home for Chudleighs at four for a penny, 2 oz. of cream 2d., new milk at 3d. a quart in the summer, and skimmed milk at 3 pints a 1d. Butter 1/- a pound in May and June, never higher than 1/6, eggs at 6d. and the most 2/- a dozen. The fattest chicken for 2/6, rabbits for 9d. dough cake 3d. bread 2½d. a loaf.

Before the advent of gas cookers, many families took their Sunday dinners to be cooked at Clode's bakehouse (now Broughton's). Charge 2d.

Items from advertisements of 50 years ago :—

In 1901 Trumps advertised

Picnic Hams @ 5d. per lb.

Prime cuts of bacon @ 8d. per lb. Streaky 5d.

Cream Cheese 6d. each.

Old Scotch Whiskey	@ 2/8 per bottle.	
Rum	@ 2/6 ,,	,,
Port	@ 1/6 ,,	,,
Claret	@ 1/- ,,	,,
Sherry	@ 1/10 ,,	,,
Champagne	@ 4/6, 5/-, 7/- per bottle.	

and Messrs. John Field & Sons,

Blankets   @ 5/11 to 21/- per pair.

Down Quilts   from 2/6½ to 37/6 each.

Winter dress material from 6¾d. to 1/11 a yard.

All-wool flannels   ,,   ,, ,, 1/3½ ,,   ,,

OLD CUSTOMS AND NEW

"*ONE* a penny, *two* a penny hot-cross bu-uns" was the welcome sound which awoke us in the early hours of Good Friday. The cry came from boys employed by local bakers, who had been baking all night. Buns never tasted better than when we were allowed to eat them before breakfast. That old custom has gone, but a wonderful idea presented itself to a popular member of the Council. Mr. J. P. Millen.

On Good Friday of 1900 the distribution of hot-cross buns on the Bedford Lawn was introduced by him when the bakers of Sidmouth "struck" against making buns on Good Friday. Mr. Millen went to Newton Poppleford and obtained a large supply. On his death the custom was taken up by the local lodge of R.A.O.B.

On Good Friday of 1958 I watched over a thousand children gather there, coaches being lent to convey them from our outlying parishes of Sidbury, Sidford, Woolbrook and Salcombe Regis. Their happy little face makes one's heart go out in grateful memory to J. P. Millen and "Bert" Goodwin.

PEACE CELEBRATIONS

WHAT a day of rejoicing when Peace was celebrated on Saturday, 19th July, 1919.

The town was be-flagged and decked with bunting. The Church bells rang out. Everywhere there were tokens of joy.

Celebrations started at 10 o'clock with a Marathon Race from the Beacon Lamp, around Sidford via Primley Hill, High Street, ending at the Bedford Hotel. The honours were won by two Sidmouth men, Gigg and Pile, a Canadian coming third. Gigg traversed the four miles in 26 minutes ! The Victory March of the local naval and military forces was a sight which lingers in many minds. Headed by a band, the procession was as follows :—P.C.s Moore and Kiff, Col. J. E. H. Balfour, C.M.G., Capt. Greenwood Standard Bearer, Band, Crimean Veterans, Old Comrades, Men of the Navy, Officers and Chaplains, Men of the Army, Devon 25 V.A.D.s, Army Veteran Association, Land Workers, Church Lads Brigade, Boy Scouts, Girl Guides. The procession formed at Exeter Cross, proceeded through the town across the Esplanade, and was dismissed at the Triangle.

Every window was filled *en route* and crowds massed in the streets. It was good to hear the boys, sickened by the sights of war, breaking forth in their old jests and songs as they marched. They sang the songs they must have sung to keep their courage up when marching to face death.

Wreaths and an immense cross were placed at the foot of the Memorial. Tea was given to the children in the Manor Hall and Victory mugs were presented to 1,000 children up to the age of 14.

In a large marquee in Barton Close old people were given a meat tea. Bedridden pensioners had parcels of good things sent to them. There was a grand Cinema Show and a Dance at the Manor Hall, and afterwards a firework display on the Front, which was decked with lanterns and fairy-lights.

All along the coastline from Portland Bill to Berry Head and Start Point could be seen flashing lights, "Cape beyond cape, in endless range those twinkling points of fire".

Sports were held on the Monday. Trump's Stores gave an impromptu supper to their employees and a week's extra wages.

On the following Thursday 600 Service and ex-Service men sat down to a Victory Dinner in the Manor Hall at the invitation of the Comrades of the Great War Association and the Peace Celebrations Committee. Regimental Sergt.-Major Colwill and Corporal Snelgrove spoke for the Devons. Capt. Maitland Payne and Mr. Ivan Sparkes responded for the Air Force.

WATER CART

I REMEMBER the water cart, in the shape of a barrel, on two wheels, with a long pipe across between the two back wheels, which sprayed the roads. Reg. Holland was the driver. The cart was filled from hydrants placed in various parts of the town.

On 5th May, 1914, "The roads committee instructed the Surveyor to draw up a scheme for street-watering by means of a hose and stand-pipes". The water cart was still being used in March, 1918.

Soon after the first edition of my book had come out, I was hailed by Mr. Reg. Holland, who told me that I had made a mistake in saying that Joey Lightfoot drove the "water cart", as he (Reg. Holland) was the driver, and as Joey had lost one ear, the boys would call after him: "Happy new yur" (ear). He told me that "Joey" drove the dust cart, and I had quite forgotten its existence, as I was only a child.

DUST CART

THE dust cart was a two-wheeled horse-drawn cart, which used to collect and empty the dust-bins, also shovel up the heaps of dust, left by the roadside by the crossing sweeper, unlike the present day, one man for each job ! That was before tar macadam roads.

Our Fishermen

ONE notes with regret and sadness the passing away of our old Fishermen. Fortunately, most of them have left children to carry on the old names.

In my childhood days it was a delight to go down by the sea. The foreshore was in those days the undisputed domain of the fisherman, who could keep his boats and bathing machines there, without hindrance. Terraces of shingle enabled them to beach their boats, and dry their nets all along the shore.

Beginning at the Bedford steps, each family had its own pitch. Old Sam Ware and his sons, Fred and Bill, have gone and sad to say none of their family are there; and so have the Hooks, Jim and Dan. Dan was a popular character, with his dark beard, hairy arms and hands and the far-away look in his eyes, as he related wonderful tales of the sea.

I like to recall George, father of the Woolleys, a fine figure swinging along, his handsome wrinkled face and blue eyes, the colour of which the Woolleys seemed to have borrowed from the sea (his brother, "Uncle Sam", was greeted by all). There were several sons; some joined the Navy, but Bob and Tom ("Neebie") joined their father, and were always ready to welcome and be welcomed by all.

Dear old Bob is sadly missed, and, although over 80 when he died, could be seen busy with his boat to the end.

Happily I can still see "Neebie" from my window in the early morning, walking over to "Chit" collecting sea-gulls' eggs in their season, gathering driftwood or beach-combing. Though his step is slower, his smiling greeting is always there.

Mr. and Mrs. Tom ("Neebie") Woolley, who were married on 1st June, 1898, celebrated their Golden Wedding in 1948.[1]

Next came John and Bill Farrant, refined friendly men who confined most of their activities to taking visitors sailing and rowing. I can just remember old John, their father. The Farrants were very popular, and it was a sad day when they passed on.

"Gully" Bartlett or "Red Cap", who confined most of his energies to his lobster pots, was an irascible character, who "shooed" us away when we got near his boat, and had a monkey ready to snap at anyone who ventured near. Then came "The Smiths",

---

[1] 21st January, 1953. My heart is very sad, for "Neebie" died this morning, just before taking his walk across the Front. Sidmouth mourns the loss of another of her popular stalwarts.

Old Ben, a gentle character, and his son Toby, big and blustery.

Another family of Smiths, better known, were Jack and "Scrummer". Scrummer passed away a short time ago and is sadly missed from the York Steps, where he and his pal, "Stan" Harris, did a thriving trade conveying passengers for trips in the Bay in their Drifter. Happily, Stan still carries on.

The Harris family came next, "Uncle Bill", Jim, "Tink" and "Tuzzy". All now gone, but happily leaving many sons who carry on. "Tuzzy" took the prize for the number of his progeny, with a family of fifteen much respected sons and daughters.

"Tink" will be best remembered for his "husky" cry, "Veesh all alive-o", as he pushed his barrow along the streets.

Hayman Salter is still there, a member of a popular old Sidmouth family, and so are the Bagwells. The old families of Beavis, "Gibberick" Bastin, John Rugg, George Horn, Pursey, "Dickey" Bird, Bob Stone, Pike and Tapley have gone. Last, but by no means least, comes "Dappy" Pinn. Being blind, he could not catch fish, but he hawked them, pushing his barrow all over the town and his fine voice singing "Crab-o, Crab-o, Crab-o-o" or "Herrings all alive-o", could be heard from one street to another. He was also a keen "spectator" (?) at all Football matches shouting encouragement to the players. Alas, "Dappy" passed away a few years ago.

The fishermen families lived near their "pitches". The Hooks, Woolleys, Conants and Wares lived in Bedford Square. The garden-fronted cottage with trellised porch, mentioned in "A Poor Man's House", the home of Bob and Mam Woolley has gone, and so have the homes of the Woolleys.

Other families lived in "The Marsh", now known as York Street. An extract from a journal of 1883 runs:—

"'Frederick Bartlett' of Western Town (Osborne House) and George Horn, both fishermen of this town (Horn coxswain of the Lifeboat) through the kindness of Dr. Pullin, Mrs. Floyd and Sir John Kennaway, not only shared in the ceremonies and enjoyments liberally provided, including visits to the Queen, Etc., but were fortunate enough to receive the commemoration medal of the event. As but 400 of these were given for the United Kingdom, and 16 for Devonshire, the two Sidmouthians may be congratulated on their success."

CHAPTER XX

WOOLBROOK

WOOLBROOK, Walbrook, Wallabrook, or Wellabrook, means "Brook coming immediately from the fountain, and not yet joined with any other". There is a stream that rises in the hollow between Core and Beacon Hills, which passes down by Stowford Gate, then by a hamlet called Higher Woolbrook, then by Lower Woolbrook, and proceeds between the grounds of Livonia and Lime Park (Lymebourne) falling into the river Sid. Just below Lower Woolbrook this stream throws off a gutter that once passed down by the side of the road to Sidmouth and finally all through the town by way of High Street and Fore Street (the leat ran through the town until 1873, when it was covered in) until it finds its way through the main sewer to the sea. At Mill Cross (High Street) it is supposed to have been used by the monks of old to turn their Mill.

At f. 80 of the Otterton Cartulary there is a grant of Woolbrook to Adam de Radway by the Abbot of St. Michael's Mount bearing date 15th August, 1272. There is no evidence to show how the Abbot got Woolbrook originally.

It may have been handed over in the lump along with Otterton. The grant is of 2 ferlings which Christopher had held for the rent of 20 pence; and the ferling which Richard Harding had held for 2 shillings, Adam de Radway to hold them to himself and his successors for all services except what he owed to the King. The Otterton Cartulary shews that Robert de Cottematone held a ferling of land and Tholomen also held a ferling of land about this time at "Hallebrok", which Robert altered to "Dollebroke" paying 12d. rent to the monks.

Anne Britton
Nov 1953

In the Churchwardens' accounts dated 1706 is the following entry:—"to waning at Woolbrook –00–02–0"—meaning repairing parts of banks of the stream.

Several portions of Lower Woolbrook belonged to Sidmouth Manor and Higher Woolbrook to Sir John Kennaway, but since Woolbrook has been so much built upon the land is entirely split up.

At the same time that Tholomen held land at Woolbrook of the Abbot, a change took place which appears in the Cartulary under the head "Sydemue". In English it reads:—"Tholomen for one ferling which Robert of Cotmaton held of our lordship in Woolbrook which William Wise now holds. He was of the tenants of Robert of Ascerton". This gives the transfer of Woolbrook through the hands of Robert of Ascerton, Tholomen and William Wise.

My first memory of Woolbrook is of pasture lands, orchards, fields of corn and root-crops, covering the entire area from the entrance at Alexandria Road reaching to Bulverton, Bowd, Core Hill, High Street, along the Sidford Road, down Manstone Lane.

Dotted with thatched farm buildings and cottages, is the lovely little hamlet of Lower, Middle and Higher Woolbrook. It was peopled by the families of Lawrence, Gigg, Churchill, Ebdon, Parsons, Gooding, Mitchell, Pyle, Pratt, Deam, Bastin, Barratt and later Hill and Dommett. Members of these families are still there, many occupying the houses in which they and their parents were born. Newcomers occupy the farm where lived Farmer Ned Lawrence and Butcher Ebdon opposite. Farmer George White lived at Manstone.

Mr. Usher's shop occupies the lower part of Jack Gigg's lovely old cottage, built in 1705, of which the upper storey is well preserved. Frank Churchill and the families of Parsons and Gooding are still in the cottages at the corner of what I remember as a lovely country lane leading into Middle Woolbrook.

My memory carries me back to my childhood days, picnicking in the hay-field, riding back to the field in the empty hay-cart, or being held on the horse's back along through this lane, so narrow that wisps of hay were caught on the brambles on both sides, where we gleaned armfuls of fox-gloves, honeysuckle and dog roses. Farmer Gigg was at Middle Woolbrook Farm in those days. Soon after came Farmer Hill and his family, the latter now grown up and carrying on in the fine old farm buildings. All the old thatched cottages and buildings are well preserved, and mostly occupied by the families whose parents and grandparents were born there. The group of thatched buildings known as "The

Square", the home of the Churchills and Ebdons, I am told, is to
be preserved as an ancient monument. Across the road from there
stood the little village school, used also on Sunday for services
and entertainments. This building stood on a spot which is now
the middle of the road, for the road has been widened, and a fine
new hall built. Next to this school was Daniell's Smithy and Forge,
later moved to Holmdale.

An extract from a journal reads:—

"On Monday Nov. 17th, 1873 a Tea-meeting was held in
the wooden structure erected at Woolbrook. Each child received
a woollen garment, a piece of cake and a penny, the gift of a few
friends present. After an address and dedication prayer, by the
Vicar, the Rev. H. G. J. Clements, the room was declared open.

"It is intended to hold Divine Service every Sunday afternoon
for Woolbrook, Bulverton and the neighbourhood. In a short
time it is intended to establish a Sunday School."

A fine modern Council School with spacious playgrounds was
amongst the first buildings, and was erected at the cost of £7,000.
Later a Church and many good houses were built. Despite this,
the delightful "atmosphere" of Woolbrook remains, and evidently
emanates from the old Woolbrook people—a delightful community
—pulling together and ready to welcome all who come to live
amongst them. Their Fêtes, Garden Parties, Sales and Entertainments, and work for their Church are fine outstanding efforts.
The land for Woolbrook Church was given by the late Col. J. E. H.
Balfour, D.S.O., C.M.G., and dedicated on 16th May, 1931.

Boughwood or Bowd Inn, built in 1651, was the centre of much
smuggling activity for about 200 years. It is a favourite "rendezvous"
with well-preserved old buildings in the Harpford Parish.

Bulverton can be reached from Woolbrook by way of Greenway
Lane, at the top of which stands the old Turnpike Cottage.
The family of Churchill were born and still live there. Bulverton can
also be reached through Ice House Lane. Robert Genever (Otterton
Cartulary, f. 26) held one ferling of land at Bulwint, Boluorton
or Bulverton, for which he paid twelve pence. The same person
held houses and land in several parts of the Manor. At f. 27 the
following entries occur together:—

(Translated). "Eddvart of Boluorton, one ferling; to plough
one acre (for the Prior without pay) to help at the Mill; to do
5 days work and to pay eighteenpence.

"Richard de Boluorton, the same service, one ferling to pay
eighteenpence.

"William de Boluorton three ferlings and a half; half an opus or piece of work; to plough 1 acre and 1 perch; to cut or mow one perch; to do 5 days work and pay 3s. and 8d. or farthing & half a farthing."

These menial services without pay were often complained of as grievances in the nation, and raised a spirit of rebellion.

Bulverton is rarely mentioned otherwise. The hamlet of Bulverton, which lies a mile inland, was in the early days approachable only by a rough narrow lane, until the new Ottery road was made. Before this the only road to Ottery was by Woolbrook, right up to Core Hill and down into Ottery. I cannot find when a road was made, but I think it must have been after the Railway came. At this time the road from the Bedford Hotel past the Fort Field and Rosemount, now known as the Station Road, was made. I first remember Farmer Robert Coles at Bulverton Farm. The fine old cob barn, known as "Bulverton Well", stands, but the cottage and other farm buildings are evidently of much later date.

At present Councillor Hill occupies the farm. At the lower farm I remember Farmer Bobby Gigg. The old thatched farm house remains, but across the road are new cow-sheds and stables.

1956. February. A petition against suggestions to change "Ice House Lane" to "Bulverton Lane" was received and signed by fifteen residents in the area, offering strong objections to a change from a name which was a reminder of Sidmouth's past history.

At 3 Bulverton Cottages, during repairs, a chimney was uncovered, 15 ft. wide and 4 ft. deep, dating about 1300.

CHAPTER XXI

SIDMOUTH URBAN DISTRICT COUNCIL

SIDMOUTH is fortunate in having a good governing and progressive Council, most of the members born in Sidmouth and Sidbury. Mr. E. Hill is a son and Mr. J. Skinner nephew of former Councillors.

The first Local Government Board was sanctioned and confirmed by the Head Board in London on 20th May, 1863, and held its first meeting in Hope Cottage.

The Local Government Board became Sidmouth Urban District Council, with the late Mr. T. Kennet-Were as Chairman, a position he held until 1914. He was succeeded by the late Mr. J. G. H. Halse, who continued as Chairman until 1923. It was then decided to elect the Chairmen by rotation, so that all Councillors may hold that honoured position.

The names of Mr. Charles Colwill, Mr. John Skinner, Mr. Morrish, Mr. Ford, Brigadier Crick, Mr. E. Whitton, the late Mr. T. E. Fitzgerald and the late Mr. Walter Martin, must be mentioned as Chairmen who served on the Council many years.

1959. The present Chairman is Mr. F. A. C. Pinney, J.P., member of an old Sidmouth family. He was returned for a further 3 years in May 1959, and Mr. Pickard was elected as Councillor.

Mr. J. A. Orchard became Clerk to the Council in 1880. He was succeeded by Mr. P. H. Michelmore in 1916. On the latter's resignation, Mr. R. Pickard was appointed in 1937, and held the post until 1958. A keen advocate of everything dealing with the welfare and advancement of the town, his wise counsel has helped to steer our governing body through very troublous times.

Miss Chilton was the first woman to serve on the Council. Later Mrs. Butteris and Miss Tyrrell served at the same time and together did good work where a woman's counsel was needed. Mrs. Gibbens gave wise counsel during her term of office and was responsible for many improvements in the town.

CHAPTER XXII
INTERESTING HAPPENINGS
THE MEN OF THE TREES

THE MEN OF THE TREES is a fellowship founded by Richard St. Barbe Baker thirty-four years ago. It has enlisted the co-operation of men and women with vision and determination to work for large-scale tree planting throughout the world.

Many trees and woodlands have been saved for posterity that would otherwise have fallen to the axe, and large-scale reafforestation has been encouraged during the thirty-four years' existence.

In response to a small advertisement in the "Sidmouth Herald" by Mr. Cuthbert Brown, Lyndale, Sidford Road, in September, 1954, a small group was formed, who campaigned against the felling of trees in Arcot and Station Road. The first meeting in Sidmouth was held by kind invitation of Mr. Dore at his house in Redwood Road in March, 1955. The late Mr. Chipperfield was also a strong supporter—a tree was planted in Sidbury Churchyard in his memory.

In March, 1957, Sir Shane Leslie, Bart., lectured on Trees at Sidford Alexandria College and Woolbrook School, under the auspices of our local "Fellows of the Trees".

A branch was formed in June, 1957, called "East Devon". Sidmouth U.D.C. became a corporate member, and many new Fellows were recruited by the secretary, Mr. T. R. Woods, of Kore Bank, Sidford, and the present Hon. Secretary, Mrs. Evans, of Frys Lane, Sidford.

A Spring Conference was held at The Knowle Hotel, Sidmouth, on 18th April, 1958, to be followed later by a personal visit of Mr. St. Barbe Baker—the President and Founder. On behalf of the S.U.D.C., Councillor F. A. C. Pinney, J.P., opened the Conference. He told how, in the past three years the Sidmouth Council had saved some of the finest specimens of the oldest trees and had planted 7,000 trees in the Sid Valley. A Norway Maple Tree was planted in Blackmore Gardens to commemorate the Conference.

May many beautiful old trees (mostly on new estates) be saved by all our efforts and many more new trees planted. We will still hope for a broad Green Belt.

THE ALMA BRIDGE CENTENARY, 1855–1955

9th July. It is 100 years this month since the first Alma Bridge was erected at the east end of the Esplanade, and so giving access to the cliff walk over Salcombe. It was called "Alma Bridge" after the Battle of Alma, where the British and French allies gained a victory over the Russians.

Before the bridge was made, the only means of reaching Salcombe was either by way of Salcombe Road (after 1817 when Salcombe Road bridge had been built) or over the footbridge near the old mill, turning left leading into Milford Road.

In 1846 a public meeting was called "for the purpose of proposing plans" for the general improvement and for securing to the public the existing walks on the cliffs of Salcombe Hill and the paths leading thereto.

At the meeting held on 9th September, 1846, a Committee was formed called the Sidmouth Improvement Committee, the meeting being presided over by Sir John Kennaway. Mr. Paul Hayman was elected Secretary and the twenty-seven members of the Committee included the names of Lousada, Carslake, Radford, Trump, Harris and Hook.

After protracted negotiations with Mrs. G. Cornish, owner of the land between the bridge and the sea, eventually a compromise was reached over the claim of right-of-way, and Mrs. Cornish agreed to the erection of the Alma Bridge. The bridge to be made of the planks of the wreck of the late ship "Laurel", the cost being £26. 10s. 0d.

It was open to the public in July, 1855. It was damaged by a severe storm in 1877 and cost £34 for repairs.

The present bridge was erected in 1900 by the Urban District Council.

"MR. FREDDY DREWE'S BOYS"

1955. 24th December. Former pupils of Sidmouth Boys' School (now Messrs. Potbury's Auction Rooms) and All Saints' Church School held an enjoyable Reunion Dinner at The Anchor Hotel, when reminiscences of school life of 60 years ago were recalled. The dinner, arrangements for which were made by Messrs. S. A. Bartlett, A. E. Slade, L. Badcock and G. Basten, was presided over by Mr. J. W. Skinner, and the company of nearly fifty included Sidmothians who had travelled from as far as Altrincham, Cheshire (Mr. Reg. Snelgrove), Bristol (Mr. Eric Mills), Totnes (Mr. Ivor Sparkes) and Branscombe (Mr. R. Bingley Pullin).

At the beginning of the century Mr. Freddy Drewe and Miss Dolly Edwards were Heads of the two schools (with Miss Marsh at the former girls' school) and many amusing tales were exchanged. Mr. Gene Gerrard was among the guests, who entertained the company, and it was decided during the evening that an "Old Boys Association" should be formed, Mr. J. W. Skinner being invited to become President.

SIDMOUTH'S FIRST WATER WORKS

THE plans for the construction of the Reservoir for the first Sidmouth Water Works were prepared by Mr. T. Whitaker of Exeter, Surveyor, in 1843, and the reservoir was built the following year, in Cheese Lane. There was a passage 3½ ft. wide and 11 ft. long from the edge of Cheese Lane and the outer gate; this passage may still be seen abutting on the lane in front of the house called "Enslie".

In a book, "The Climate & Medical Topography of Sidmouth", published in 1843, "The waters in about Sidmouth is of pure and excellent quality and is brought from Cotmaton Hill. This water has its source from various springs."

An Act of Parliament obtained in 1886 soon resulted in great extension and improvement and more springs on the hills were utilized, two filter beds and a reservoir, capacity 750,000 gallons, were constructed by the Water Company in 1894. The water supply was materially extended.

The Water Undertaking was taken over from the Company in May, 1933, by the U.D.C. at a cost of £48,250. Since then the supply has been largely augmented by a bore hole at Sidford, and a scheme for a reservoir on Core Hill has been adopted.

1958. October. The old reservoir has been removed this year and many bungalows have been erected on what is known as The Cottington Estate.

Extract from a journal, 1916:—

"THE WRECK OF THE 'GRINDON HALL'"

On Friday, Oct. 21st, a disastrous gale, thunder, lightning, rain and wind; a storm such as we never remember. A hurricane, such as blew the whole of Saturday night and Sunday morning. Chimney pots and slates were carried off in all directions.

Captain Brewis, bound down channel from France to Barry Dock, Cardiff.

Mr. Ernest Bonner, on seeing the distress signals from his home at Barclays Bank, hurried out . . . . .

Volunteers were asked to go with Mr. Stephen Reynolds to lower a rope over the cliff (as the 'Grindon Hall' had drifted into the cliff at the mouth of the River Sid), with a view to hauling the men up, but, owing to the violence of the wind, that means of rescue had to be abandoned. Mr. W. Govier produced a rope, which Mr. Tom Harris tried to throw across; this he failed to do. Mr. Bonner then volunteered to take it across the river; the rope was tied around his waist; crossing the river he reached the men (a crew of 27, including 6 men of colour); they were brought safely across. Mr. Yeo also went out to the boat.

Those who helped to land the crew were Messrs. Skinner, Haselock, J. Hayman, W. J. Govier, A. L. Smith, 'Nobby' Hamson, Pring, W. Turner, A. C. Drewe, Tom and Bob Woolley, T. P. Syres, W. Hook, W. Ware, T. and J. Harris, D. Hook, J. Tapley and J. Cordey, etc. Mr. Yeo successfully applied for a medal. Captain Brewis and the crew presented Mr. Bonner with an inscribed silver-mounted walking stick and a letter of thanks."

CHAPTER XXIII

ITEMS OF INTEREST
(in brief)

1776	"Journals and letters of Samuel Curwen" state:— In August, 1776, situated very low in a bottom or vale Sidmouth consisted of about a hundred houses, built with mud walls and thatched roofs, except for a very few built with Cornish tile and some of shingles.
1790	Fortfield Terrace built.
1800	Bath Chapter and Manors were sold.
1802	Samuel Cawley exchanged land by the Mill for dilapidated Poor House in High Street (Lloyds Bank).
1803	Theatre built in East Street.
	Sidmouth's first Guide published.
1805	"The Shed" (now Bedford Hotel) and Knowle Cottage (Hotel) built. This seems to be the beginning of Sidmouth becoming a fashionable watering place, visited by nobility, who from this date proceeded to build their own houses.
1809	Inhabited houses rose from 310 to 562 in 1811.
1811	A Protestant Dissenting Chapel was built on the Marsh.
1812	York Terrace built.
	Marsh School established.
1813	Denby Place, Fort House and Sea View built.
1815	Belgrave (Council Offices), Blackmore Hall and Amyatts Terrace built.
	Guns removed from Fort and Signal Station dismantled.
1817	Waterloo Bridge at entrance to Salcombe built by Mr. Pinney.
1819	Their Royal Highnesses The Duke and Duchess of Kent, with their infant daughter, Princess Victoria, came to stay at the Woolbrook Glen.
1820	Clifton Place, Bedford Place, Coburg Terrace and Cotlands were built.
1824	Great storm destroyed Chit Rock and Cottages on the shore.
1826	Houses built in Elysian Fields.
1827	The Fort Field (Cricket Field) enclosed.
	Hall's Pannusborum Works burnt down (Skinner's Yard).

1831	Petty Sessions were held every month by 2 resident Magistrates for Sidmouth and several neighbouring Parishes.
	Court Leet and Court Barons were held.
1835	The Sea Wall was built at the cost of upwards of £2,000; completed in 1838.
1837	The town first lit by gas.
	All Saints' Church erected.
1839	The Market re-built. Dues granted to the Lord of the Manor.
1841	Claremont burnt down, leaving only walls standing.
1847	Big fire destroys row of houses at Mill Cross (opposite Sidlands).
1848	All Saints' School built.
1851	Flagstaff at Signal Station, High Peak, struck by lightning.
1852	Greenwich time adopted at Sidmouth.
1859–60	Parish Church rebuilt. "Old Chancel" built.
1863	On the 20th May the Local Government Board formed, sanctioned and confirmed by the head Board in London. The first members were: Mr. Alexander, of Woolbrook Glen; Mr. Arnold, Core Hill; Mr. S. Chick; Mr. Hodge, Chemist; Mr. J. Newman; Mr. F. Pyle; Mr. R. Searle, The Brewery; Mr. Wm. Till, 2 Seafield Place; Mr. W. B. Webber.
1866	A big fire in Western Town.
1867	23rd Nov. Sir John Kennaway elected first M.P. since Sidmouth became a Polling Station.
1869	Lifeboat presented by Mr. Rimmington.
1870	5th Nov. "Bonfire Night"—Great disorder in the town, houses nearly set on fire by blazing tar-barrels, which were rolled down the streets.
1873	Local Board enforced By-laws to secure proper use of Bathing Machines and to ensure proper bathing.
	Asphalt paths laid costing 1/– per yard.
1874	Railway opened. Cambridge Terrace buildings started.
1875	Gas Works removed from Landpart to the Ham and plans produced for Harbour by Mr. Dunning. Serious breach in Sea Wall.
	A Petition sent to the Vicar urging that Sunday evening services be held in consequence of overcrowding at All Saints'. Vicar points out the expense of fittings for lighting and pipes for heating.
1876	Storms and sea-water flooding caused milk to be delivered by boat.

1877   Fortfield House (now Church House) was offered for sale; withdrawn when highest bid was for £200.

1878   Honiton and Sidmouth Turnpikes sold.
        Cemetery consecrated.

1879   A large fire occurred at The York Stables. The new Fire Engine, manned by 24 vigorous men, speedily extinguished the fire. The Fire Engine, supplied by the W.E. Insurance Co., was fitted with recent appliances and about 300 ft. of hose.
        Cricket Pavilion built. Mr. Hine-Haycock Lessee of Cricket Field.

1880   A decision was made to revert to Oil Lamps for town lighting because of disagreement with Dunning, owner of Gas Works.
        First Amateur Theatrical Performance held at The Knowle.

1881   Fortfield Place was built.

1882   The Knowle becomes a Private Hotel.
        Alexandria Road opened.

1883   M.O.H.'s Salary reduced from £35 to £20 per annum.
        The Convent built.

1884   Methodist Chapel and Sleep's Factory built.

1885   Cottage Hospital opened at May Cottage.

1886   Y.M.C.A. opened 11th January. A Tea Meeting was followed by a discourse.
        Smith's Music Saloon opened at Sphor House, Fore Street.
        Coastguard houses built on Alma Hill.
        Thatched buildings in Market Place demolished.
        Visitors conveyed to Sir Walter Raleigh's Birthplace by donkey chaise.

1887   Sale of land in Knowle Grounds to open up a road.

1890   Masonic Hall built.

1891   Bill for "Free Education" came into operation.
        In the Spring of 1891 Sidmouth was honoured with a visit by The Empress Eugenie, who travelled incognito and resided at the Knowle Hotel.
        March. A blizzard occurred which left snow lying about for 6 weeks.
        Decision to hold Athletic Sports. A Town Band formed.
        Clerk of Local Board has salary raised from £35 to £45 per annum.
        July. Manor Concert Hall opened.

1893   Constitutional Club opened at Town Hall.

1894	The Local Board became the Urban District Council.
1895	The Drill Hall opened. Liberal Club opened at Canister House.
1896	The Ham presented to the town by Mr. J. G. Radford.
1897	Celebrations of Queen Victoria's Diamond Jubilee.
1898	The Opening of Bickwell Valley, a lovely expanse of green fields and orchards. There was no access to the Golf Links (then a 9-hole course) except by the Convent Road, then through a lane on the left of Jenny Pine's Corner. The proposal made to Major Balfour to open up a road did not materialize. In 1908 the first sod of the Bickwell Valley Road was cut by Mr. J. P. Millen.
1899	The Three-cornered Plot presented to the town by Major Balfour.
	Part of Salcombe Regis civil Parish added to Sidmouth.
1900	April 7th. Mr. J. P. Millen elected unopposed to fill the vacancy on the Council, caused by the retirement of Mr. Orchard.
	May 1st. Visit of Major-General Baden-Powell to Sidmouth.
1901	A petition signed by 250 persons for widening Turnpike Lane, as there was no road leading from Landpart to the Station.
	Observance of Market Act enforced after being extinct. Sidbury applies for telegraphic service and guarantees the Post Office Authorities half of the loss if the Office does not pay.
1902	The first Cinema introduced by Mr. A. W. Ellis at the Drill Hall.
	Members elected to the Council: Mr. James Pepperell 219, Dr. Bingley Pullin 198, Mr. Albert Maeer 196.
1903	The Victoria Hotel opened in March. Mr. J. Maguire Manager.
	Peak House rebuilt.
	Turnpike Lane becomes Winslade Road. Brewery Lane widened.
1905	Major Balfour offers "The Little Glen" to the town, affording a through track from Manor Road to Seafield Road.
	Fort House bought by Mr. R. H. Wood.
1 Mar.	A proposal to build workmen's houses lost.
8 ,,	Plans from Messrs. Baker for erection of houses in Winslade Road passed.

April, 1905	U.D.C. Election resulted in J. Pepperell 324, B. G. Pullin 291, Albert Maeer 286.
26 April	Blackhawk Minstrel Performance.
July	Suggestion that Bathing in the Western Bay be prohibited between the hours of 11 a.m. and 4 p.m.
2 Aug.	Decision to hold a Regatta and Sports.
8 Aug.	Coburg Field bought by Mrs. Scott of Blackmore Hall.
5 Oct.	Mr. R. H. Wood presented Fort House to the Church, and the land in front to the town.
5 Dec.	Death of Mrs. Brembridge in her 105th year.
1906	Market dues bought by the U.D.C.
1910	Major Morrison-Bell succeeds Sir John Kennaway as M.P. for Honiton Division.
1912	Permission was granted for Abernethy House to be transformed into the Westminster Bank.
1913	Telephones introduced into Sidmouth. Horse Ambulance bought for £20. The Council take over the Gas Works. First proposal to buy Blackmore Hall.
1914	
13 Jan.	The L. & S.W. Railway ran a special half-day trip from Sidmouth to London, leaving Sidmouth at 11.45 a.m., arriving at Waterloo at 3.45 p.m., returning at midnight. Tickets—6/3d. each.
24 Jan.	Mr. Guy Shorrock of St. Helens is starting from Calcutta to England in a 100-ton yacht.
5 April	54 Motor vehicles passed through the town between 2 and 4 o'clock on Sunday.
26 „	Mr. James Pepperell re-elected President of Sidmouth Development Society, Mr. Halse Vice-President.
1 May	Prince and Princess Arthur of Connaught concluded a fortnight's stay at The Victoria Hotel. They made several motor trips in "The Puffin", operated by the Woolley family.
June	There were steamer excursions by "The Duke" and "Duchess of Devonshire" to Torbay to witness trials of the Americas Cup challenger "Shamrock".
1 July	Much excitement was caused in the village of Otterton by the arrival of an Army Aeroplane which had left Netheravon at 11.30 a.m., and had travelled 120 miles to Otterton by one o'clock. It required two starts before the "take-off". Sidmothians had an excellent view of the novel visitor.

1 July	Mr. J. P. Orchard proposed at the Council Meeting that Council workmen should leave work at 1 p.m. on Saturdays instead of 4 p.m. It was stated that the usual daily hours were from 7 a.m. to 5 p.m.
2 Sept.	Plans passed for erection of 6 houses in Vicarage Road. Devon County Council approve increase of number of Councillors to 12.
	Plans passed for Mr. Carter of Exmouth to erect 48 houses on Salters Meadow at a cost of £9,255.
	Mr. W. Dingwall appointed Clerk of the Works.
25 Nov.	Headquarters of Boy Scouts opened by Mr. Johnson of "Littlecourt".
1915	
1 Jan.	Belgian guests were welcomed by Mr. and Mrs. Kennet-Were at the Winter Gardens.

THE WAR PERIOD

1918	
16 Jan.	Major Gilbert Davidson awarded the D.S.O.
28 Jan.	At a Council Meeting a Councillor proposed moving at the next meeting that Coburg Field be ploughed up.
30 Jan.	At a Meeting of the Council in answer to Mr. Fry, Mr. Pickson said that the break-up of Coburg Field for allotments was definitely moved and seconded at a recent Committee meeting. (This was never carried out.)
June	Open Air Nurseries provided on the Ham, sponsored by Lady Lockyer and helpers.
	Miss Leigh-Browne was asked to grant permission for a footbridge from Water Lane to The Byes. (Not granted.)
4 Sept.	The Surveyor was instructed to open the Three-Cornered Plot to visitors and place seats therein.
	The Council decided to purchase a Motor Ambulance at a cost of £125.
	The extension of the Esplanade at the Eastern end is completed.
11 Nov.	Surrender of Germany.
1919	
16 April	Mrs. Butteris, Mr. Lashbrook and Mr. Dagworthy become Councillors.
	Mr. H. A. Pickson keenly interested in promoting Harbour Scheme.
June	The first contested by-election since 1915 resulted in A. C. Drewe 412, W. J. Bell 142, Mrs. H. Major 27. Only 591 voted out of a possible 2,392. This was the first time women aged 30 and over had the vote.

Aug.	It was decided to fix a speed limit of 10 miles an hour for all motor vehicles in the town and Esplanade.
Sept.	Suggestion that the speed limit be reduced to 6 miles.
8 Oct.	"During the big Railway strike Mr. Dagworthy ran his motor char-a-banc to London and back every other day. Perhaps the day may come when motor char-a-banc trips to London may become popular."
	The Sid Vale Association were enterprising enough to secure the celebrated Richard Kearton, F.Z.S., F.R.P.S., to lecture on Birds and Animals.
	A suggestion is made to form a Camera Club.
19 Oct.	The King has appointed Col. J. E. H. Balfour, C.M.G., D.S.O., as Sheriff of Devon.

1920

20 Oct.	Messrs. G. Northcottes' tender was accepted for the erection of 56 houses on the Great Royals site, Winslade Road.
	£120 subscribed towards a new set of instruments for the Town Band costing £250.
3 Nov.	Castle House and cottages (3) bought by the Council. Mr. Fitzgerald outlined scheme for a Pavilion on the Bedford Lawn where people could sit and meet their friends.

1921

14 Feb.	Plans passed for conversion of Belmont into an hotel.
20 Feb.	Sidmouth Parish Church War Memorial unveiled.
10 April	The Town Band performed before H.R.H. The Prince of Wales at Bicton.
21 April	Mr. J. G. Halse elected Chairman of Council for 6th year in succession.
	Tender by Mr. Ryall accepted for 12 houses in Path Whorlands. Mr. Sampson's plans for 56 houses in Winslade Road adopted.
11 May	Suggestion for Library and Reading Room at Church House.
21 July	Ministry of Health agreed to Mr. Whitford holding the position of Surveyor and Sanitary Inspector.
15 Aug.	George Robey appeared at the Manor Hall.
9 Nov.	Mr. J. G. Halse adopted as Liberal candidate for Honiton Division. He made his first speech in Sidmouth on 7th December.
	Mr. Hill proposed the erection of a dwarf wall 18 inches high about 80 ft. eastwards of the Bedford steps. Although several members considered the proposal fantastic, the plan was passed. The wall was known as "Hill's Folly"

1922

Feb.   Extract from "Sidmouth Journal":—
            "It appears that the decision of the U.D.C. to grant a
            bonus of £50 to the Surveyor (Mr. Whitford) and £80
            to the Foreman (Mr. Pyne) for their work in connection
            with the sea-wall has given rise to a good deal of
            comment."

April   Mr. Halse elected Chairman for 8th year.
            Mr. Kennet-Were served as chairman for 20 years.

19 April   Tar Macadam is suggested for roads.
            Fore Street is flooded by sea-water as far as Trump's
            Stores. In Sidmouth murmurs are heard: "I shouldn't
            wonder if Mr. Pickson didn't turn up with a Harbour
            tucked up his sleeve."

26 „   Death of Mrs. Kennet-Were.

3 May   The Royal York Hotel is offered for sale at the Rougemont
            Hotel, but is withdrawn.

28 June   The Service Men's Club opened by Sir John Hart Dunne,
            K.C.B.

30 Aug.   Proposal to buy the Bedford Lawn by compulsory
            purchase.

15 Nov.   Death of Mr. Theophilus Mortimore, for 30 years Town
            Crier.

1923

Jan.   Sidmouth Baths closed.

„   Major Morrison-Bell presents the Football Field to the
            town.

March   Much regret expressed at resignation of Mr. J. G. H.
            Halse from the Urban District Council after being a
            Member for 20 years and Chairman for 8.

April   Mr. T. E. Fitzgerald elected Chairman of S.U.D.C.

May   Decision that each Member of the S.U.D.C. shall be
            given the honour of Chairmanship by rotation.

23 May   Mr. Thomas Clarke made hon. life member of the
            bowling club.

20 June   Decision to reopen the Baths in October.

27 „   New form of tar-spraying and chippings instead of sand
            used for roads.

30 „   Major Morrison-Bell, M.P., created a Baronet.

1 Sept.   Mr. J. G. H. Halse elected County Councillor unopposed.

24 Oct.   Col. Balfour offers to give land for widening road to
            36 ft. at Woolbrook.

1927

2 Feb.   Suggestions made for removal of Gas Works to the Station.

22 Mar.	Christabel Pankhurst addressed meetings at Manor Hall.
30 ,,	Prince and Princess Bibesco and Lady Oxford and Asquith come to stay in Sidmouth.
6 April	A meeting at Manor Hall to promote a branch of St. John Ambulance Brigade.
13 ,,	Sidmouth's G.O.M., Mr. W. H. Lamb, of "Brooklands", celebrates his 100th Birthday.
26 May	Arcot Park house and Longpark playing fields opened by Mr. Arthur Neville Chamberlain, M.P.
23 July	Fête at Bicton addressed by the Rt. Hon. Winston Churchill, M.P.
15 Nov.	Our late King George and Queen Elizabeth, then Duke and Duchess of York, visit Lord and Lady Clinton at Bicton.
5 Dec.	Leff. Pouishnoff gave a Piano Recital in Manor Hall.
12 ,,	Old houses in Church Street burnt down.

1928

16 Jan.	Castle House pulled down for road widening.
20 ,,	The Council holds first meeting at Hope Cottage. (The old Local Board met at Hope Cottage for many years before moving to the Masonic Hall, and later to Castle House.)
21 June	The New Radway Theatre opened.

1929

6 Nov.	Sidbury decides for Amalgamation with Sidmouth, voting 321 for and 167 against.
23 ,,	First sod of Woolbrook new Church cut by Sunday School Children.
4 Dec.	At the Annual Meeting of "The Baths" it was stated that during the year 3,350 treatments were given.
12 ,,	Woolbrook Church corner-stone laid by Col. J. E. H. Balfour and dedicated by the Lord Bishop of Exeter.

1930

12 Mar.	A new Fire Engine bought.
April	Result of Council Election: J. G. H. Halse, W. Martin, A. W. Ellis, W. Dagworthy, T. Sisterson, V. G. Horton.
7 May	Proposal for Croquet Ground on Coburg Field.
28 ,,	First negotiation to buy "Sea-view" at the cost of £3,500.
4 June	Purchase of "Sea-view" confirmed.
Nov.	Electricity Undertaking acquired by East Devon Electricity Co.

1931	Mr. Cedric Drewe elected M.P. for the Honiton Division.
Oct.	H.R.H. The Duke of Connaught comes to winter at Sidmouth.
1933	Mr. James Pepperell advocated that the cliff at Jacob's Ladder be sloped back, a chine-way cut in the Cliff Field, seats placed at intervals and certain plants planted to save cliff erosion. Other Councillors did not favour this scheme. (1958. A great part of the cliff has gone).
	A protective "apron" and wall was built, and this year (1958) large-scale operations are taking place, a wall being built extending to Clifton Place.
1936	The Council Offices moved to "Belgrave".
	Purchase of Cricket Ground.
1938	General Post Office opened by Chairman of Sidmouth U.D.C., Mr. T. E. Fitzgerald.
1946	Sidmouth Youth Choir formed by Mr. Clifford Brown.
1952	Television comes to Sidmouth.
	Mr. Cedric Drewe, Member of Parliament for Honiton Division, knighted.
1953	
1 Feb.	Arcot House opened as "The Eventide Home" for residents.
	The Manor Hall purchased by the Town.
	Blackmore Hall Coronation Gardens opened to the public by the Chairman of S.U.D.C., Mr. Owen Ford, on 18th July.
1954	
Nov.	"Any Questions?" by the B.B.C. was broadcast from the Manor Hall.
23 Nov.	Mr. Robert Mathew, prospective Conservative candidate for the Honiton Division, who recently purchased Paccombe House, Sidbury, arrived to-day. A special train conveyed the livestock and farmyard equipment.
1955	Sidmouth Veteran St. John Ambulance workers, Mr. Quaintance, has done 21 years and Mr. Chick 17 years; they both hold the Meritorious Certificate of the St. John Ambulance Brigade as well as R.S.P.C.A. Rescue Certificates. Up and down the cliffs they are hauled and lowered rescuing people stranded, cut off by the tide, etc., and many a dangerous rescue of terrified dogs. Sidmouth is proud of these men.
Sept.	Miss Kilgour, of "Hills", Sid Road, who died in March, aged 103, bequeathed Woolcombe House and gardens to Sidmouth Council for voluntary social effort purposes.

1956

Feb.   Miss Jane Cox gave a Luncheon Party at Westcliffe Hall
              to celebrate her 104th birthday.

1957

Sept.   The Autumn Carnival was revived for the first time since
              1938 (19 years). Mrs. Gibbons crowned the Carnival
              Queen on The Ham.

24 Sept.   A Film Unit visited Sidmouth.

26 Oct.   There was a large congregation present at the Parish
              Church at the Funeral Service for Prebendary Edward
              Foley Ball, M.A., Vicar of the Parish from 1938 to 1954.
              Prebendary Ball was a Chorister at St. George's, Windsor
              Castle. He took part in the Diamond Jubilee Service of
              Queen Victoria in St. Paul's Cathedral.

Dec.   Col. Edmund Perry, who was Medical Officer of Health
              for Sidmouth for 21 years, died at the age of 85. The
              Council decided to plant a tree in the Sidmouth Cemetery
              to his memory.

19 Oct.   A clear view of the first Russian Satellite was seen from
              his garden at Woolbrook by Mr. S. Uglow and his father,
              Mr. Alan Uglow, who saw it appearing as a small ball of
              fire at 5.18 a.m. It passed rapidly across the sky and
              disappeared in a S.W. direction. It was also seen at
              Hillside, Sidbury, by Mr. and Mrs. B. King.

Sept.   Sidmouth British Legion's Standard Bearer, Mr. L. T.
              Smith, is also the Bearer of the Southern Area Standard.
              At the Annual Meeting of the Sidmouth Branch of the
              British Legion Women's Section, Mrs. Sinnot, Chairman,
              announced that Poppy Day Collection for 1957 was
              over £400.

HONOUR FOR SIDMOUTH

1958   British Legion Chairman. Described as a man who
Nov.   exemplified the spirit of The British Legion's motto:
              "Service Not Self". Dr. R. G. Michelmore, who has
              been Chairman of the Sidmouth branch of the Legion
              since 1946, was, at the Annual Meeting on the 12th,
              presented with the Gold Badge of the Legion, awarded
              by the National Executive for services of a very high order.

1958

4 Jan.   Death of Sir Archibald Bodkin at the age of 98.

15 Mar.   Sidmouth Devon 28 Red Cross, Nursing and First Aid
              Competition; won the Fortescue Cup.

10 May   Council buy "Trump's Yard".

16 Aug.   The sale of jointly Sidmouth and Salcombe Regis for United Missions to Central Africa, organized by Miss Gilbertson, realized £140.

3 May   Eight delegates from all parts of Devon came to Sidmouth for the Annual Meeting of the Devon Congregational Union. The Local Minister is the Rev. Francis Gibbons.

16 May   Death of Mr. Alan Uglow in his 85th year. A much respected Sidmothian. Mr. Uglow cared for and wound the church clock for more than half a century, as his father had done before him. He also looked after the clocks in Sidmouth Manor and Peak House, and installed the clock on the tower at Connaught Gardens, when it was a private residence. Sidmouth mourns his loss.

2 June   Miss Barnard of Sidmouth gave a talk on B.B.C. Television on Honiton Lace-making.

3 June   A much respected resident, Mr. Alfred John Mountstephen, died at his home at Moor Court.

7 Oct.   The Council approved a Resolution under the Housing Act of 1957 to acquire "The Old Malt House", one of the oldest buildings in Sidmouth, situated in "The Marsh"—re-named York Street.

20 Oct.   The Bishop of Crediton (the Right Rev. W. A. E. Westall) consecrated the extension to Sidmouth Cemetery.

At Exeter Carnival, Sidmouth's Carnival Queen tableau, Miss Elizabeth Vincent of Sidbury and her attendants Maureen Pike and Shirley Perry, won the Bruford Cup for the best Carnival Queen tableau in Devon.

Sidmouth Carnival was a great success. There was an entry of nearly 50 items with five bands. Hundreds of youngsters among the onlookers waved coloured balloons as the procession made its way through the town, headed by Sidmouth Fire Brigade, Sidmouth Town Silver Band and the Carnival Queen.

Seated under a graceful canopy on a setting of red velvet, the Carnival Queen was accompanied by her attendants, Shirley Perry and Maureen Pike and the Carnival Prince and Princess, Andrew Caswell and Adrienne Hughes.

An escort was provided by a posse of mounted riders, led by Misses Hilary and Gillian Blackmore (Sidbury). Prizes were distributed by the Carnival Queen in the Market Square.

The Present Day
CHAPTER XXIV

Having drawn attention to ancient Sidmouth, where the pains-taking antiquarian may look for its old monuments, we arrive at the present day.

One of the charms, if indeed not *the* charm of our compact little town, lies in the absence of the restlessness so apparent in most watering places. There is nothing to remind the visitor of town or city.

"The leafiness" of the surrounding country spreads, unmolested into the town. Trees are everywhere; at every entrance to the town are shady avenues.

Walks and Excursions

If the sunshine of the sea-front becomes excessive, or the breezes in winter too strong, it is easy to retire to a sheltered corner of Connaught Gardens, or find seats tucked away on the cliff side facing west, up on the winding path of The Hanger or in the shelter of The Ham, overlooking the pool where children can sail their boats in safety.

Taking a delightful walk from there, pass across the wooden bridge into Milford Road and within five minutes you reach the Old Toll House. Enter the little wicket gate by the river and find yourself in "The Lawn". In this lovely green pasture, the most weary visitor from town or city can find peace, or a tired mother can sit under the big spreading trees surrounded by seats, whilst the children play at ball on the grass, or feed the ducks in the river.

Cross the little bridge[1] into Temple Street or if a longer walk is desired, pass along through Lover's Walk into the fields where seats are placed at every few yards, when another wooden bridge is reached. Just pause awhile, and look up and down the river; the beautiful picture of overhanging trees and foliage reflected in the water will fill you with delight.

Either pass up Lymebourne Lane and reach Landpart or proceed along The Byes, through the fields and arrive at Sidford. A tea garden is just there waiting, where either morning coffee or a delicious Devonshire tea can be obtained.

---

[1] When this bridge was built in 1936, the inhabitants of Lawn Vista were so elated that they held an opening ceremony. On its completion a bottle of wine was broken, and the bridge named "Heart's Delight".

Turn to the left, if wishing to return through the village, where many delightful old buildings can be found, or to the right passing the old Blue Ball Inn. At St. Stephen's Cross a gallows once stood.

Again turn to the right along the old Roman road passing some fine old cob buildings known as Grigg's Farm, the old house Sid Abbey, and at the corner Bird's Nest Cottages.

If desiring to return by the river from here, turn right into Sid Lane, passing rows of old cottages. At the bottom are two charming houses with old-world gardens sloping down to the river. Or if proceeding along the Sid Road look beyond an old lawn and trees where can be seen the charming old Salcombe Lodge, with "Sid House" across the road. Further down past Hill's Cottage and Salcombe House two old cottages stand at the entrance to Redwood Road, where charming modern houses have been built on either side. Passing along with Brooklet Cottage at the corner, we arrive again at the old Toll House. Having taken up so much space, I can only touch on many delightful excursions that can be made.

A great charm in all these excursions is the beauty of winding lanes, relieved at intervals by thatched cottages. Wooded hills rise up on either side where the lane winds along the bottom of one of the many valleys that run inland from the sea.

Frequently these valleys become Devonshire "coombes", and then the riot of ferns and wild flowers is a sight for the gods.

Another walk is by way of Glen Road through the Bickwell Valley. Turn into a lane by the old thatched building, "Bickwell Cottage", proceed past the entrance to the Golf Links, arriving on the Moor and Kebel's Seat, there sit and rest. What a wonderful panorama meets the eye. Space will not permit me to point out the beauties of this view, but just go and see !

Muttersmoor is delightful at all times of the year, either when yellow with gorse, or sprouting with bracken, with here and there primroses peeping out. Later there is the fairy-like blue of bluebells, and in the summer a glorious mass of purple heather, with the red cliff of High Peak and the sea in the distance. No artist could describe its beauty. Crossing the Moor take a turning on the right leading past Pinn Farm into Otterton and Ladram. Or on the left, down the road one must pause to peep through every gap and gasp with delight at the view of our lovely valley.

For those not fortunate enough to possess a car, excursions further afield may be taken by buses which convey passengers to Exeter, Exmouth, Budleigh Salterton, Ottery St. Mary, passing Harpford Woods on the way. It is well worth while to pay a visit to these delightful woods, and to visit the old Church at Ottery

St. Mary and (if fortunate) hear the chimes of the Clock. Or pay a visit to the gardens at Bicton, the village of East Budleigh, and to Sir Walter Raleigh's birthplace at Hayes Barton. These places all lie on the road to Budleigh Salterton and Exmouth.

Going through Harcombe and arriving at Sidford, continue through the village and out along the old Roman road of High Street, emerging into Stowford, through Woolbrook, where amid well-planned modern houses, lovely old thatched buildings remain. Arriving at Exeter Cross and the town, pleasantly tired, you can mount a bus and be "dropped" from here (or Sidford) at any bus stop *en route* to the terminus at the Triangle.

Sidmouth—The Present Day

To sum up, our little town has all the amenities—first-class Hotels and Boarding Houses, good shops to supply our needs and nice friendly shop-keepers, Concert Halls, Libraries, Cinemas, the finest Cricket Ground in the County, with good tennis and croquet courts, Cumberland-turfed Bowling Green, a Golf Course and Club House, and last, but by no means least, a Football Ground with a team to be proud of, well supported by enthusiastic followers, a Swimming and Sailing Club, a bathing beach at Jacob's Ladder, fishing and rowing, excursions by Drifters. There are no Pierrot or Concert Parties to destroy the peace, but excellent Musical and Amateur Dramatic Societies, and a fine Town Band with Concerts and Folk and Square Dancing in the beautiful surroundings of the Connaught Gardens.

Sidmouth people have passed through varied experiences, some happy and some sad—nature has been so kind.

On occasions, the waters of the English Channel have been unduly boisterous dashing upon the sea wall and destroying it, and causing havoc in many directions. Yet who would live away from the sea? The whiff of the briny is a tonic in itself. The grandeur of the rising waves and the intensity of the storms—then comes the calm and peace! The nights when the moon is up, lighting the water with a shimmering path of gold, when people can stroll along in luxury, with the beautiful scene, and revel because they are of Sidmouth.

When Spring comes wrapping the countryside in a mantle of green, where else is it possible to behold such beauty?

Sidmouth is typical of Devon and Devon is typical of all that is good!

PORT ROYAL

SALCOMBE REGIS, BRANSCOMBE, SIDBURY AND SIDFORD

THIS is by no means a history of these villages, but to record old memories, to add to my "Story of Sidmouth" which, I am happy to know, has fulfilled the purpose for which it was written and given pleasure. At the request of many I have included Salcombe, Branscombe, Sidbury and Sidford.

Salcombe Regis, Sidbury and Sidford have amalgamated with Sidmouth, and are represented on Sidmouth Council. Farms and lands belonging to these villages are so intermingled that (in the case of the farms and farmers) I must write of them collectively.

SALCOMBE REGIS

CHAPTER I

SALCOMBE REGIS "UP OVER"

THE Parish of Salcombe Regis shares with Sidmouth the seaward end of Sid Vale (their common boundary being the River Sid) and extends eastward between Salcombe and Dunscombe Hills, seaward to the western side of Weston Combe.

The Parish Register dates 1586.

The Manor of Salcombe Regis was bestowed on them by a Saxon King, and later included amongst those belonging to the See of Exeter. The Court was held at Thorn. The Michell family were there in 1611. Slade House was built by William Leigh on the estate which formerly belonged to the Michell family. Before this the Slades lived for nearly two centuries at Sea-side House, Branscombe. The Manor of Salcombe was held on lease by Mr. Kestell, and was purchased by his son-in-law, Mr. George Cornish, in 1801, since when many acres have been split up.

Every entrance into Salcombe Regis is beautiful, and our gratitude must go out to Sidmouth Council for their keenness in meeting the requirements of the late Cornish family and thus together preserving the amenities.

Salcombe Regis lies in one of the loveliest "coombes" on the coast. The hill can be ascended either by the cliff path or by road and from the top the panorama is one of great beauty. The view eastward extends right along the coast. Beyond Beer Head, Portland can be dimly seen.

The view westward of our little town, nestling between the two hills, is even more beautiful, and over the cliffs of High Peak and Ladram Bay it extends to Otterton point, while the "tors" of Dartmoor can be seen in the blue distance. Cross the plateau, and as you descend the other side, the Church comes into view. A path on the left leads to the village, and a winding path leads down to the sea.

At the entrance into Salcombe by the cliff path is Southcombe Farm; the late owner, Dr. Vaughan Cornish, and the late Rev. George Cornish, who owned North Coombe Farm, signed an agreement with the Sidmouth Town Planning Committee, under The Town and Country Planning Act of 1932, that parts of these lands should remain an "Open Space" and so preserve its amenities for ever.

Some years ago when Salcombe Valley was threatened by a hutment invasion Sidmouth Council bought Combe Wood Farm, which comprises cliff fields on the western slopes of Dunscombe Hill. All those fields of Combe Wood have been reserved from building by the Council, so that the whole coastal front of the valley is now preserved.

Recently when the plateau was threatened by invasion by caravans, Sidmouth won a long hard fight and purchased thirty acres of land on the plateau. All this land was costly. Thus the sky-line from the Sid Vale should never be cut, and on the plateau and entrance to the valley one can enjoy the beauty and solitude of cattle grazing on pasture land, fields of corn, arable land, and not a building in sight !

Before 1852 there was a race-course on the plateau.

Mr. Boalch tells me there was a horse-trough on the bend of Salcombe Hill, where horses stopped to drink and draw their breath, as Salcombe Hill is steep, but one is encouraged to face the climb by passing through a lovely avenue of trees and mossy banks, beautiful at every season.

The Salcombe Thorn Tree, enclosed by a fence, stands near the house. It is said that the superstition is that the welfare of the village depends upon the tree, so when it dies another is planted.

On the east side of the road is the meadow called Long Stone, situated on the crest of the plateau. This commands a clear view of the V-shaped valley which slopes down to the sea.

No trace exists of the salt works, which gave Salcombe (Salt combe) its name, nor of the Fort, which is said to be the last to hold out for King Charles.

CHAPTER II

THE CHURCH

AT the top of this lovely coombe, nestling between banks carpeted by primroses and daffodils, stands the Church of St. Peter, built about 1107, restored in 1845, the chancel rebuilt in 1869. In spite of restoration, the church retains its ancient beauty. Space will not permit me to give its history. Entered by a Lych Gate beneath an old yew tree, on the right a seat has been placed by Mr. Rupert Nicholls, a fitting memorial to his wife, "Winifred Anne Nicholls", a much-loved friend of mine. As I sat on this seat overlooking a most beautiful "Garden of Rest", I felt what comfort could be given to those who have stood on the hallowed ground in times of tribulation, and knew how sorrow could be softened by the peaceful beauty of the surroundings.

Some of the oldest monuments are of the Michells, later the Cornishes, and the much-revered Anderson Morshead family, Sir Ambrose Fleming, Sir Norman Lockyer and family.

CHAPTER III
THE VILLAGE

TURN in on the left for the Norman Lockyer Observatory. A bus takes passengers to and from Sidmouth to the village at frequent intervals. If refreshment is needed, turn right at the hilltop, for morning coffee, teas, and best of all a most wonderful view of our beautiful valley.

There has been no school in the village for some years since the death of Miss Woolnough. The first schoolmistress was a Miss James. There is no Nonconformist Chapel and no public house, but in very early days there was a "Kiddly Wink" or cider house known as "The Cat and Donkey" at Trow.

A tea garden is situated next to the church and across the road is the Vicarage, a charming, old-world house. Just pay a visit to this charming village and you will be well rewarded.

CHAPTER IV
THE OLD FAMILIES

I HAVE very little personal knowledge of the villages "Up Over" as, in my young days, our only means of transport was by cycling and walking; but I have many happy memories of the families from Salcombe and Branscombe, who came over the hill to bring their produce and do their shopping in Sidmouth; Farmers Hill from Woodhead Farm, Bishop from Thorn, Richards from Slade, Ellis from Lower Weston, Northcott from Trow, Pike, Blackmore, etc. I remember other familiar names, some from the other villages around, especially the wonderful contents of their baskets when they arrived in Sidmouth; and what delicious contents! scald-cream butter in layers of $\frac{1}{2}$ lb. pats, in yellow curly rolls covered with spotless butter muslin, with a wonderful slightly smoky flavour made from cream scalded in wide open pans over a wood fire in the wide hearth and chimney corner. (I can remember seeing this somewhere);

baskets of new-laid eggs; chicken at 2/– and 2/6 each (plucked and also wrapped in white cloths). The contempt we felt for "factory butter" sold at the grocers, and, when later, "Stores" were opened selling margarine—*well*, words failed ! How good it is to have known those days and those dear old people.

CHAPTER V

"DOWN UNDER"

SALCOMBE Parish boundary "down under" lies along the east side of the River Sid, from Alma Bridge extending to Sidford Bridge. I have such happy memories of this part of Salcombe parish (which we have always looked upon as part of Sidmouth) that I feel I must write of the district, not only for my grand-children and the old families and their descendants who continue to live "Up Sid", but also for the many families who have come to reside there and become "One of us".

CHAPTER VI

I REMEMBER

I REMEMBER the Alma Bridge as a narrow plank bridge, the only approach to Salcombe by the cliff walk (no winding path). There was a flagstaff encircled by seats at the top of the steps. It has gone.

Passing along The Ham or The Marsh (now renamed York Street, a real misnomer) through Mill Street, cross the Mill bridge into Milford Road, through an avenue of trees; on the right you arrive at the lovely old Myrtle Cottage, for many years the home of Colonel and Mrs. Mewburn. "Egypt" and "Woodbine" are approached by the same path. "Egypt", built for a member of the Cornish family, when they returned from that country, acquired the old Toll Gates and placed them at the entrance. Pasture lands extended to the entrance to Beatlands Drive and Salcombe Hill House, which is now a hotel but still retains its old-world charm, and so does the lovely old cottage Mount Pleasant, overlooking a sloping lawn surrounded by old trees. It has been renamed Cote Lawn. All the gracious old houses remain well preserved. A row of villas have replaced the hedge and modern buildings stand on the site of the old pasture (see sketch Milford Road). I remember great excitement was caused when a Circus came to the field and we saw elephants going to bathe in the river. The old Toll Cottage remains at the entrance to the Byes (once known as By-side).

SALCOMBE ROAD (NOW MILFORD ROAD)

CHAPTER VII
PARISH BOUNDARY

SINCE Sidmouth Council bought the Lawn some years ago and the fields extending to Sid Lane were acquired by The National Trust, the boundary passes along the Sid Road. Here I must turn aside at Brooklet (once the home of Mr. J. A. Bellamy), walk up the road, where stands the charming Salcombe Cottage, still with green shutters, as when it was the home of the Burroughs, and Mrs. Spence, and now the Huckers. The fine Old Farm House, said to be Elizabethan, well preserved in its old-world beauty. I like to picture hearty, grey-bearded Farmer Russell and his two rosy-cheeked daughters Lucy and Sarah (still living) followed by Farmer Williams, and lastly by blue-eyed, cheery Farmer "Danny" Tedbury. What tales could be told of the happenings in that old house; smuggling "Hideouts", illicit distilled liquors known as "Grammers Pins"; also a Ghost ! Since becoming a private house it has given much happiness to children from London, who have spent happy holidays there.

CHAPTER VIII

HILLSIDE ROAD

A COUNTRY lane with a five-barred gate led into Salcombe farm-
lands. I remember being scolded when, with my sisters, we plunged
into a field of corn to pick poppies. Never were there such black-
berries or primroses and white violets as were found in those hedges.

In those days the only buildings on the land were the Coastguard
Cottages, built in 1886, which have now been converted into private
houses. The lane once known as "School Lane" is now Hillside
Road and many fine houses and gardens have been built on the farm
land. Happily fields of corn and arable land remain to gladden the
eye.

CHAPTER IX

"EXTRACTS FROM A JOURNAL"

PROPOSAL FOR HOUSES ON HILLSIDE

On 18th March, 1921, a proposal was made to build sixty-one
houses on about four and a half acres of land on Salcombe Hill.
As this was thought to be an excessive number, a meeting was held.

6th July: "A deputation from The Sid Vale Association with
regard to the erection of houses on Salcombe Hill .... They
thought it would be serious if the beauty of the hillside was spoilt.
Some members of the Council objected to the desire to keep the
hillside for "the sweet selected few". Although Sidmouth owned
a great part of Salcombe, the village was then governed by Honiton
Rural District Council, who refused to pass the plans. A Local
Government enquiry was held and a deputation invited a representative of Sidmouth Council to attend the enquiry. Sidmouth Urban
District Council declined."

At the enquiry a Salcombe Councillor wished their hillside might
be left as nature endowed it.

I am sure these people who fought against the hillside development would have approved of the fine buildings erected there.

CHAPTER X

SID ROAD

THE approach to the hamlet of Sid is along what is said to be an old Roman Road.

The Marquis of Bute and Dr. Cockburn, Dean of York, once lived at Salcombe House, which I remember as the home of the Rev. and Mrs. G. Cornish. Its character has completely changed since it has been converted into Bishop's Court Hotel.

CHAPTER XI

"THE BAD OLD DAYS"

SID OR SEED, once known as Mill Town, was a very old settlement, and an important one, too. As long ago as 1086 out of a population, Bondmen and Free, of about 160 for Salcombe Regis Sid accounts for 90, but this would probably include all the inhabitants of that side of the hill.

The name Mill Town was given to it about 1281, when a mill was erected there, at the bottom of Sid Lane, on part of Sidcliffe Farm (now occupied by Mr. Fry). Mrs. Fry tells me there is still evidence of the Mill being there. T. Holway worked the Mill and thereby bought himself free from slavery under "Bloody Mary". At that time all the tenants had to work for their holdings and were obliged to grind their corn at the Sid Mill, and turn out with their ox team whenever a new millstone was ordered. Trow remained "Trow" and Sid got the name of "Mill Town" and Salcombe "Church Town". All the people from "Up Over" had to bring their corn down Mill Town Lane to be ground. The name still exists. G. Gilbert held an acre of land rent free at Sid House, on condition that he kept "a cage for felons". They did not stay long in it, however, for there was a further remedy—a gallows at Stephens Cross. The Canon was Judge, the tenants Jury and the Vicar said "Amen"!

163

CHAPTER XII

THE PRESENT DAY

RETURNING to the entrance to Sid Road, the dignified Brooklet Villas remain unchanged to gladden the eye.

Miss Cornish's Farm is now the Redwood Road Estate. The Redwood tree continues to flourish. There is said to be a fine Redwood tree across the road at "Hills", occupied for some years by Mr. Aylmer and formerly owned by the late Miss Leigh Browne, a great benefactor to Sidmouth. Miss Kilgour died there at the age of 103, since when it has been converted into Flats without changing the character of this fine old house.

The two little cottages, once the home of the Woodleys and the Salters, remain unchanged. Some attractive houses have been built on either side of the entrance to Brownlands. Sid should now be known as the "*District of Good Works*" in these "Good Days". Mrs. Brown in opening her Zoo to the public on Sunday afternoons during the summer, where beautiful exotic birds and animals can be seen, has raised large sums of money for various charities. Mrs. Sinnott has lent her beautiful home of Sid Lodge and its lovely grounds for Fêtes and Entertainments, benefiting the Church and the Women's Section of The British Legion, of which she is Chairman, and has done wonderful work whilst she has lived there.

Built on the stables of Sid Cliffe many years ago by a Captain Clarke, Sid Abbey has no connection with an abbey or church. It is very appropriate that Mrs. Gilchrist, its present owner, should be a great church worker. Sid Abbey is a "Hive of Industry" and many meetings in connection with Salcombe Church are held there. I have been told that when Miss Skinner lived at Sid Abbey, "School Treats" were held there, and children conveyed in farm wagons, carrying their mugs and singing, had a wonderful time.

Along the road at Fortescue live Miss Gilbertson and Miss Sibley who work for, and organize sales and entertainments, reaping rich rewards for the U.M.C.A. The late Mrs. Trepplin lived at Sidgard and was the Founder of our Cottage Hospital.

CHAPTER XIII

SID LANE

THE family of Melhuish lived at Greenmount. The fine old house standing in spacious grounds is now Clevedon School for boys. The charming Lodge still stands at the entrance.

We have now arrived at Sid Lane. To me the name of that delightful vicinity conjures up two words: "Peace and Beauty". The beautiful old-world Sid Lane Cottages on the right were built of cob by a Mr. William Pinney, great-great-grandfather of Councillor F. A. C. Pinney, J.P. Six cottages stand on both sides of the lane; those on the right have gardens in the front, always a blaze of colour —flowers at all seasons. With gabled roof at each end, although attached, not one of the cottages are alike; each one has a different porch. Mr. Pinney lived at Tower Cottage at the end, so named because a pseudo tower stands outside the front entrance. Slates have replaced the thatched roofs and the two pumps (one on each side) which supplied water to the cottages, have gone. One stood in the garden and the other in a hollow built in the wall. The cottages on the left are much older and have their gardens behind but Mrs. Dingwall has found room for a narrow border of pansies, stocks, etc., and a clematis climbs over the end of her cottage. A large pot of geranium now stands in the hollow. Passing down the lane, modern houses have been built during the past twenty years. On the right stands "River Close", an attractive house with a lovely garden; across the lane looking through the open entrance to Salcombe Close can be seen a fine herbaceous border of flowers, and rose-covered pergolas. A lawn and fine trees lead to an attractive house on the river bank. We now arrive at the bottom of Sid Lane. Although I have described this delightful spot in my early edition, I cannot resist writing again of the joy of standing on the bridge and facing the lovely old-world Sid Bank Cottages, with gables at each end, a little thatched summer house perched on the top corner, the green shutters, steps leading down from the terrace to gardens filled with choice flowers and shrubs, evidence of the great care bestowed upon them by their owners, Mr. Hall and Miss Green. Added to this, the soothing sound of the river, falling over the weir beneath the bridge, further up-stream the tinkling little waterfall; look up, then down at the beautiful old trees reflected in the water. Oh, the peace of it!

165

CHAPTER XIV

OLD FAMILIES

How much I have enjoyed "looking in" on some of the old people, families who have lived in Sid Lane as long as they can remember. I had such a happy "chat" with Mrs. Stretton and her sister, Miss Taylor, in their home at Tower Cottage. It is quite possible that the Taylors' ancestor followed Mr. Pinney. We recalled old families who have lived "Up Sid" and continue to do so: Davies, Gorman, Yeolden, Hiscox, Harding, Richards, Churchill, Gigg, Denner, Melhuish, Spencer, Sweetland, Webster, etc. There were several families of White, which reminds me that I must proceed up the lane, where stands Sid Cottage, the most inviting and suitable entrance to Sid Lane.

CHAPTER XV

OLD HOUSES AND FARMS

As a child I remember being taken for walks along the Sid Road I used to like to stand and enjoy the picture made by the cottage. Sid Cottage is built in triangular form, like outstretched arms: gables at each end, once covered entirely by Virginian creeper (now clematis, jasmine and ivy); the front door with pointed wood porch, stands between two windows which seemed to be peeping through the creeper to see whoever might be coming through the wicket gate and along the flower-bordered path. The cottage is a gem, and to me always resembled a Dutch doll's house. I remember Farmer John White living there many years ago. He farmed Sidcliffe Farm. His great niece, Miss Molly White, lives at "The Orchard" next door where an old-world garden is a delight.

Miss Maunder tells me that her grandfather, Mr. Winsley, built the delightful Birds Nest Cottage about 150 years ago. There they stand to greet you, well preserved and unchanged since, as a child, I stood patiently waiting to see birds fly out from the thatched nest porches.

Around the corner there was once an old saw pit, which has now been filled in. For generations the Davies family had their carpenter's shop there. Mrs. Davies still lives in the cottage.

We now arrive at Sidcliffe. In 1760 Baron was the name of the occupier and later Chanon, Tyrrell, Coney and lastly Gray, whom I remember living there. The house was first turned into flats. The estate has recently been developed and some fine well-planned houses and bungalows have been built which, with their colourful gardens and terraces, commanding a beautiful view overlooking pastures in the Sid Valley, are an asset to the neighbourhood.

It is comforting to know that some of the old farms and cob-walled homesteads remain and are well preserved. I remember Farmers Sam White at Skinner's Farm (now Lavers), Darke at Fortescue Farm (now Clarke). Happily Mr. Darke, who was born at Fortescue Farm, continues to live near. Farmers Horn, later Pike (now Hamlin) at Higher Griggs, Rowland at Champs (now a private house renamed Mead, owned by Mr. and Mrs. Crane). This house has a tablet dated 1688 built in a wall.

The hamlet of Sid has been developed in recent years. Modern houses have been built on farm lands. It is now known as Fortescue, but to me and to the old people it will always be "Sid". Along the right bank beyond Fortescue, some fine houses were built about 1914. Standing in spacious grounds surrounded by beautiful trees, with an uninterrupted view of pasture land and the River Sid, these houses are a wonderful acquisition and lend a pleasing dignity to the end of Sid Road and Salcombe "Down Under", bringing us to Stephens Cross and the old Roman Road which to me is the heart of the farming district and the villages of Sidbury, Sidford, Harcombe. Trow Hill on the right leads to Branscombe; facing is the entrance into Harcombe, thence to Sidbury and left to Sidford.

CHAPTER XVI

Items of Interest

(in brief)

In 1309 J. Warren was copy-holder of the farm (now occupied by Mr. and Miss Dyer at Sidford) and sub-let it to Nytheway.

In Queen Elizabeth's reign, Katherine Robins was jilted by William Grigg after the banns had been three times called.

Cider was sold at "The Green Dragon" at Sid and at "The Cat and Donkey" at Trow. Chief manufacture in Salcombe is cider.

Mammoth bones were found at Paccombe.

J. Baron, in ye reign of James I, did blasphemously baptise a mare in the Sid.

In resisting the Puritans who were advancing from Lyme five Salcombians were slain on Sidford bridge.

Vicars of Salcombe

In 1307 the new Vicar of Salcombe allowed tench and carp to escape from his pond at "Spring Combe".

1353 T. Hert "allowed tithe stock to be rescued from the Pound" (beside the Thorn).

1453 T. Bastard is said to have "worn out the Parish Lantern".

1517 T. David "Oxford Scoller: got the 3/6 for Chelson".

1589 F. Pring "wrote all Parish Wills".

1728 Joseph Hall "tithed every black fleece for wool for his stockings".

Mr. William Pinney was Parish Clerk at Salcombe Regis for over forty years. He had a pet raven who used to accompany him perched on his shoulder. Mr. Pinney taught the raven to talk; unfortunately, the bird acquired some language unsuitable to his master's "calling". When it became the habit of the bird to perch on an open window, or in the doorway, and pour forth strong language during the service, the poor bird had to be destroyed!

In 1958 Sidmouth Council leased land in Salcombe to The Forestry Commission to protect the woodland.

BRANSCOMBE

CHAPTER I

ORIGIN OF THE NAME BRANSCOMBE

A FEW miles from Sidmouth is the village of Branscombe, a sprinkling of picturesque old cottages that "winds somewhere safe to sea".

There are many suggestions as to the origin of the name of Branscombe. In the "Western Antiquary", Exeter Museum, Friar John Burgess of Exeter wrote that there was a King's son named "Sanctus Brandwellanus". He is said to have come from Sicily or Calabria, and to have landed in England A.D. 300. His interment in Branscombe would account for the name "Bran" the saint and "Cwm" the valley, where he was buried. In the Domesday survey of 1086 the Manor is called Branckescombe or "Brannois Vale" which means "The place of the branching combes", and this, I think, is a most delightful description of the lovely village.

Branscombe is about six miles from Sidmouth; great cliffs rise above the coastline to a height of over 450 feet; entered by a steep dip, into a delightful jumble of little valleys, the horizon hidden on three sides by escarpments of surrounding hills.

At a spot known as Branscombe Mouth, the cliffs are broken by a deep and narrow valley through which a little brook flows swiftly through green fields to the sea. The lovely valley winds inland amid scenery of the greatest beauty and here and there little combes give rise to the saying that Branscombe was made up of odds and ends which were left over at the end of Creation, or, that it was "the virst place to be made in the world avore they knawed how to do it, lookee".

CHAPTER II
THE MANOR

THE Manor of Branscombe was one of the estates belonging to the Kings of Wessex and is mentioned in King Alfred's will. In Domesday surveys it is included amongst those belonging to the See of Exeter. It appears to have been given before the Conquest by Thomas de Branscombe and was then appropriated to the maintenance of the Canons. For several centuries the Church authorities seem to have managed their own estates at the "Church Living". Here the Canons of Exeter had some sort of country house and one of their number would act as Chaplain, but it was never the Vicarage. Early in the 13th century the Manor Estate of Edge was rented to a "firmarius" (factor or Farmer) and probably at the same time the movable Chaplain became Parish priest.

The first note is found in the register of Bishop Walter Bronescombe, who built the beautiful Lady Chapel, and its adjoining chapels in Exeter Cathedral. King Alfred's will suggests that the first Hundred Court was held at Branscombe.

CHAPTER III
ANCIENT HOUSES

PERCHED high on the hillside, Egge or Edge Barton Manor, as it is now known, was the seat of the Bronescombes. Sir Richard Bronescombe resided there; a family of great distinction who gave three Sheriffs to the County of Devon in the reign of Edward III. Before the end of that reign it had passed to Sir John Wadham; after remaining in the Wadham family for eight generations, it passed with two of the co-heiresses of Nicholas Wadham, founder of Wadham College, Oxford. The families of Strangeways and Wyndham inherited it.

The Dean and Chapter had held the Manor for a thousand years, but it was sold to H. Ford, Esq., in 1865 and remains in the family to the present day (1959). A John fford married Agnes Walsh in Branscombe on 29th November, 1551.

The Fords resided at the charming "Lower House" from the 16th century. In one of the bedrooms can be seen a plaster-cast bearing the double-headed Eagle of the Tsars. This commemorates a visit of the Grand Duchess Helene of Russia in 1831. She was at the time residing at Fortfield Terrace for several months. "Lower House" is still owned by the Fords, but Mr. Ford is at present residing at "The Outlook".

1958.

I had the pleasure of visiting Edge Barton this year with the Devonshire Association and we were favoured with a most interesting talk by its present owner, Mrs. Blackburn. Some parts of the house may date from the 13th century. Many interesting features remain, some unearthed and restored by Mrs. Blackburn and her late husband. The restoration has been carried out with great care and includes the corkscrew stairs (now covered with wood) and the Priest Hole. The present dairy is said to be part of the ancient chapel, which was desecrated before 1772. A tunnel is supposed to extend beneath Edge to the Church, probably used by smugglers. Edge is a truly beautiful residence.

After leaving Edge Barton the party proceeded to "Hole", where we were received by the present owner, Mr. Lethbridge. Mr. Lethbridge is a keen archaeologist and has dug up a remarkable collection of Roman-British pottery and other objects since coming to live at Hole.

Hole was the ancient inheritance of the de la Holes, afterwards for seven descents of the Holcombes, until in the 17th century it passed as a lady's portion to the Stuckeys and was then sold to the Bartletts, whose many monuments can be seen in the Church of St. Winifred's.

The Bartletts resided at "Weston House", where they administered the estate. A fine old house built by the Stuckeys, Weston House was burnt down in 1810. The name Bartlett exists to the present day.

Berry Barton (or Bury) mentioned in 1307 as "la Berry" stands at the top of a steep hill close to the edge of the cliff. A tumuli and the remains of a Roman Camp stand near. Bury was burnt down in a disastrous fire and the present house was built in 1887. The ghost of a little old lady in steeple crowned hat and buckled shoes, is said to have haunted the old house in search of hidden treasure. About a hundred years ago money was found at the spot. Since then she has not been seen.

"Barnells" (or Barnwell) was built by Captain Ewell, Nelson's Captain of Marines on the *Victory* at the Battle of Trafalgar, and was at one time known as "Trafalgar House". It stands in a magnificent situation and is now occupied by Major and Mrs. Bucknell and family.

"Margel's Cottage" at the upper part of the village is a charming survival of the past. A very fine and ancient oak ceiling can be seen in a room on the ground floor.

CHAPTER IV

THE CHURCH

How fortunate Branscombe is to have its fine old church of St. Winifred's so wonderfully preserved; unlike some other churches which had many of their beautiful old features destroyed in the urge for reconstruction.

Space will not permit me to give many details of the Church itself, which has been adequately described in other books.

Architecturally the Church is of exceptional interest, with its fine Norman tower built about 1160 and Saxon masonry can be found at the base of the turret staircase and in part of the tower. An outstanding feature is the carved oak gallery.

There are many interesting memorials, one of which I must mention; it is that of Joan Wadham, mother of the founder of Wadham College, Oxford, who had twenty children, fourteen by her first husband and six by her second marriage. These may be seen in the memorial. There are memorials of the Holcombes, and many of the Bartlett family. One is of Anna Bartlett, inscribed: "Here lieth a blossom of the world's great tree, which was as fare as buds of roses be. She died an infant. Heaven was made for such." A stone was raised to John Perryman, who was well beloved in the Parish. He was shot (presumably by accident) as he was returning from work on 8th September, 1883.

The new Vicar of Branscombe, the Rev. A. T. Allwork, was inducted by Prebendary T. G. Shelmerdine on 26th September, 1958.

CHAPTER V

THE CHAPEL

THE Methodists were introduced in the 19th century with the goodwill of the Vicar; Services were held for years in Bury Farm house, then occupied by Samuel Chick and his wife Abigail Chick.

Chiefly by their aid a Chapel was built in 1832, which has sacred happy memories for many old people. A new Chapel was built in 1900, when the old one had fallen into decay. I must write of a "happening" of the old days. A good but uneducated brother (Local Preacher) was appointed to preach at one of the chapels, and was warned to use his best English, so, to use his own words: "In the morning I took up the silver trumpet but 'twas no good, I coulden make 'en zound no how. I axed the Lord to forgie me that once an I zaid I'd never try un no more, and in the aivening I took th'ole rams horn once more, and I *did* blaw a blast I tell ee."

CHAPTER VI

THE VILLAGE

EVERY time I visit Branscombe I liken it to a "place of enchant- ment"; passing along the narrow lanes and hedgerows, past the groups of well-preserved old thatched cottages, with flower beds in front and plants in the windows, down through the winding lanes where a few years ago while strolling down the valley, one would meet a string of donkeys winding their way leisurely up the road bearing panniers of new potatoes. Donkeys are still used to bring these potatoes up from where they are grown on the cliff side.

Deep down in a hollow there is, what appears to be, a Lilliputian homestead set in a patchwork of fields, in the most beautiful scenery; then, perched high on the hillside appear other farms and cottages, and a long way down the valley is the sea. The Smithy is still there and so is Harry Layzell! For over one hundred years that good old family have been there; as long as the Layzells are there the Smithy will carry on. Once upon a time the clang of the hammer on the anvil was heard in every town and village. Now most of the Smithies have been converted to other uses. Fortunately there are still horses and donkeys in Branscombe. They must be shod; also many visitors like to drop in and buy a horse-shoe for luck. Unlike so many other Devon villages, Branscombe remains unspoilt and un- commercialised (like Sidmouth). The aim of the inhabitants is to retain its old-world peace and beauty, even if that is looked upon as "snobbery"—a name that has been recently applied to my beautiful home town, and I sincerely hope that Branscombe people will remain "snobs", for it is that quietitude that encourages some of the old families to come back. I rejoice when I see the names of "Pullin" and a member of the Shorrock family (Mrs. Bucknell) coming to live so near "home". They will be glad to be amongst the old families and (like me) will recall some of the parents, also grandparents, of the present generation.

CHAPTER VII

OLD FAMILIES

I HAVE so much enjoyed meeting some of the descendants recently (November, 1958). When I want to glean news of old happenings I go to meet them in the places where they regularly deliver their goods. Mr. Perryman tells me that his father used to walk into Sidmouth carrying his wares in two baskets, later driving his pair of donkeys; he no longer comes, but his sons bring their motor vans filled with everything of the best. How proud he must feel at the happy results of his early efforts.

I enjoy meeting and talking to Mr. Woodrow (who tells me that he has been coming into Sidmouth for fifty years). He still lives at Grape Vine Cottage, where he was born. In his early days he used to take potatoes into Exeter by donkey trap, leaving at 2 a.m. and returning at 9 p.m. Although his age is now the wrong side of seventy, he still works his two donkeys down on the cliff "plats", where the earliest and well-known Branscombe "taties" have been grown ever since the old, old days when the toilers were only allowed "to parsue the soil that had slipped". Mr. Woodrow's dear old white pony Topsy has replaced the donkeys, and is rewarded by "tit-bits" as she stands outside the houses of delivery.

I do not remember Mr. Woodrow's parents, but I can recall the dear old wrinkled faces of Mr. and Mrs. Dowell, Mr. and Mrs. Gosling (the old ladies wearing bonnets and shawls), coming over the hill into Sidmouth in their donkey traps, filled with vegetables, fruit, rabbits and eggs. I met their son Mr. Gosling this week, bearing a strong resemblance to his mother. He tells me that he also made the early journey into Exeter by donkey trap, this was in order to avoid paying toll. They stopped for breakfast at Half Way House and bought a 4d. loaf which they soaked in a pint of ale (2d.) for the donkey's breakfast. He still works two donkeys down the cliff but no longer brings his potatoes into Sidmouth. I forget that I am recalling the old days of fifty and sixty years ago!

CHAPTER VIII
INDUSTRIES

IN the old days whilst the men worked on their potato "plats" on the cliff, their wives worked at the fine art of Lace-making. In most cottage doorways the women could be seen, working the little wooden sticks weaving the most delicate lace on their round pillows.

Many years ago a Mr. Chick did a thriving business as a "Lace Manufacturer", both in Branscombe and Sidmouth. In Branscombe he engaged a Mrs. Dean to collect the lace from the cottagers. Instead of paying them with money, he traded groceries and household articles; it is not surprising that his business was successful!

I was glad to hear that a few women continue to bring their lace into Sidmouth. This week I saw fine specimens of "Branscombe Point" and Honiton lace.

A wonderful instance of Mrs. Dean's thrift and perseverance has been related to me. She wanted a cottage of her own, so she, with her children, toiled to get it by going to and fro collecting waste stone from outside Beer quarries, and carrying it to a piece of land, where they built their cottage. Her little boy aged seven was "lent" to a farmer at Slade Farm, Salcombe. His duties were to pick up stones, also scare birds from eating the crops. When he knew that his mother was passing through he would run out and give her 3d. which he had earned, saying: "Here, Mother, is money to buy our cottage." What a gallant woman, and what an inspiration to her children. She lived to be over eighty in the same cottage.

Some years later her daughter, Miss Dean, together with her brother who had returned from serving in the Navy, built their own house, brick by brick, and later catered for Guests. Descendants of a married daughter are living in Sidmouth.

November, 1958.

Dairy and poultry farming, and horticulture continue to be the main industry.

Although Mr. Temple-Cotton is not an old "Branscombian", he has for some years brought his well-filled van of vegetables, fruit and flowers into Sidmouth.

In recent years another enterprise named "Repeatavision" has been introduced which dispenses with television masts, invented by Mr. Fielden. We congratulate him and wish him every success. Mrs. Fielden is a member of an old Sidmouth family.

CHAPTER IX
THE PRESENT DAY

ALTHOUGH Branscombe remains "old world" and unspoilt the inhabitants have a very happy social life. Women's Institute, Men's Club, Youth Club, etc., all made enjoyable by well-appointed committees, and many people from all around the district are attracted to their entertainments. The Branscombe Players came to Woolbrook and gave two One-Act Plays, produced by Mrs. Bellchamber, on 21st May, 1958.

The week of the year is Carnival Week and Branscombe Apple Pie Fayre. This is an annual proceeding. This year from Monday, 15th September, to the 20th was a week of gay festivities. Twelve huge pies were baked and Messrs. Stuart and Gerald Collier spent all day making pastry and baking the pies in a brick oven heated with faggots of wood. The twelve pies, each weighing about half a hundredweight, were carried on a decorated farm waggon through the village. Led by Sidmouth Town Silver Band, the procession included a float carrying the Carnival Queen and her attendants, the Misses Jill Read and Una Lock. Escorting the waggon-load of pies were members of the British Legion, Men's Club, Parish Council and Youth Club, wearing countrymen's smocks and hats. There were also several attractive tableaux.

Arriving at the Square, the first slice of apple pie was cut by Mr. C. Ford and handed on a cardboard plate to the Carnival Queen, after which crowds of adults and children filed past trestle tables, each carrying their own spoons. In addition the organizers prepared a substantial meal consisting of "Hot Dogs" for those who were hungry. The proceedings ended with dancing in the Social Hall.

Although the village of Branscombe is not attached to Sidmouth (being under another Governing Council), I feel I must include the village when writing of Sidmouth. Branscombe people bring their business into Sidmouth and join in our social life, musical societies, etc., that I feel they are "one of us". They are a happy and progressive community, and evidently greatly changed since the days when old John Dean of Sidford remarked: "Branscombe people begined wi' nowt and have bin losting every zaison zince!"

CHAPTER X

ITEMS OF INTEREST

December, 1958.

Miss Ethel Butter, who was postmistress at Branscombe for 21 years, has retired. She was presented with a cheque for £40 by Mr. P. W. Perryman (Chairman of the Parish Council). She is succeeded by Mr. Poulton.

In the New Year's Honours List, 1959, Mr. Kevin Tallent Spencer, of Wootans, Branscombe, was awarded a Knighthood; he is a Knight Bachelor. Mr. Kevin Tallent Spencer is Chief Scientist at the Ministry of Power. He won the M.C. in the 1914–1918 war and received the C.B.E. in 1950.

Just where Branscombe, Beer and Southleigh meet, is a large boulder, partly sunk in the soil, and called Hangman Stone. The tradition is, that a man having stolen a sheep sat down with his back to the stone, and drew the rope used to bind the animal's feet, around him; the rope tightened around the man's neck and choked him.

THE WINDING LANE OF BRANSCOMBE

SIDBURY

CHAPTER I

EARLY HISTORY

KING ALFRED'S will 901 suggests that Sidbury and Salcombe Regis were annexed. The Saxon advance was supposed to have stopped at Sidbury.

In 925 the Saxons turned Christians and King Athelstan gave Sidbury, Salcombe and Branscombe with twenty-three other Manors to Exeter Cathedral.

The Father of Alwyn and Goodwyn at Sidbury may have been a Danish wrongdoer, but he was allowed to retain three-fifths of the land as a compromise. During the Mediaeval and Tudor periods from William the Conqueror to Queen Elizabeth, the manorial or feudal system of administration was in existence as in Saxon times. In 1269 Lawrence de Sydebury was instituted by Bishop Bronescombe. 1050–1072 *Sidebury* means "the burgh on the Sid". The burgh is the earthwork known as Sidbury Castle.

Sidbury is blessed by beautiful surrounding countryside; hills and valleys, a cluster of delightful old Tudor and Georgian houses and cottages; the eminence of Evergreen Hill; the woodland of South Lincombe (house built 1610), farms and pasture land, with the River Sid running through.

The Celtic earthwork of Sidbury Castle was once the outstanding feature of historic interest and remains a landmark for miles around. When there was a fear of invasion by Napoleon, and soldiers were quartered in the villages along the south coast, we know that Sidbury women were given red cloaks, and used to parade daily on the top of Castle Hill to represent a regiment of soldiers, when any French ships came in sight.

CHAPTER II

THE CHURCH OF ST. GILES

THE church is picturesque and interesting. The tower is Norman; the south porch with its battlemented turrets is of a later date, but the chequer work at the east end is unmistakably Norman. Many memorials and windows to the Huyshe Cunningham, Bayley Hunt and Cave families have been placed within.

Quoting Mr. Ralegh Radford:—"The Saxon crypt in the Chancel would have been the burial place or repository of relics of a local chief perhaps, and had become a relic of some 200 years before Sidbury Saxon church was built. There are only two in this country."

The Rev. Henry Taylor, B.A., L.TH., Rural Dean of Ottery, was inducted as Vicar in 1945.

CHAPTER III

MANORS

MANORS were granted to men of power and importance. The Lords of the Manor became vassals and rendered services in return for the land allotted to them. They in their turn made grants of land called a holding or fief, with certain commonage rights to lower vassals, who were called the customary tenants of the Manor. They were permitted to cut heather and bracken for bedding their cattle and allow their pigs to go into the woods to pick up acorns. The tenants or bondmen in return rendered the lord certain services by helping to cultivate his farm and give him some livestock as part of the rent. Until the 16th century the lords were lessees.

Then came the wealthy merchants, Huyshe, Cawley, Isaacke, Michell and Lacy, who bought lands at Sidbury, Sidford, Salcombe and Branscombe. They grassed down the best land into sheep-runs, and replaced the old wooden buildings of Sand, Manstone, Radway, Dunscombe and Edge, with fine new stone houses. Bullock teams were still turned out on task work, the new-fangled iron plough was forged and lent from farm to farm and things gradually improved.

We have to thank those good men for making it possible for the agriculturalists to become free to rent the lands and become tenant farmers.

CHAPTER IV

THE MANOR OF SIDBURY

THE Manor was held by the Dean of Exeter until the 19th century. The names of what appear to be the first Lady and Lord of the Manor after the See of Exeter had ceased to be Lords, are inscribed in a calf-bound manuscript book entitled "Manor of Sidbury Presentments Begun 22nd April 1778".

In beautiful copper plate handwriting the first entry reads:—

The Manor of Sidbury { The Customary Court Leet and Court Baron the said Manor there held for Susanna Duke widow in her own right, as to one moyety thereof and John Stuckey Esquire, as to the other moyety thereof.

On trust for the only benefit of John Pearse Esquire, on Wednesday the twenty second of April, in the year of Our Lord, One thousand seven hundred and seventy eight—Before—

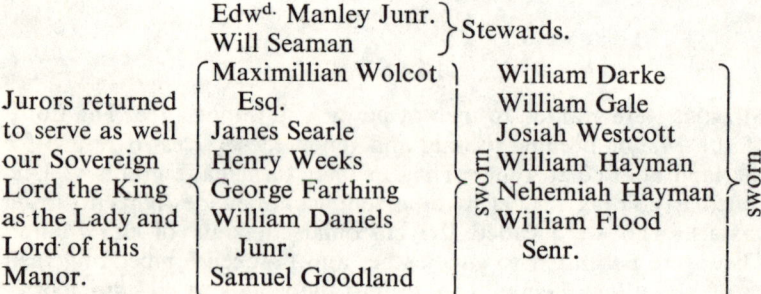

Edwd. Manley Junr. ⎱ Stewards.
Will Seaman ⎰

Jurors returned to serve as well our Sovereign Lord the King as the Lady and Lord of this Manor.

{ Maximillian Wolcot Esq.
James Searle
Henry Weeks
George Farthing
William Daniels Junr.
Samuel Goodland } sworn

{ William Darke
William Gale
Josiah Westcott
William Hayman
Nehemiah Hayman
William Flood Senr. } sworn

CHAPTER V

FINES IMPOSED AT COURT BARON AND COURT LEET

WE present the death of William Symons a Customary Tenant of this Manor and as for the Heriott wee refer to the copy.

We present that if any Tenant of this Manor dyes and a Heriott becomes due to the Lords of the Manor upon such Death That in such Case the Reeve is to seize the said Tenants Best Beast in Liew thereof with two Customary Tenants if the same shall become forfieted who are to value the same and that sum is to be payed to the said Lords in respect of such Heriott or Heriotts. We present that if any Tenant of this Manor dyes between either of the Quarters Days in the Year and their Estates shall fall on the Lords Hands by such Death that their Exors. or admors. shall hold and enjoy the said premises till the next Quarter Day after such Death without doing any spoile wast thereon.

We present the Manor of Sidbury to be a free Warren. (Signed as above).

FINES IMPOSED AT COURT BARON AND COURT LEET

WE present William Burrough to doe the office of a Beadle by desire of the Lord.

We present William Rockett to doe the office of a Reeve for Clayhouse Estate.

We present Pyle's well where the inhabitants of Sidbury formerly fetched their water to be out of repair.

We present Mr. Richd. Buller, and Mr. John Guppy, Mr. Edwd. Holwell and Mr. Wm. Smith for cutting turves within this Manor and selling the same.

We present the Common Pown belonging to this Manor to be out of repair.

We present Math. Clark for not scouring up a ditch adjoining to John Pearse's orchard, etc.

In 1784, on the death of John Pearse, the Manor is divided. Susanna Duke still holds one moiety and the other is divided between five parties: Pearse, Guppy, and four members of the Manley family. In 1807 Robert Hunt Esq. became Lord of the Manor until 1837. James Cunningham Esq. became Lord of the Manor 1834 to 1853 Daniel Cave Esq.   „   „   „   „   „   1854 to 1871

Right Honble. Stephen Cave became Lord of the Manor 1872 to 1879
Charles Daniel Cave Esq.   „   „   „   „   1880
Sir Charles Daniel Cave Bart.   „   „   „   „   1896 to 1922
Sir Edward Cave Bart inherited   1946

This completes and fills the entries in the Presentments of Sidbury Manor, kindly lent me and permitted me to copy by the courtesy of the present Lord of Sidbury Manor, Sir Charles Cave.

CHAPTER VI
THE CAVE FAMILY
LORDS OF SIDBURY MANOR

MR. DANIEL CAVE, a Bristol Banker, began to buy land in the Sid Valley and Sidmouth, and in 1854 purchased Sidbury Manor from the Cunningham family.

In 1856 he bought Witheby, Sidmouth, and a lot of land around Sidbury. He died in 1872 and was succeeded by The Right Hon. Sir Stephen Cave. In 1878 Sir Stephen Cave commenced to build Sidbury Manor House but died in 1880—the year it was finished— leaving no children. He was succeeded by his brother, Mr. Charles Daniel Cave, who was created a Baronet in 1896. He resided at Sidbury Manor for three or four months of each year; until in 1921 his son, Charles Henry Cave, came there to reside permanently. He succeeded to his father's title in 1922 and died in 1931. His son, Sir Edward Cave, succeeded him and died in 1946; he was succeeded by his son, Sir Charles Edward Coleridge Cave, who is the present Lord of the Manor.

Much gratitude must go out to the Cave family for bringing prosperity to Sidbury, buying much land, surrounding farms, improving and restoring old houses and beautifying the whole district, planting woodlands and some fine specimen trees in the Manor gardens, and carefully controlling development. The Manor Estate provided water supplies from three mains for the village, coming from Filcombe, Ridgway and Hatway, which is still maintained by the Estate.

A considerable acreage was sold for Estate Duty following two deaths and much house and cottage property has been sold during the past ten years, and the deer herd has been reduced.

The Village Hall and site was given by Sir C. H. Cave, costing £3,000, built in 1925 to replace the Iron Hall.

The Manor House was let to Alexandra College School for girls in 1939 and the family now reside at Castle Hill.

There was much rejoicing in the village at the birth of the present Lord of the Manor on 28th February, 1927, when bells were rung at Sidbury Parish Church.

In February, 1928, a silver bowl was presented by tenants on his first anniversary. May the Cave family long remain the Lords of Sidbury Manor.

Sir Charles Edward Coleridge Cave married Mary Elizabeth Gore, on 5th June, 1957, at Rogate Parish Church.

John Charles Cave, their son, was born on 5th September, 1958.

CHAPTER VII

ANCIENT HOUSES

SAND BARTON.   ELIZABETHAN

SAND OF SAND, a family of ancient repute, possessed the name before the time of Henry V. It passed to Tremayne, then to Ashby, then to Huyshe. The house is reported to have been built in 1594 by Roland Huyshe.

This fine old house, rich with oak-panelled walls, sculptured stone windows, bearing the arms of Catharine of Aragon, and arched doorways leading into wonderful gardens. For a period it was occupied by the family of Dymond, who farmed the land. In later years it was restored by the late Roland Huyshe of Clyst Hydon, and let as a private residence to Mr. Ormiston, followed by Mrs. Sheldon, who did much in restoring the beautiful gardens. Sand is now occupied by Mr. and Mrs. Campbell.

KNOWLE, COURT HALL AND MANSTONE

Knowle is reputed to have been built by a "Bold Buccaneer" over 400 years ago. In George III's reign a Mr. Wolcot migrated from Sidbury to Knowle.

My ancestors, the Cawley family, were there when my great-great-grandmother, Anna Cawley, celebrated her 21st birthday in 1820. My mother stayed there as a child with her uncle, Thomas Cawley.

In 1866 Mr. Daniel Cave bought the Estate, consisting of Buckton, Harcombe, Boswell and Knowle, from the Countess of Egremont.

Court Hall, situated opposite the Church, is an old Elizabethan mansion with an Italian portico. Sometime used as the Manor House by the Cunningham and Hunt families, it was nearly re-built in 1856; the latter sold it to Mr. Cave in 1871. Members of the

Cave family have frequently occupied it. I remember the much revered Young family and Elton Young being there, who did much good work for Sidbury. Without in any way detracting from the exterior of this lovely building, the house was reconstructed in 1930 and has recently been divided into flats.

Manstone, dated 1369, mentioned in Parkers Mediaeval Domestic Architecture, has massive timber work in ceilings, a large room probably the Chapel, restored with much care by the late Sir Charles Cave.

CHAPTER VIII
I Remember
The Village and Old Families

My first memory of Sidbury was in my childhood days when I went with my sisters to stay at Barnards Farm, first with the Collins family, later Goodland, and when older at Springfield. I like to remember the daffodil field at "Capern's Bottom" (Plyford), which continues to flourish.

Farmers Dymond, Snell and Blackmore were at Sand and Sand Barton. (The Blackmore family now have a Riding School there.)

Cotford Lodge remains, but modern buildings occupy the site of Cotford House, which the Bayley family are reputed to have bought from Dr. Cockburn, Dean of York. The Horton family were its last owners. Denner was at Cotford Dairy, Mr. Nicholls at Brookdale.

Steps led up to Mrs. Norsworthy's house, known as Mount Pleasant; the steps have gone and the entrance is at the side; now known as Rose Hill it is delightful. Alwyn Baker's Smithy is now a garage.

What tales the fine old one-arched stone bridge could tell !

Happy entertainments were held at the Iron Hall; outstanding in my memory was Farmer Blackmore's singing: "Has an-ny-budy-see our c-a-a-t". He was called upon to sing it on every occasion and brought down the house ! What fun it all was.

Seawards were grocers, Frenches butchers and at Mrs. Pearson's emporium everything from boot-laces to beautiful Honiton lace could be bought. It was also the Post Office. Mr. Turner was landlord of "The Royal Oak" and Mr. Yeo at "The Red Lion". Hoskins followed by Langdon and Froome were at The Rivulet Bakery (now an antique shop). The Rev. J. A. Prendergast was Vicar and Mrs. Prendergast was an indefatigable social worker. The Rev. F.

and Mrs. Spray, assisted by Miss Lewis, did wonderful work during the many years as Pastor of the Congregational Chapel. An organ was placed there in 1910. Mr. Knight, assisted by Miss Webber, was Schoolmaster; Mr. Champernoun Manor Estate Agent.

The names King, Pidgeon and Parker appear in old documents. Other old names that I can recall are Hamlin, Northcott, Elliott, Skinner, Pinn, Morrish, Hull, Records, Quick, Chown, Thorn, Maeer, Vinnicombe, Lee, Wood, Palmer, Summers, Barden, Vincent, Finlayson, Thornton, Morey, Kerslake, Earland, Mitchell, Selway, Heywood, Lockyer, and last but outstanding was Mr. Charley Selley. More recent names are Lt.-Col. Harvey at Court Hall, Mr. Clarkson at Buckley, Mr. Bourne at Rose Hill, Dr. St. Cin, Mr. Mathew, M.P., at Paccombe, all active members in the social life of Sidbury.

HARVEST HOME

THE Harvest Festival was a whole day of rejoicing, ending with a church service.

When we were older we used to cycle from Sidmouth for the evening service. The church was always packed and never were Harvest hymns sung more heartily. Fair Days and holidays were entered into with such gusto. All these traditional entertainments continue. What a happy village!

CHAPTER IX

TRANSPORT

BEFORE the advent of the motor car the only public conveyance to and from Sidmouth was by wagonette, driven by Mrs. Alwyn Taylor every Friday. Otherwise older folk travelled by pony and trap or governess car.

CHAPTER X

HIGH DAYS AND HOLIDAYS

THE MANOR COURT LEET

THE MANOR COURT LEET and annual rent audit dinner, held in November since 1461, commences with the tolling of the church bell at 11 a.m. to call together the jury at the Estate Offices in the presence of the Lord of the Manor, Foreman, Pig and Duck Driver, Beadle, Reeve, Town Crier, and two constables. The customary oaths having been taken, the payment of the Michaelmas rents proceeds until 6 o'clock. The whole party adjourn to the Royal Oak for dinner, ending with a concert.

SIDBURY FAIR

SIDBURY FAIR is opened on the second Tuesday of September. Before 12 a.m. a large crowd gathers to see the white gaily-decorated Glove hoisted from an upper window of The Royal Oak, to denote the opening of Sidbury Fair, which takes place on Wednesday. Cattle, sheep, pigs, etc., are sold by auction in the street. (In the old days there were one or two stalls, and children crammed into carriages for 1d. rides, driven by Mr. Skinner.) At 12 noon the younger children race from school to scramble for hot pennies thrown from a window of The Red Lion. Skittling for a live pig takes place on the Rifle Range. The Fair terminates at 12 o'clock after a dance in the Village Hall, when the Glove is taken down.

FOLK DANCE FESTIVAL

AUGUST, 1958: ENGLISH FOLK DANCE AND SONG SOCIETY FESTIVAL was opened by the Vice-Chairman of Sidmouth Urban District Council, Mr. George Hamlin, and much enjoyed by a very large crowd of spectators. The opening programme included a traditional dance originating in Sidbury—"Hunt the Squirrel".

HARVEST HOME

1958: Sidbury and Sidford continue to hold their HARVEST HOME. Sports, organized by Mr. Lloyd, took place in Daniel's Close, with Sir Charles Cave, Bt., as starter. Tea, organized by Mrs. Anstis, was provided free. In the evening a Thanksgiving Service was conducted by the Rev. H. Taylor in St. Giles Parish Church. This was followed by a Dance in the Village Hall.

BRITISH LEGION

22nd November: SIDBURY BRANCH OF THE BRITISH LEGION held a "Dug Out" at the Royal Oak. Visitors from Sidmouth, Exmouth, Branscombe, Ashburton and Newton Poppleford attended. Present were Sir Charles Cave, President, Lt.-Col. Harvey and Chairman. The "Bread and Cheese with Pickles" supper in the candlelight, and war-time songs played during the meal, were much enjoyed; also the "Sing-song" which followed. Mr. H. H. Palmer was Master of Ceremonies and Mr. Seaward acted as pianist.

ANNUAL PANCAKE RACE

10th February: The Annual Pancake Race created much excitement.

CHAPTER XI

ENTERTAINMENTS

SIDBURY folk work well and play well. There is a Rifle Range, Football, Cricket, Boxing and an active Branch of the British Legion. The Women's Institute was opened in 1952 with Mrs. Tucker as President, where Evening Classes in Handicrafts of all kinds, including Honiton Lace, are taught. There are Whist Drives and other entertainments.

May, 1958: EAST DEVON HUNTER TRIALS, held at Otterton Barton, were highly successful and good riding was witnessed. David Baldwin (Sidbury), under 12, won the cup for the best rider in East Devon, while Miss Caroline Fogwell (Sidford) won the cup in her class for ages 13 to 15.

Pairs Awards: David Baldwin and Terry Hamlin; Caroline Fogwell and Pam Masters 2nd. In the Associates Class, Miss Hilary Blackmore and Miss Marion Slowcombe were awarded first place.

10th May, 1958: THE MAY DAY REVELS, in which residents of Furze Hill estate took part, was held on the Recreation Ground and arranged by two school girls, Sheila Quick and Jacqueline Vanstone. Carol White was crowned May Queen. Her two attendants were Pamela Nicholls, Jennifer Shepherd, and John White. Maypole Dancing and races were much enjoyed by children and parents alike.

A party of Exeter Morris Dancers visited the Revels and danced around the maypole.

Fellow members of Sidmouth Council honoured Mr. G. Morrish at a reception to mark a completion of fifty years' service and also to commemorate his Golden Wedding. A silver salver was presented by Mr. J. W. Skinner.

Mr. Morrish was first elected to the Parish Council in 1907 at the age of twenty-two, was Chairman for five years. When the Parish Council ceased to exist, he was representative of Sidford.

CHAPTER XII
THE PRESENT DAY

February, 1959.

What a happy time I spent walking through Sidbury Village this week (February, 1959) to make enquiries and recall old days. I was impressed to find old buildings so well preserved, retaining the old-world atmosphere. I called upon Mrs. Bishop (née Layzell) at Hillside and spent a happy hour renewing acquaintanceship after an interval of over fifty years.

In the High Street the shops have been carefully modernised without detracting from the old structures, and well stocked to supply all needs. I called at the butcher's shop (Anstis & Pike) to make an enquiry. When I said that I remembered French as butcher, the attendant remarked: "Madam, you wear well." What a compliment ! The charming "Cherry Tree" cottage is there to offer refreshment. The Royal Oak and Red Lion; the gracious old building Court Hall. It was all unchanged. Turning into Church Street I found the same dignified old houses with grey stone Tudor windows, old brass knockers and bell-pulls; Rivulet Cottages with the same trellised porches, the thatched creeper-covered porched cottages in Queen Street, unchanged since my childhood days. Arriving at the old stone bridge and looking up and down stream, the cattle grazing on the hillside, nothing to disturb the peace and beauty—I was just overjoyed !

A myrtle tree grew outside Myrtle Tree House. Thinking it could *not* be the same tree of over fifty years ago, and as the door was ajar, I tapped, and Mrs. Hamlin invited me to meet Mr. Hamlin, whose father, Mr. George Hamlin, I well remembered. It *was* the same tree. During our interesting talk Mr. Hamlin told me that the house, built in 1614, was once a Coaching Inn and behind were old Tithe Barns. His small son proudly showed me a sword worn by a Hamlin ancestor when escorting the body of the Duke of Kent to Honiton, who died at the Royal Glen, Sidmouth, in 1819. Another ancestor, Joseph Hamlin, farmed "Barnards" in 1810 and was distressed on discovering hidden casks of brandy in a loft; also that his son was hired to warn smugglers at the approach of the Excise Officer. Mr. Hamlin encourages the Sidbury folk to keep up old customs and is a member of Sidmouth Council.

Next to the imposing entrance to Alexandra College, the lovely white porched Rose Cottage stands as of old, also in contrast, the dignified old Chapel, built in 1820, both a fitting picture to welcome incomers to the village. On the left is other evidence of the care which has been taken to preserve the row of old cottages in Chapel Street; the constabulary has gone, but a "Baby Parlour" and Drug Store have been developed with such ingeniousness, that the structure of the exteriors remain unaltered. Miss Jackson invited me into her Drug Store and I was amazed to find it fully equipped and modernized.

Some of the old families were there to greet me in the cottages where they have always lived. Farmers Clake and Denner have gone from Furze Hill, but the Coles family remain at The Mill. At Burnt Oak a row of modern buildings and shops have arisen and Mr. H. H. Palmer (Bunny) has opened as newsagent, bookseller and stationer. Many blocks of buildings have arisen at Greenhead and Furze Hill. These overlook lovely pastures with the Sid flowing through. May they long be preserved.

CHAPTER XIII

ITEMS OF INTEREST

(in brief)

IN 1642 Parliament issued a warrant for Richard Clap of Sidbury, also for Mrs. Searle, and they must appear at London and must now christen their child again because he could not say the Epistle and Gospel fast enough.

Richard Babbington was Rector of Sidbury Church 1630 to 1645.

Fines imposed *at the Court Leet* and Court Baron:

1788 Mr. Wolcot   fined 5/– for not attending Court Leet.
       Mr. Stone   „   2/6 „ „   „   „   „
       Mr. Welsman   „   2/6 „ „   „   „   „
1789 Mr. William Carslake to do the office of Tythingman at the Court Leet held in the house of Thos. Cawley.
1792 Thos. Wolcot fined 10/– for non-attendance.
1795 Manor Mills burnt down.
1798 Fines of £2 and £5 for premises not repaired after deaths of tenants (at Court Leet).
1854 Mr. Daniel Cave began to buy land in the Sid Valley. In the same year he bought Sidbury Manor from the Cunningham family.
1871 Court Hall bought from Mr. R. H. C. Hunt.
1875 A new public road was begun behind Evergreen Hill and completed in 1877.

1878   The Right Hon. Sir Stephen Cave commenced to build Sidbury Manor. He died that year leaving no children.

1879   Sidbury House, known as the old Manor House, demolished.

1880   Manstone new farm house built.

1882   (Aug.) Charles Daniel Cave and family came to live at Sidbury.

1882   Land given for the Cemetery.

1886   Herd of fallow deer put in park.

1896   Charles Daniel Cave created Baronet.

1901   Death of Daniel Addington Cave, eldest son of Sir Charles.

1901   Sidbury applies for telegraphic services and guarantees the Post Office Services half of the loss if it does not pay.

1908   Buckton rebuilt.

1912   New house built under Castle Hill on site of Sidbury Castle House.

1912   Death of Lady Cave, wife of Sir Charles. Memorial window placed in Church.

War Years

1918   Part of Deer Park ploughed up and sown with corn. Herd of deer reduced.

1918   (June) Forty German prisoners arrived and billeted in stables with English warder.

1919   (Sept.) Electric Light driven by power at Sidbury Mill.

1919   (March) German prisoners left.

1922   Edward Cave married Miss Betty Coleridge.

1922   (29th Oct.) Death of Sir Charles D. Cave.

1925   (March) New Village Hall opened by Sir Charles Cave.

1926   (July) Four concrete Block cottages built at Greenhead.

1927   (28th Feb.) Birth of Charles Edward Coleridge Cave. Bells rung at Sidbury Church.

1927   (3rd March) Charles Edward Coleridge Cave christened.

1928   (28th Feb.) Silver bowl presented by tenants, Mr. George Hamlin, the oldest tenant, making the presentation, on 1st anniversary of Charles Edward Coleridge Cave.

1928   Land sold for Trow Road deviation. Building site sold in Brook Field to Honiton R.D.C., also part of Furze Hill field for building.

1929   (Nov.) Sidbury decides for amalgamation with Sidmouth; 321 for, 167 against.

1930   Hamlin's Orchard sold to Honiton R.D.C. for building. South end of Court Hall reconstructed.

1930   Paccombe enlarged. Electric light installed.

1931   Automatic telephone exchange installed.

1932   (26th July) Death of Sir Charles Henry Cave.
1932   (Oct.) Sir Edward Cave and family move into Manor House.
1933   Land for new Cemetery given.
1934   Manor gardens visited by Duke of Connaught.
1935   Jubilee celebrations in Jubilee Field.
1935   (18th July) Unionist and Imperial League at the Manor attended by Lord Burghley, J.P., M.P., and Mr. Cedric Drewe, M.P.
1939   Paccombe let for a girls' school.
1939   The Manor House becomes Alexandra School for Girls.
1957   (5th June) Marriage of Sir Charles Edward Coleridge Cave to Mary Elizabeth Gore.
1958   (8th Sept.) Birth of John Charles Cave.

CHAPTER XIV

Mrs. Pearson

The Grand Old Lady of Sidbury

Mrs. Susan Pearson, of Sidbury Post Office, was in her early life a school teacher. She later became Postmistress for Sidbury and carried out this office for fifty years, when she resigned in favour of her niece, Mrs. Kerslake.

She was also widely known as a Honiton lace-maker. Her work was acknowledged by experts as among the best in the kingdom. She was engaged on this work a week before she died, at the age of 89, in September, 1929. When well over 80 Mrs. Pearson conducted the whole of the work of Sidbury Post Office.

I remember Mrs. Pearson when I stayed in Sidbury as a child. Her shop was well stocked with haberdashery, wools, notepaper, in fact one expected to find everything in that emporium; but the outstanding feature was her window display of beautiful Honiton lace.

———————————

Lace making was universal in the old days; the greater proportion of women and girls could be seen sitting in the doorways with pillows on their laps happily employed in making this gossamer handwork, with the greatest ease and rapidity. A lady, when once describing the process to a friend, remarked: "They twiddle about a few little sticks and out comes a lace collar."

This is not in any way intended to be an accurate history. Having spent such happy visits over many years, re-visiting and calling on some of the families and recalling old days, I have endeavoured to impart some of its history which I have gleaned, some from old manuscripts and some imparted to me by old and new Sidbury inhabitants. If a few inaccuracies have occurred, please excuse, hoping that I may have given as much pleasure to the reader as it has given me to record it.

In order to recall nostalgic memories, I will pass along Buckley road and old farmsteads, through lovely Harcombe lanes, where primroses are already blooming, which brings me to Stephens Cross and Sidford.

SIDBURY

SIDFORD

CHAPTER I

OLD DOCUMENT

THERE is in the Parish Chest a document of 1656 which mentions some places in the vicinity, difficult to identify now. It declares that "John fforce appeared and demanded against Harry Pease and Andrew fforce, one messuage and certain lands in Salcombe Regis and Pydden Hill, Snodbrooke Meadow, otherwise Darneford Meadow in the parish of Sidbury and Hitways, as their right; the claim was allowed".

Snodbrooke, or Snogbrooke stream rises in the hills above Harcombe, comes down by Knowle and Boswell and falls into the River Sid just above Sidford Bridge. The source of the stream is known as Roncombe Girt (Sidbury) and sends down a large stream of water. Pydden or Bidden Hill is thought to have been part of Trow Hill.

193

CHAPTER II
The Present Day
Farms and Excursions through Lovely Scenery

This seems to be a suitable place to mention the farms in the vicinity mentioned in the document, taking Sidbury as the focal point in the surrounding farms.

From Stephens Cross, bounded on the left along the old Roman Road through Sidford village, High Street, extending to Core Hill, are: first, Warren and Stone farms (much of the latter in High Street has been recently developed), Brook, Ebdon and Sidford farms.

From Stephens Cross turn right, ascend Trow to Orleigh's Hill. Here the most wonderful panoramic view greets one. Looking through the wooded slope overlooking the valley lies Paccombe, Chelson, Knowle and Boswell, with Buckton Hill on the north; across Sid Valley to Sidbury Castle looming in the distance.

Continue along the old Roman Road, passing the fine old "Three Horse Shoes" Inn, to Blackberry Castle camp and nearby the old mansion of Bovey House. These historical landmarks need a chapter of their own.

Turn left, passing through the most glorious wooded lanes of Southleigh, beautiful at every season. In spring the trees appear as overhanging lace, the banks and hedges carpeted with primroses, followed by bluebells, foxgloves, dog roses and honeysuckle. Later glorious autumn tints. On to Farway, Gittisham, Roncombe, passing down the lane encircling the farms of Mincombe, Sand, Goosemore and Burscombe to Sidbury Castle. Again return to Stephens Cross. Go directly forward through the lovely lanes of Harcombe, dipping down to Snogbrook, the lane skirts the side of Buckton Hill, descending Hitway Hill into Sidbury, passing the farms of Buckton, Buckley Higher and Lower Sweetcombe.

CHAPTER III
Porch House

Descending Stephen's Cross passing the Blue Ball Inn, cross the old pack-horse bridge, built about 1100 and rebuilt in 1930, and enter the village of Sidford.

There is a tradition in the village that, after the battle of Worcester, Charles II passed through the village and slept one night at a house called Porch House. This house lies on the south side of the street going down the village to the river. The room reputed to have been occupied by the King is at the north-west corner, with the window looking into the street. There was a projecting chimney in the front of the house, in the middle of which there was a stone tablet bearing the date 1574. Sad to say, the chimney has been removed, but the date appears on the outside with the letters N.I.E.

It is said that when the King left he forgot one of his gloves, which was cherished afterwards as a precious relic; also that the old lady of the house never entered that room without making a profound bow. It is also said that his horse lost a shoe and the blacksmith who was asked to make a new one, noticed that the shoes of the horse were put on the wrong end before—that is with the toes behind—so that when the King was fleeing eastward, his enemies might think he was going in the wrong direction.

One can imagine the joy the old lady experienced as she pounced upon the glove, and cherished it as a memento of her royal visitor. There appears to be further evidence that he passed through the district, as Charles II coins have been discovered at a cottage in Sid Lane, and at Salcombe Regis, where it is said he unsuccessfully tried to procure a vessel to Lyme. I like to think that the horse might have been shod at the old smithy where I remember Mr. Teed as blacksmith.

CHAPTER IV

FARMS AND FARMERS

AT this point I feel I must digress and recall old memories, related to me by my father between fifty and sixty years ago, and speak of the occupants of the farms mentioned.

The annual Agricultural Dinner held at The Blue Ball was the day of the year for the farmers; silver cups and prizes were distributed for the best cultivated farms and crops. Attended by the Lords of the Manor of Sidmouth and Sidbury, entertained by Mine Host, Mr. Tom Reed, all the farmers from Sidmouth, Sidbury, Sidford and Salcombe met. First and foremost to be mentioned is that fine upstanding character, the late Farmer Richard King of Buckley, the father and grandfather of many sons and daughters, some of whom continue to occupy the farms. He was always called upon to open the programme by singing his famous song, "A Hunting we will Go", and one can imagine how the chorus joined in by all the farmers resounded and rang out, to be heard throughout the village of Sidford. The silver cups would be filled and refilled and passed around.

There were farmers Maeer of Chelson, Hartnell at Buckton (followed by Clode), Tom Lawrence at Stone, Tilk at Paccombe, Dyer at Warren, Elliott at Sidford Farm, Collier at Boswell, Reed at Knapp, Summers at Ebdon, Pile at Brook, Northcott at Sweetcombe, Northcott at Trow, Langdon at Wragg, Hallet, Sage, and from Sidbury farmers Blackmore and Dymond from Sand, Goodland, Clake, Spiller and Denner, etc. Descendants of many of these families continue to occupy the farms.

Another day of rejoicing was on the occasion of the 21st birthday of my great-great-grandmother, Anna Cawley, in 1820, when there was dancing on the green outside The Blue Ball by all the villagers. She was then at Knowle. The top of her birthday gown is in Sidmouth Museum.

CHAPTER V

ANCIENT BUILDINGS

STONE FARM has sometimes been mentioned as Stone Manor. The De la Stone family of Sidford, mentioned in ancient writings, appear to have been seated at Stone Farm in the time of Henry II. Again it is said to go back to 1066. Walls vary from twenty-four to twenty-seven inches in thickness and are built of flints bonded with mixtures long fallen into disuse.

WARREN'S FARM. In 1309 Warren was the copy-holder—hence the name. The old farm house with stone porch remains unaltered, and is still farmed by the Dyers family, who have been there for many years.

THE BLUE BALL INN. This fine old cob-walled thatched Inn is a "welcome" picture at the Stephens Cross entrance into Sidford. Unchanged since the days when the coaching horn resounded in the courtyard.

The present landlord, Mr. H. W. Newton (born at Dunscombe), kindly showed me the interior. A stone tablet in the chimney corner bears the date 1369–89. The fine old oak surround and beams are well preserved.

The horn of the huntsmen is still heard at the gathering of the Meet.

Vallances are the earliest owners that I can trace—from 1832 to the present day. Jeremiah Layzell was landlord in 1884, followed by Daniels, Tom Reed, John Bolt, Ernest Spiller. The present landlord, H. W. Newton, has been there twenty years.

SCHOOL STREET. A row of lovely old cottages with the school house in the centre, remain well preserved. The outstanding features are the old stone chimneys of the Stuart period. One bears the date 1633, another 1641.

CHAPTER VI

I REMEMBER

THE VILLAGE

PLEASE pardon me for becoming personal, but it is necessary in describing life in the village over fifty years.

In my childhood days it was the greatest thrill for my two sisters and myself to go to stay at a farm at Sidford and run wild (usually to recover from, or avoid childish ailments), and run wild we did !

Every day was filled with fresh excitement. The joy of sitting in the chimney corner; we sat on stools, the older folk sat on the tall wooden "settle". There was a little square window on one side, and the chimney was so wide that we could look up and see the sky. The wood fire on the hearth had large logs laid across on fire dogs. Hams were hanging up to be smoked. The kettle was boiled by hanging on an iron suspended from the chimney, meat and poultry roasted in a Dutch oven facing the fire, girdle cakes baked on a trivet standing on the embers, but the biggest thrill was baking-day, when bundles of wood were thrust into a large hole at the side of the chimney, set alight, and after the ashes had been raked out, loaves of bread, in tins, thrust into the oven on long spatulate poles. Never since those days have bread and cakes tasted so good as those. Large pans of cream were scalded over the fire and the next day skimmed, and when large basins had been filled, the cream was poured into a churn which was attached to a long pole, a horse was harnessed to the pole and walked round and round in a circle churning the cream into butter. Watching the work in the farmyard, the milking, feeding hens, collecting eggs, etc., picnicking in the orchard and finding that a pig had strayed in and was eating our tea; every minute of the day was happily filled.

There was no difficulty in getting us to bed, climbing narrow stairs leading from the kitchen, the sloping floors of bedrooms which led one into the other and the doors fastened by pieces of wood raised by pulling a string and dropping into a wooden socket. Best of all was the novelty of sleeping in a nest of feather bed, and being wakened by the farmyard noises.

Oil lamps and candles were the only lights and a lantern for outdoor use. The freedom of "running wild" in the village, with no restrictions, paddling in the river and swinging on the gates beneath the bridge, making our first and only mud pies in the lane leading to Hawkin's Mill. It was quite worth the scolding !

Sunday was strictly observed, the villagers attending either Church or Chapel. We were taken to the little chapel, quite a different service to our church. Mr. Bertie Radford played the harmonium and swaying as he joined in the singing of Sankey's hymns, and how heartily they sang; outstanding in my memory was Mr. Haycraft. I was fascinated and impressed by it all as a small child. In the afternoon we were taken for a walk in the lanes or along the road leading to Sidbury, where we picked watercress from the roadside. There were no houses beyond Country House to Sidbury. Such a happy care-free community. The only entertainments I can remember were "Tea-Meetings" held in a field, with sports and competitions.

CHAPTER VII

The Old Families

OUTSTANDING in my memory are Mr. Freddy Hawkins and his sister and Miss Martha Reed, who produced from her capacious pocket either sweets or a penny ! Also Miss "Honny" Maeer. These kindly folk always had a smile. Mr. Hawkins was Church Organist. Other names I remember are Pring, Haycraft, Layzell, Langdon, Fry, Fowler, Venn, Small, Solman, Perry, Thomas, Joyce, Godfrey, Fayter, Cudmore, Bishop, Vincent, Pile, Wagstaff, remembered over many years. Another Hawkins' family lived in School Street—Bessie, Lena, Mabel and Charley. They now live in Sidmouth. The Irish family were Blacksmiths at Harcombe for over 100 years; they continue the business in Sidford today.

It is good to see the old names of Reed and Northcott appearing at Harcombe Harvest Festival, 1958.

CHAPTER VIII

THE VILLAGE OVER FIFTY YEARS AGO

THE quaint little village consisted of two long streets, both main roads, one leading from Sidmouth to the north through Sidbury and Honiton, the Lyme Stowford road extending from Trow Hill through High Street, entering the Exeter road at Stowford.

There were no houses along High Street and only three along the Sidmouth Road from Primley, Malden, Ragg Farm and Finlayson's cottage at the old brickfield.

A suitable entrance to the village was the little cob chapel on the right and two thatched cottages, and the Cyclists' Rest on the left. Next came Teed's Smithy, "The Rising Sun" (Mr. Helman) and a row of lovely cottages, with the village school in the centre, extending to Country House, with Sidford Farm across the road, happily still farmed by Elliotts. An old cob thatched farmhouse stood on the corner (now Sewards and Post Office) and below was creeper-covered Stone Farm house. Farmer Tom Lawrence lived there, followed by Oscar Summers. The old cob farmstead still remains across the road.

With the exception of the Church, erected in 1868, and some villas beyond at the entrance to the Mill, the whole village consisted of lovely old buildings with front gardens and trellised porches. A stream ran down on the right which was crossed by a stone slab to enter the cottages, some built back to back facing up and down. Mrs. Strawbridge lived at Applegarth. Its exterior is unchanged.

The one village shop was Horn's, Baker and Post Office; this shop was taken over by the Vinnicombe family in 1912. Meat and fish was brought in and sold from vans.

CHAPTER IX

INTERESTING HAPPENINGS

SALCOMBE REGIS, Sidbury and Sidford were administered by Honiton Rural District Council before being amalgamated to Sidmouth in 1929.

In 1912 first suggestions were made by Honiton Housing and Town Planning scheme for the development of land in the Sidford district. (Apart from Malden, Ragg Farm and an old brickfield cottage there were no houses along the Sidford road between Primley and Sidford).

Extract from a Journal, 1912

"It was suggested that the main road from Sidmouth to Sidford may be widened and straightened. Also that blocks of two, four or six decent looking dwellings—twelve to sixteen to the acre—each with a garden and a yard, pleasant and useful adjuncts which the Act will gently, but firmly, insist on being clean !

"A new road may one day replace Byes Lane.

"The attitude of those attending the meeting at Sidford was, on the whole, friendly enquiry and interest. The chief opponents to the scheme did not put in an appearance to ask questions and to have their manifest ignorance of the Act and scheme exposed and enlightened. Amongst those were Thomas Cawley of Kensington (owner of the land), who sent out a circular to everybody supposed to be principally concerned."

This land and property at Sidford has been in my mother's family (the Cawleys) since the early 16th century. My second cousin, Thomas Cawley, and his father before him, strongly objected to buildings appearing on his pasture lands, which occupied both sides of the Sidmouth–Sidford road, preferring to keep the district rural. Honiton Rural District Council's project was not carried and the land remained rural for twenty years until 1931–32, when Thomas Cawley died suddenly, leaving an elderly unmarried sister. The whole of this land and other land in Sidford, including Stone Farm, extending along High Street, was privately sold *en bloc* (I am told within a week) mainly to one purchaser, after which the land was sold piecemeal and development went ahead, seemingly unrestricted. Some fine old buildings were replaced by shops. Although much of the old Sidford remains, I feel saddened at the irreplaceable loss of some ancient monuments in the village.

CHAPTER X

The Present Day

The old chapel has gone, and a modern one erected on another site. The main part of Stone Farmhouse was demolished and replaced by a Baker's Shop; one wonders why its destruction was permitted. I have been shown a photograph of the exterior previous to this, as I remember it. The frontage appears to be Victorian (evidence that the frontage had been already replaced). It is now Myrtle Guest House and the present owner has built in a chimney corner in order to recover some of the old-world atmosphere.

The fine attractive houses erected on the pasture lands are a great improvement on those suggested twenty years ago and have brought prosperity to Sidford.

The first garage was opened at the bottom of the village by Mr. Lavers. A VILLAGE HALL was built in 1907 and tennis courts opened providing happy entertainment. Drama Groups formed; EVENING CLASSES; Handicrafts provided by the WOMEN'S INSTITUTE OPENED IN 1919; Ladies' Choir formed, Exhibitions, FLOWER SHOWS, etc., in fact everything to entertain old and young. With up-to-date shops to supply all requirements, attractive cafés and guest houses, Sidford is a happy progressive village.

Happily many old families remain and it is for that reason I have written so much of the early days of the old village where I spent so many happy holidays. Please forgive me for being somewhat garrulous, but it is a failing of the elderly, and, after all, I *am* a Great Granny of another little Anna.

CHAPTER XI

INTERESTING DOCUMENTS

COPIED from an old manuscript in Exeter City Library dated 1290:—
"J. Ffarewaye in Myncombe 1394 12/6
J. Trevet and J. Crosse, Isabella in Stone 12/6
J. Ffarewaye in Cotteforde 1 mess and 4 ferl
T. Bampfilde in Wolton 1 mess and 3 ferl 7/–
B. Pile in Saunde 12/–
J. Hittewaie tenet in Saunde 1 mess and 8 ferl 20s.
R. Bishop in C. Cote 5/–
J. Roche in Harecombe 1 mess, 1 ferl, Redd 5/– (Fauet ut supra etc.)
S. Potel in Potel 1 mess, 1 ferl 4/8
W. Bonnuyle 1½ ferl 6/– in Hittewaye
R. Lapplod in Harecombe 1 mess 1 ferl
J. Wonard in Manstone 3½ ferl. 30/–
J. Atwodhous 1 mess and 3 ferl 14/– (Firmarii ad term: vite)
J. Farewaie in Roncombe 1 parellum de vasto 6/–
J. Rawlyn Vicar 10 A 10/–
Yarde is 2 ferl and S. Lencombe 4 ferl."

It will be noted that some of these family names have become place names to-day. (A. S.)

CHAPTER XII

OLD DOCUMENT

GRIGGS, Orleigh Hill and Skinner's Farm are probably associated with the families of Henry Grygge 1524, William Orley 1780 and Richard Skynner 1333.

ORIGIN OF THE PLACE NAMES AND OF
SIDBURY, SALCOMBE AND HARCOMBE

Chelson is Chevelston 1154, Chevestun 1175, Chevelstun 1301.

Paccombe is Pecombe 1369.

Trow is Trowe 1282 and was the home of Agnes atte Trewe and John atte Trewe 1333.

Knowle and Slade House were the homes of Adam de la Cnolle 1282 and Juliana atte Slade 1333, le Knolle 1420.

Dunscombe 1249 probably Dunn's coombe.

Buckley Farm is Boughcleve 1301, Boheclyve 1307, Bowclyve 1369. It is compound of O. E. boyer 'bow' and 'clif' referring to the steep curved hill.

Buckton is Buckadun, 1200 Bukedune.

Burscombe is Berrdescombe heuford 1067, Bridescombe 1333, Burdescombe 1394.

Brook Farm is la Broke 1283, Broke 1350.

Sweetcombe possibly associated with family of Thomas Suetle or Suete, who was living in the parish in 1260.

Mincombe Farm is Myncombe 1313, Myncomb 1325. It is suggested derived from O. E. Minte—hence "Mint Valley".

Ebdon Farm is Yebedon 1280, Ybbedon 1501, Ebbedon 1510, Ybbedon 1524, "Ibbas Hill" and dun.

Hatway Hill and Cottage is Hittewye 1301, 1308, 1330, Huttewye 1330 is possibly associated with the family of William Huythe 1260.

Knapp Farm is la Crappe 1280, la Knappe in Manerio de Sydebire.

Bernards Farm and Clapps Hill. Associated with family of Thomas Barnarde 1612 and Roger Clappe 1333.

Harcombe is Harecumbe 1200, juxta Sidemuth 1340, 'Hare cumb'.

Plyford is Pleyford 1330, Pleyeforde 1333, Playford possioly referred to the spot where animals, such as young otters disported themselves.

CHAPTER XIII

ITEMS OF INTEREST

(in brief)

1066	Stone Farm or Manor reported to have been erected about 1066.
1100	Sidford Pack Horse Bridge built about 1100; rebuilt 1930.
1309	Warren appears as copy-holder of farm.
1369	The Blue Ball Inn built 1369–89.
1574	King Charles II is said to have slept at Porch House. Tablet bearing date 1574 N.I.E. appears on outside wall.
1633 } 1641 }	Old houses in School Street bear dates 1633, 1641.
1868	Sidford Parish Church built.
1899	11th August: A new organ was placed in Sidford Church.
1907	Village Hall built and tennis courts opened.
1912	Suggestion by Honiton R.D.C. for blocks of houses on Sidford Road.
1927	New bells at Sidford Parish Church dedicated by the Bishop of Exeter.
1932	Large sale of land, Sidford, Sidmouth Road and High Street.
1958	18th May: The Women's Institute celebrated its 39th Annual Birthday. Sidford, Sidbury Horticultural Show attracted 550 exhibits. Mr. and Mrs. Haycraft celebrated their Golden Wedding.

MARCH 1959

A SPARKLING Spring morning creates a vision of the country and the river, and invites me to visit my favourite haunts. An early bus takes me in a very short time to Stanhope. Walking down Livonia Road, entering Byes Lane the enchantment begins. In the hedges the dew is still on the ferns and foliage, little tufts of green on the strands of honeysuckle, dog-roses and bushes, waving catkins and "Pussy willows" and at the end of the lane our river! Not a soul in sight. With the lull of the stream and the stillness the enchantment begins and I day-dream and return to memories of my childhood days. On the right the sloping meadows of Livonia are carpeted with daffodils, before me the old chestnut trees over-hanging on both sides of the river. Messrs. Underdowns Nursery Gardens occupy the site of Sidpark Road. Crossing a narrow plank bridge, passing through a meadow into Lovers' Walk, I sit on a tree trunk and listen to the cheep of the birds and the soothing sound of "Mother Sid", picturing her flowing down from Roncombe uniting our villages on her way to the sea.

Cattle are grazing on the Lawn Pastures amid our grand centuries-old trees. I awaken to find that a little bridge named "Heart's Delight" enables me to cross into Temple Street, facing the lovely entrance to The Elysian Fields where (again reminiscing) I see massive wrought-iron gates. I pass along Vicarage Road through an avenue of trees, old stone walls enclose Culver Park on the right and lovely pasture land extending to Enfield Villas on the left, where cattle are grazing peacefully. The fine old Vicarage with Regency porch stands amid lawns and flower beds. Massive cedar trees can be seen above the cob wall of "Radway", the home of Major Walker. (A seat now replaces the entrance to Sidlands Lodge, formerly Radway Manor, but the grand old Regency porches of the house remain.)

Crossing the road to the Blackmore Fields, passing the Unitarian Chapel, an old garden wall extends to charming old May Cottage, with the little green wicket gate outside the front door and the climbing Passion flower. A wall encloses the gardens at the back of Pike's Court.

Arriving at the path leading to Coburg Field, I find the high garden wall of Blackmore Hall has been lowered, and a seat placed upon it. The garden has been planted with rose-beds and flowering shrubs and seats placed against a sheltering wall. A lovely stretch of green playing field covers the Coburg pasture land where cattle once grazed, but the gracious old buildings of Coburg Terrace, the Old Chancel and Amyatts Terrace remain unchanged.

Iron gates stand at the entrance to Blackmore Hall. The old house has gone, but the lovely massive old trees stand amid beautiful lawns and surrounding flower beds; a true haven of peace can be found there. With our grand old Church Tower before me over-looking the Resting Place of our ancestors, as I turn the corner and gaze at the picture framed by the Lych Gate, high in the chestnut tree two thrushes send forth a song of joy, telling us: "Spring is here". With their song echoing in our hearts, looking forward, looking upward, let us rejoice that we *are* of Sidmouth.

EPILOGUE

AND now my tale is told, of my beloved birthplace, the home of my Ancestors, and the dear people I love—for them I have written this book.

At Port Royal our fishermen are preparing to put out to sea. Looking across our beautiful Bay, as I see the sun going down, a wonderful peace descends upon me and my heart is filled with thankfulness as:—"I lift up mine eyes unto the hills, from whence cometh my help."

ANNA SUTTON

THE BEDFORD HOTEL,
    SIDMOUTH.

THE LYCH GATE